HOUSING AND THE CUSTOMER

Understanding needs and delivering services

Edited by Joanna Richardson

Chartered Institute of Housing Practice Studies

in collaboration with

the Housing Studies Association

The Chartered Institute of Housing

The Chartered Institute of Housing (CIH) is the professional body for people involved in housing and communities. We are a registered charity and not-for-profit organisation. We have a diverse and growing membership of over 22,000 people – both in the public and private sectors – living and working in over 20 countries on five continents across the world. We exist to maximise the contribution that housing professionals make to the wellbeing of communities. Our vision is to be the first point of contact for – and the credible voice of – anyone involved or interested in housing.

Chartered Institute of Housing
Octavia House, Westwood Way, Coventry CV4 8JP
Tel: 024 7685 1700
Email: customer.services@cih.org
Website: www.cih.org

The Housing Studies Association

The Housing Studies Association promotes the study of housing by bringing together housing researchers with others interested in housing research in the housing policy and practitioner communities. It acts as a voice for housing research by organising conferences and seminars, lobbying government and other agencies and providing services to members.

The CIH Housing Practice Studies are published in collaboration with the Housing Studies Association and aim to provide important and valuable material and insights for housing managers, staff, students, trainers and policy-makers. Books in the series are designed to promote debate, but the contents do not necessarily reflect the views of the CIH or the HSA.

Cover photographs: Affinity Sutton

ISBN: 978-1-905018-79-6

Housing and the Customer: Understanding needs and delivering services
Edited by Joanna Richardson

Published by the Chartered Institute of Housing
© 2010
Printed on FSC stock from sustainable sources by Hobbs the Printers Ltd, Totton, Hampshire SO40 3WX

Whilst all reasonable care and attention has been taken in compiling this publication, the authors, the publishers, the Editorial Team and its advisers regret that they cannot assume responsibility for any error or omission that it contains.

All rights reserved. No part of this publication may be reproduced, stored in a retrieval system or transmitted in any form or by any means, electronic, mechanical, photocopying, recording, or otherwise without the prior permission of the Chartered Institute of Housing.

Contents

List of figures	iv
List of acronyms	vi
Acknowledgments	vii
Notes on contributing authors	viii
Foreword	xi

PART ONE: CONTEXT — 1

Chapter 1: Setting the context: the need for a customer-focused approach in social housing — 2
Joanna Richardson

Chapter 2: Customer voice: the changing context for listening to and involving service users — 16
Tim Brown, Joanna Richardson and Nicola Yates

Chapter 3: Customer models and their application to social housing: a marketing approach — 32
Tony Garry and Joanna Richardson

PART TWO: POLICIES AND ISSUES — 49

Chapter 4: Who is the customer? — 50
John Bloxsom and Joanna Richardson

Chapter 5: What do customers want? — 68
John Perry

Chapter 6: The revolting customer? – the meaning of customer satisfaction — 87
Tim Brown and Nicola Yates

Chapter 7: Customer Relationship Management and Customer Insight: knowing and satisfying the customer — 105
Joanna Richardson

| Chapter 8: | Brand: new products and new markets | 125 |
| | Kerry James and Joanna Richardson | |

| Chapter 9: | Putting the 'social' into marketing | 145 |
| | Joanna Richardson | |

| Chapter 10: | The power of communication – talking and listening to the customer | 161 |
| | Kerry James, Joanna Richardson and Nicola Winn | |

| Chapter 11: | 'Selling' social housing: marketing campaigns and advertising | 185 |
| | Kerry James and Nicola Winn | |

| Chapter 12: | Change management | 206 |
| | Joanna Richardson | |

PART THREE: CONCLUSIONS — 223

| Chapter 13: | Conclusions and next steps | 224 |
| | Joanna Richardson | |

Index — 231

List of figures

1.1	Housing in England by tenure type	4
1.2	House repossessions	5
1.3	New-build completions	6
1.4	Citizen/consumer – binary distinctions	8
3.1	Spectrum of public services	35
3.2	The consumer decision-making process	37
3.3	Categories of consumer-provider relationships in the public sector	39
3.4	Primary and secondary decision-makers within the public sector	40
3.5	The seven Ps of the housing marketing mix	44
4.1	Economic status by tenure type for 2008-2009	51
4.2	Diversity within diversity	54
4.3	Social tenants by age	58
5.1	Top ten reasons preventing a homebuyer settling on a house	70
6.1	Customer satisfaction and performance	101
7.1	Don't be a DRIP	108

7.2	Decision-making processes	110
7.3	Key strands of Customer Insight	112
7.4	Framework for improving research and intelligence management	115
7.5	Mosaic public sector 15 groups and types	117
7.6	Profile of resident groups	120
8.1	Perceptions of brand	127
8.2	Expression of the brand	127
8.3	Kinds of place	140
8.4	City decay dynamics	141
9.1	'Selling' new affordable housing development to a local community	149
9.2	Factors influencing behaviour	150
9.3	Cognitive dissonance (or the value/action gap)	152
9.4	Nudge/Think	157
10.1	Communications model	162
10.2	Government priorities and role of communications	163
10.3	Communications triangle	164
10.4	Harvest Housing Group customer involvement mechanisms	166
10.5	Winn's wheel: different approaches to communication and engagement	174
10.6	Me and my network community	179
10.7	Types of crowd-sourcing	181
11.1	From point A to point B	187
11.2	Flow chart for creative brief	197
12.1	Individual responses to change	210
12.2	Force field analysis	217
12.3	Snakes and ladders of change management	221

List of acronyms

ALMO	Arms length management organisation
BANANA	Build Absolutely Nothing Anywhere Near Anyone
BME	Black and minority ethnic (groups)
CBL	Choice-based Lettings
CI	Customer Insight
CIH	Chartered Institute of Housing
CLG	Department for Communities and Local Government
CRM	Customer Relationship Management
CSE	Customer Service Ethos
DRIP	Data Rich Information Poor
DIY	Do It Yourself
DMU	Decision-Making Unit
HCA	Homes and Communities Agency
HECS	Housing and Employment Connections Service
ICT	Information Communications Technology
LAA	Local Area Agreements
LGA	Local Government Association
LCHO	Low Cost Home Ownership
LSP	Local Strategic Partnerships
LULU	Local Unwanted Land Use
NHF	National Housing Federation
NI	National Indicator
NIMBY	Not In My Back Yard
NIMTO	Not In My Term of Office
NTV	National Tenant Voice
PSE	Public Service Ethos
RP	Restorative Practices
STATUS	Standardised Tenant Satisfaction Surveys
TQM	Total Quality Management
TSA	Tenant Services Authority
WIIFM	What's In It For Me?
WIMBY	Welcome In My Back Yard
YIMBY	Yes In My Back Yard

Acknowledgements

The editor would like to thank all of the contributing authors for their expertise and insight, and their good humour in meeting deadlines. Special thanks are due to Kerry James for her infectious enthusiasm and hard work and to Tim Brown for advice. Thank you to John Perry at the Chartered Institute of Housing for support and guidance throughout the writing and editing of the book, and to Jeremy Spencer for design and production. Also, thank you to Deborah Bennett at Seven Locks Housing Association and Lourdes Sharpe at Solihull Community Housing for inspiration and insight. All of the contributors to the book would like to acknowledge the interesting examples provided from a range of housing and other organisations which help to illustrate key points.

The Chartered Institute of Housing thank Affinity Sutton for their sponsorship of this book.

Notes on contributing authors

Joanna Richardson is Principal Lecturer at the Centre for Comparative Housing Research, De Montfort University. She has been a member of the Chartered Management Institute since 2001 and is also a fellow of the Chartered Institute of Housing. Jo has written a variety of publications, including a (2006) book *Talking about Gypsies: the notion of discourse as control* as well as a report published by the Joseph Rowntree Foundation and the CIH in October 2007 *Providing Gypsy and Traveller Sites: Contentious Spaces.* Her most recent publication (2010) is a book for Policy Press *From Recession to Renewal: the impact of the financial crisis on public services and local government.*

John Bloxsom is a Service Director for Housing and Planning in Leicester, Leicestershire & Rutland. He is a former head of housing and homelessness manager. John has developed housing and regeneration partnerships and programmes and established Derby Homes, one of the first high-performing ALMOs to deliver decent homes. He has undertaken consultancy, research and interim management projects for a wide range of national, regional and local clients including the Housing Corporation, Government Offices, local authorities, housing associations and ALMOs. He has written studies on the accommodation needs of BME groups, refugees and Gypsies and Travellers. He is a Fellow of the Chartered Institute of Housing and holds the Public Services MBA with distinction from the University of Birmingham. John is a registered PRINCE2 Practitioner and an independent Board Member of Derby Homes Ltd.

Tim Brown is Director of the Centre for Comparative Housing Research at De Montfort University. He is a Corporate Member of the Chartered Institute of Housing. Tim is course leader for the MSc in Business for Housing and teaches on a wide range of undergraduate and postgraduate programmes include MBAs. He has written widely on choice-based lettings in academic journals and has contributed to two government good practice guides on this topic. Tim has spoken at national and internal conferences on the challenges of adopting a customer approach in social housing. Currently he is working on a project that is investigating the advantages and disadvantages of the new policy and performance framework of Local Area Agreements and national indicators.

Tony Garry is a Senior Lecturer in Marketing in the Department of Management at the University of Canterbury, New Zealand. Having worked in both the public and private sector with organisations as diverse as Hewlett Packard, BT and the Greater London Council (GLC), Tony is able to bring both experience and understanding of industrial work practices to his work. He is a Chartered Marketer and a member of both the Chartered Institute of Marketing and the Academy of Marketing. His research interests are wide and varied and include services marketing, relationship and network marketing and consumption communities and tribes within both offline and online contexts. His research outputs have been published in journals such as the *Journal of Marketing Management*, *Journal of Services Marketing*, *Journal of Consumer Behaviour* and the *Journal of Business and Industrial Marketing*. He has also co-authored a book on relationship marketing.

Kerry James is Marketing Director at The Bridge Group. Kerry is a full member of the Chartered Institute of Marketing and fellow of the Chartered Institute of Housing, Kerry holds a first-class honours degree in housing and has more than 20 years' sector experience. She has provided marketing and communications support to more than 40 housing organisations, including the CIH, HouseMark, TPAS and a range of RSLs and local authorities across England and Wales. She has also spoken at numerous CIH, National Housing Federation and Community Housing Cymru events on issues such as targeted publications, e-communications and the secrets of successful campaigns.

John Perry was Director of Policy at CIH for twelve years until early 2003. He took the lead on a range of issues including housing investment, housing strategies and welfare reform. Since March 2003 he has been based in Nicaragua, where he helps co-ordinate projects with low-income farming families, including the installation of solar panels in homes without electricity (see www.cih.org/nicaragua for further details). He is now part-time Policy Adviser to the Institute, and his recent UK work has been on housing finance and the future of ALMOs, community cohesion, refugees and migration, and housing and climate change. He has co-authored books such as *Housing Finance* and *Housing, the Environment and Our Changing Climate*.

Nicola Winn is Managing Director at The Bridge Group, a leading marketing and communications consultancy which specialises in housing. A Fellow of the CIH and former branch committee chair, Nicola's housing career spans more than 20 years. Her experience includes developing and accrediting qualifications within the sector, pursuing business development opportunities for a large Midlands RSL and providing communications advice to the UK's first community gateway association. She also provides strategic communications input to housing groups pursuing merger and transformational change.

Nicola Yates is Chief Executive of Kingston-upon-Hull City Council and was previously Deputy Chief Executive. Prior to this, she was Chief Executive of North Shropshire District Council and Services Director at Harborough District Council. Nicola is also an Honorary Research Associate at the Centre for Comparative Housing Research at De Montfort University. Kingston-upon-Hull City Council was rated as the most improved local authority in England in 2010. At North Shropshire, she led on the delivery of a programme of service improvements. The Audit Commission in its new Comprehensive Performance Assessment in 2008 rated the local authority as 'good' compared with 'poor' in 2004, and highlighted the significant improvements in services outcomes for customers and local communities. At Harborough District Council, Nicola led on the development and delivery of the first district-wide choice-based lettings scheme in Britain. She has written articles and chapters for books and good practice guides on a wide range of subjects include partnerships, choice-based lettings and supporting people. In 2010 Nicola was awarded the OBE for services to local government.

Foreword

We are all familiar with the mantra that the 'customer is king' but how many in the social housing world actually believe or practise it? As a sector, we have been somewhat in denial, telling ourselves that our tenants are not customers because they don't have customer choice – well that is changing as we look to better understand the needs of our tenants/customers. It's not just people power that we need to respond to though. The political landscape is changing at a pace, while the economic environment means we are all looking at how we operate now and in the future.

Affinity Sutton was one of the first housing associations to adopt a customer-focused approach. My inspiration came from an unlikely but incredibly powerful source, a family holiday to the States in the early nineties. As well as being impressed by the general level of service and attentiveness, it was the systems behind it that intrigued me. How was it that they knew so much about me? I compared this with how we delivered services. Although individual colleagues knew customers well, we worked in isolation. We didn't have any way of understanding what worked and didn't work for our customers. And so our journey to get 'closer to our customers' began.

This journey took a mish mash of inconsistent, uncoordinated services provided by a myriad of local offices and replaced it with a planned, monitored and consistently good level of service led by a contact centre. But this still does not take into account the individual needs of our customers, nor the range of products we now provide. So we are developing a more marketing-based approach and improving our Customer Insight.

We want to get a better understanding of the real needs and views of our customers and move away from the 'one size fits all' approach. A better understanding of specific needs will make it easier for us to develop distinctive, innovative products aimed at particular groups. It's not just about new products though, a better understanding of our customers will mean we can work with them to better manage issues like arrears – something that will be increasingly important as the benefit changes come into effect.

And at Affinity Sutton we strongly believe in investing in our communities. Using Customer Insight we will be able to allocate our resources more effectively by focusing on those most likely to benefit. We will also be better placed to deliver messages on key issues like carbon reduction through developing different approaches to behaviour change.

For me this book is particularly timely as at Affinity Sutton we seek to get even 'closer to the customer'. This is not an academic exercise but about our desire to both *be* the best and *do* the best for our customers.

Neil McCall
Group Director of Operations
Affinity Sutton

PART ONE

CONTEXT

CHAPTER 1:
Setting the context: the need for a customer-focused approach in social housing

Joanna Richardson

Introduction

It is important that social housing organisations understand the needs of their existing and potential customers – who they are, what they need, and how services can best be delivered. This is particularly so following a recession and financial crisis, whose impacts will last well into the future, and that for some will result in unemployment and repossession of their homes. The book will examine the notion of the 'customer' in housing and some of the challenges in using customer-focused models in social provision. It will ground itself in the wider public policy and also business literature to show that, in the right context, there are lessons for the social housing sector from customer models, such as a marketing approach. Such an approach can help organisations deliver more efficient services and meet the current and future needs of their tenants and existing and potential customers. The book focuses mainly on the context for housing in England, but most of the key points are applicable across the UK and beyond; examples are drawn from England, but also Europe and the US.

This book will help social housing organisations to understand who their customers are and what they need and want from service providers. One of the results of organisations understanding customers' needs is that they can be more efficient in targeting resources and they can keep in touch with customers. These characteristics will not only help social housing organisations to meet their social and legal obligation of involving service users; but will also help them to win new business, keep and retain high-quality staff, maintain good relationships with lenders and investors, and win national awards and recognition. The diversity and the changing nature of existing and potential users of social housing and support services will be examined. The book will also offer a customer model, particularly focusing on a marketing approach, as a framework for understanding who the customer is, what they want from social housing, and how best organisations can offer good quality services that meet need and demand. Involving service users has long been important in the social housing sector and this book will explain how taking a marketing approach can provide the ultimate mechanism to allow existing and future service users to shape products and the quality of their delivery. It will offer practical examples (from within the sector and beyond) and provide illustrations of how performance can be improved through knowing your housing customers.

Housing business leaders and decision-makers need to know exactly what the purpose of their business is, how it is positioned both in the social housing sector and the wider economy, how the organisation can grow in existing and new markets and how current and potential customers can be communicated with effectively. At a time when the government is demanding value for money and efficiency, whilst promoting choice and customer satisfaction across the public sector, many housing providers are starting to realise the importance of marketing in understanding the context in which they operate and how best to secure new opportunities and position themselves effectively with key audiences.

The recent debate on housing reform following the Hills Review, the current debate on housing finance (including council housing finance) and the emerging conversation on tenant empowerment and involvement in governance structures are all examples of the public sector, and specifically social housing organisations, concerning themselves with understanding the users of services and the processes of delivery to improve efficiency. Understanding the current and future needs of existing tenants and potential customers is particularly relevant in the current economic climate where more people may need to use the services of the social housing sector.

There is an argument for using customer models both on a business level to drive efficient delivery of services, and on a 'social' level to properly understand current and future housing needs and aspirations of a diverse population and to deliver good quality services in order to maintain and improve tenant satisfaction. Feinstein *et al.* (2008) in their examination of the public value of social housing suggest:

> *It may be that understanding how the resources, capabilities, needs and values of diverse individuals and households interact to create communities within and across physical space is key to understanding what is meant by a mixed community* (p.42).

A customer focus/marketing approach can help achieve this understanding of capabilities, needs and values of the heterogeneous communities that make up the wider social housing customer base. Investigating and profiling these aspects is not part of a commercial drive to maximise income (although increasing efficiency is a good business case in the current economic climate), instead it is part of a conversation with people in our communities to understand who they are, what they need and how we can help them as individuals and communities.

Changing context

The social housing sector in England is undergoing key changes, in line with many other public services. However there are unique challenges in the housing profession that need special attention. These include:

- The blurring between public and private provision in the delivery of social housing – councils, registered providers (or housing associations), arms length management organisations (ALMOs) and other charitable and private providers.
- The vagaries of the market economy and its effect on the delivery of housing – the financial crisis will create new customers of social housing services, and it is important that organisations make customers aware of how they can help and the housing options available.
- The government focus on choice, empowerment, efficiency and value for money in the context of huge cuts in public sector budgets following the Comprehensive Spending Review 2010.

Individuals and households fulfil many different roles and cannot be seen solely in terms of 'tenant'. They are also customers, citizens and members of the community. One can look at other areas of public service provision, such as healthcare, for examples of a customer approach through personalisation of services and the use of individual budgets. The multiple and complex functions of social housing providers, delivering not just bricks and mortar accommodation, but also homelessness advice, neighbourhood management, liaison with private rented providers, extra care for vulnerable people and in some cases now financial services and nursery day care provision. The diversity of services provided, and of people in need of those services, provides a rationale for a more customer-focused approach.

Why social housing providers need to act

Figure 1.1: Housing in England by tenure type

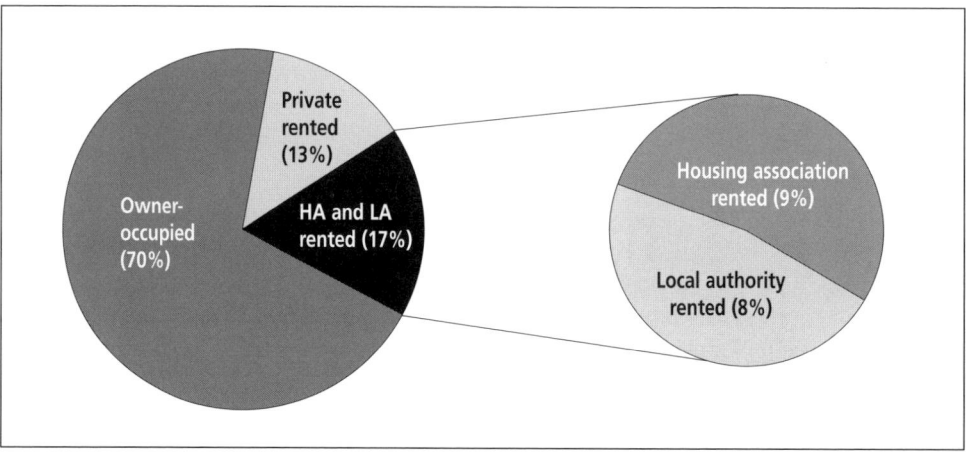

Source: *Housing and Planning Key Facts*, CLG, May 2010.

SETTING THE CONTEXT

Although the social housing sector is proportionately a small part of the total housing stock in England, there are particular needs associated with renters of social housing that have been compounded by the recent financial crisis (see further Richardson, 2010 and chapter 4 of this book).

Figure 1.2 below shows an increasing number of repossessions in recent years following the impact of the 2008 credit crunch and the ensuing financial crisis on people's ability to continue to pay their mortgage and so perhaps an increased need to provide social housing to those in need. The financial crisis clearly had an impact on homeowners, and indeed renters of private property whose landlord subsequently faced repossession – the Council for Mortgage Lenders reported in February 2010 that there had been 46,000 repossessions in 2009 and whilst this wasn't as high as predicted, it was an increase on the 2008 figure of 40,000 and a large increase on 2007 which saw 25,900.

Figure 1.2: House repossessions

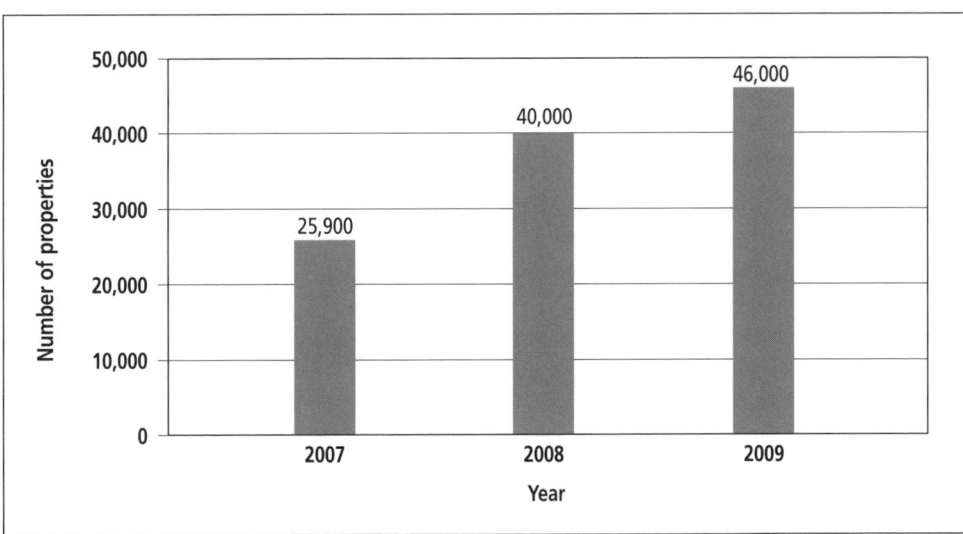

Source: *Housing and Planning Key Facts*, CLG, May 2010.

There is a recognised need for more affordable social housing (Shelter, 2008). The Housing Green Paper (2007) set targets to deliver 240,000 homes a year to meet growing demand: 2 million homes by 2016 and 3 million homes by 2020. Indeed, one can see from Figure 1.3 below that the social housing sector has attempted to increase new-build completions in recent years and has been more successful in this than the private sector. However, following the emergency budget set out by the new coalition government, and the Comprehensive Spending Review in October 2010, there will be limited funding for new house building going forward and so innovative ideas and funding streams will be needed.

Figure 1.3: New-build completions

Sector	2007-08	2008-09	2009-10
Private	144,740	108,080	88,630
Housing Association	23,100	25,510	24,740
Local Authority	300	520	300

Source: *Housing and Planning Key Facts*, CLG, May 2010.

The wider political, economic and social context has created a perfect storm of increased social need for services, but reduced resources for public agencies to deliver. Housing is such a fundamental need for people and the social housing sector such a key part of renewal and recovery in society that it is vital we do not retrench in the face of cuts, but that we continue to find innovative solutions to deliver good quality services to our housing customers.

Tenant, consumer, citizen: customer?

So, are tenants customers, really? I often ask students this question and the debate is never short and simple. Responses include issues of choice, welfare, efficiency, transaction, political ideology, resources, personal values, prejudice, access to services, need, supply and demand for housing, and so on. Some of the answers in favour of tenant as customer suggest that in the process of treating tenants as customers, efficiency and quality of service provision go up. Respondents who suggest that tenants cannot be customers usually focus on specific segments of long-term tenant who have not participated in a choice-based lettings process to select their home, are on benefits and so have no transactional process with the landlord, and have low aspirations for homeownership or employment. As we will see throughout this book, there is a huge diversity in the population of people using, or hoping to use, the services of social housing providers. Assuming tenants cannot be customers because they have no choice, is to fail to recognise the myriad different reasons people come to social housing, and choose to stay in the tenure.

Housing services as part of welfare provision, rather than customer transaction, is a powerful cultural and ideological context that explains the difficulty for some in engaging with the tenant as customer debate. Moore (1995) refers to a 'philosophy' of public service in his research in the US. In the UK, Pratchett and Wingfield (1996) discuss 'Public Service Ethos' (PSE) as having been largely resistant to pressure for change. They suggest that PSE is a political institution which structures governance and relationships between public servants across services; they underline the strength of this ethos:

> *Public servants do not simply share employment in public organizations. The nature of the employment carries with it a distinctive set of values and perceptions that shapes their attitudes and responses and provides a framework for interpreting and understanding relations with others* (p.654).

PSE and welfare provision then are important aspects of the context within which housing services are delivered; but this should not necessarily negate the social construction of 'customer' in housing services if both provider and consumer feel it drives efficiencies. The knowledge and values of people working in housing and in wider public services is embedded in everyday networks (see further Durose, 2009) and a customer service ethos (or customer focus/marketing approach which is referred to throughout the book) is a challenge to deep rooted ideals of PSE; but it should not be ignored because of the discomfort of traditionalists. Perhaps PSE has been diluted somewhat already. Clarke and Newman (2009) say that:

> *Public services have been fragmented into multiple providers, many located in the private or third sectors or multi-sectoral hybrids, whose employees are not 'public servants' in the conventional sense. Tracing publicness in these emergent fields is problematic: is it to be found in finance, in governance arrangements, in regulatory surveillance or embodied in the 'end users' (members of the public)?* (p.3).

So is it possible that Public Service Ethos (PSE) and Customer Service Ethos (CSE) are mutually exclusive opposing forces and that the challenges of bringing the two together are too burdensome to overcome? Clearly, the authors in this book do not think so. We believe instead that tenants can be seen as customers without necessarily undermining ideals of public service and welfare. Indeed 'public' service according to Newman and Clarke (2009) is itself contested and may perhaps be embodied in the 'end user'. If that is the case then a focus on the end user/consumer/citizen/tenant/customer may help to define public services themselves as they shift in changing contexts and realities. As we will see in a number of examples (see for instance chapter 9), the commercial sector is learning from the public sector in the instance of social marketing – so CSE does not have to undermine social values and PSE is not necessarily so financially draining as to be non-viable in the commercial sector – the two can live together. Indeed attempts have even been made to quantify CSE in some regards: Cole and Parston (2006) refer to public sector managers being inspired by commercial sector Shareholder Value Analysis to define and increase 'Public Service Value'.

Needham's (2006) research warned caution in the untrammelled application of 'customer care ethos' in public services. She suggested that *'...there is broad endorsement of customer terminology but inconsistency in its interpretation'* (p.857). Simmons, Powell and Greener (2009) also examine the consumer in public services, (see further Mills' (2009) chapter in their book which examines citizens, clients and consumers in housing). Clarke *et al.* (2007) set out a series of 'binary distinctions' which are embodied in the general terms 'citizen' and 'consumer':

Figure 1.4: Citizen/consumer – binary distinctions

Citizen	Consumer
• State • Public • Political • Collective • De-commodification • Rights	• Market • Private • Economic • Individual • Commodification • Exchange

Source: Clarke *et al.*, 2007.

They acknowledge that these are simplified and that there are a number of associated complications to consider. Clarke *et al.* (2007) refer to contestations not just of the label 'consumer' but also of 'citizen' which is not a straightforward concept. They also suggest that where traditional notions of passivity or activity may be ascribed to each of these labels, the reality is more varied and complex than that.

Flint (2004) discusses a politics of behaviour that has been shaping tenants into 'responsible and responsive' citizens through a wider set of rationales and processes of governance. He says:

> *In this process we are witnessing a deepening of tenant responsibility, through increasing individual agency and accountability in relation to housing allocation, rent payments and maintenance of properties. We are also seeing a widening of tenants' responsibility including engagement in community activities, greater participation in strategic housing management decisions and undertaking more active responses to anti-social behaviour* (p.907).

No matter what label is applied to the people who live in social housing (tenant or customer) there has been a shift in perception both on the part of service provider and user. Tenants are no longer seen as passive recipients of a service, but are being shaped by government and agencies to take responsibility not only for the service they receive, but for wider community cohesion and governance issues. Fung (2004) refers to 'empowered participation' as part of a changing pattern of urban democracy in the US. This reflects the growing activity of public service users and starts to chip away at the defence that tenants cannot be customers because they are passive welfare recipients.

And so, this book is unashamedly called *Housing and the Customer*. We do not trample on the ideals and values of welfare and public service – these are especially important concepts in a time of growing need following a recession. However, having debated the notion of citizen, consumer and customer, and knowing the diversity of the people that housing services aim to provide for (as is explored in chapter 4 and throughout the book) we suggest that tenants can be customers; that the people housing organisations deliver services to goes way beyond the tenant in any case, and that 'customer' is not a dirty word in the public sector. There are challenges which have been outlined in this opening chapter, but they are not insurmountable and should not result in a retrenchment to old ways, but instead should provide a platform for seeing the business and social case for a customer focus/marketing approach to service delivery in the housing sector.

Framework for the book

The book is broadly divided into three parts. Part one provides the context for examining housing and the customer, including the current political, economic and regulatory environment. Policies and issues are the focus of part two, and a range of themes are discussed throughout the book including an examination of who the customer is, what they want, what customer satisfaction might look like and how customer insight can be achieved. We also examine the importance of brand, advertising, positioning, communications and change management, as well as the merits of social marketing. The third part of the book concludes and looks at next steps for housing and the customer.

This **first chapter** has begun by setting out the context and then exploring the notion of the 'customer' in housing. Individuals and households fulfil many different roles and cannot be seen solely in terms of 'tenant'. They are also customers, citizens and members of the community. One can look at other areas of public service provision, such as healthcare, for examples of a customer approach through personalisation of services and the use of individual budgets. The arguments throughout the book will demonstrate that there is a rationale for using customer models both on a business level to drive efficient delivery of services, and on a 'social' level to properly understand current and future housing needs and aspirations of a diverse population and to deliver good quality services in order to maintain and improve tenant satisfaction.

Chapter 2 outlines the broad changes occurring in the regulatory framework for the social housing sector. The coalition government which came to power in May 2010 announced the abolition of a number of agencies (such as the Audit Commission) and the review of others, including the Tenant Services Authority (TSA) which was established following the Cave Review (2007). Government also announced the cutting of funding for organisations like the National Tenant Voice (NTV) and there is discussion of the impact this will have for 'customer voice'[1] in the sector. This chapter examines the changing policy-making and performance management framework for local government and other public service providers, e.g. Local Area Agreements (LAAs) and the need for co-ordinated approaches to service delivery. The coalition government announced its ideas including 'big society' and 'localism' and chapter 2 examines these ideas to find the place of customer voice.

Customer models in the social provision of housing services will be explored and particularly the usefulness of a marketing approach will be examined in **chapter 3**. We demonstrate that with sensitive and appropriate use (rather than just transplanting a business model into a social provision environment), a marketing approach and similar models can help social housing organisations know who their current and future customers are, and help them to involve the service user to shape the service and improve the quality of its delivery. This chapter teases out the challenges to applying marketing principles; but it will advocate that much can be learnt from them, in order to improve social housing efficacy. The chapter will include some fundamental principles of a marketing approach to provide tools that can be adapted as a framework for organisations to better understand themselves and their customers. This will include definitions and fundamental principles of marketing as they can be applied to the social housing sector, such as the marketing mix: seven Ps of services marketing. Frameworks for understanding markets, in order to position housing businesses, will also be explored.

Chapter 4 is dominated by the need to examine exactly who our customers are. The diversity of tenants and the wider existing and future customer base is further explored and there is discussion of the equalities framework and the policy context for housing organisations. Not all customers have the skills necessary to engage with customer models such as choice-based lettings for example (e.g. computer skills, literacy and knowledge of services and support that is available in the area), and they need the support and advice of public agencies, including social housing providers, to help access services. It is debated though that a customer focus should not preclude those with additional support needs; indeed this approach should enable and empower people. This approach has been used in health and social care services where users have been provided with personalised services and they have been able

---

1   'Voice' is complex and is debated further in the book. Put simply we mean the ability of tenants to be heard – this can be tied up in the systems of tenant participation, the processes of communication that a registered provider has for its customers and partners; but it also involves a level of 'agency' which relates to both the ability and skills needed for customers to have a voice, and 'empowerment' which connects to the ways in which tenants' views are allowed to be heard by those in power.

to utilise individual budgets. The diversity of need and aspiration, not just for individual services, but aspirations for diversity of tenure, income and ethnicity in neighbourhoods in order to avoid residualisation within, and social exclusion of, some areas is also debated. The diversity of services provided, and of people in need of those services, provides a rationale for a more customer-focused approach.

What do customers want and how do social housing providers respond? **Chapter 5** explores customers' needs and demands. The author examines how organisations respond to tenant aspirations and the individual and collective choices that can be offered; and the development of ideas on choice generally within public services and housing is investigated. International examples are provided, most particularly a comparison with the Netherlands. Whilst much can be learnt from abroad, the author cautions the need to look at examples to provoke thought, rather than as an idea which can be directly transplanted.

Chapter 6 examines the concept and reality of customer satisfaction, which is explored through a focus on quality of product/service, process and the image of the organisation. It is argued that high levels of customer satisfaction will only be achieved when all three aspects of quality are addressed. Links are also apparent with the theme of 'voice' in chapter 2; in particular, Hirschman's (2007) theory on voice and exit[2] are explored and its implications for social housing businesses examined. The chapter examines existing data and information on customer satisfaction analysing a number of recurring findings from research studies. The authors suggest that significant improvements in the performance of councils and housing associations as assessed by external regulatory bodies such as the Audit Commission will be contrasted with data from national and local surveys that show at best a very modest increase in customer satisfaction. Growing satisfaction levels are evident with some specific services that customers use; but there can remain a continued dissatisfaction with the organisation as a whole in some public sector organisations; rising customer aspirations and expectations that are not necessarily matched by the services provided by organisations. The implications of these issues for taking forward the agenda for delivering better quality public services are discussed, including: the adequacy of performance indicators and customer surveys, the (ir)relevance of performance indicators and the opportunities presented by whole systems thinking (such as John Seddon's Systems Thinking approach); as well as the personalisation and choice agenda, public value and co-production[3] of services.

---

2   Again, this concept it explored in depth in chapter 6, but broadly 'exit' refers to the ability to leave the service being provided. If I don't enjoy the service provided to me by one car insurance company I am able to shop around for a better service and leave. This is not the case for some tenants of social housing – they have no option to 'exit' as there is no other home for them to go to within their means.
3   'Co-production' is another complex term. However, broadly put, it refers to service users and customers being involved in the design and delivery of a product or service. Participatory budgeting may be seen as one example of co-production and there are many examples of local services across the country where community groups and residents' associations provide a service along with the council or registered provider – sometimes this can be a step to fully devolving the service to the community and we may see more and more of this as the meat is put on the 'big society' bones.

Chapter 7 focuses on a critical analysis of the application of customer relationship management (CRM) principles to social housing organisations. Over the last decade there has been a spectacular growth directly and indirectly in a desire to put the 'customer first'. This is evidenced by the appointment of customer relations managers, establishment of call centres and one-stop shops, and regulatory requirements focussing on access and customer care. But does this and should this amount to CRM? Traditional customer relationship management models are often data rich, but information poor. Customer Insight is more about using the information that organisations have and utilising it better to understand need and demand for services. Drawing on the development of CRM in the private sector, the chapter emphasises the importance of knowing the customer in developing and delivering quality services. Chapter 7 suggests that housing organisations have a substantial amount of data on their customers but little effective use is made of it in designing and implementing a proactive approach to meet customer aspirations and expectations. Techniques for making more effective use of internal data are examined including methods such as customer segmentation. In addition, there is an examination of the relevance of commercial classification systems such as ACORN and MOSAIC.

The **eighth chapter** of the book links back to the diversity of the customer but also focuses on how social housing organisations can offer a range of products and services to people who previously may not have considered themselves to be a social housing customer. It is important in the current economic climate, for social housing providers to reach out and help people who have previously not needed the services of local authorities and housing associations, and to provide new products and services as housing needs change. This chapter explains concepts of brand development and management and their application to the social housing market. A key focus is on the diversity of service users and potential future customers. The existing customer base is already heterogeneous, but there will be more customers as a result of the recession with a differing range of needs. Chapter 8 also emphasises the challenge of the diversification of markets. For example, housing associations are not just limited to the provision of bricks and mortar housing but also associated new service provision, such as child day-care, financial packages, HomeBuy and so on. The concept of developing brands through the creation and development of markets and the targeting of new customer segments is discussed. In an economic downturn, the need to look at new products and services to meet changing customer needs is vital – for example the government fund to purchase empty homes and the scheme for social housing providers to buy back properties from people in financial difficulty.

Chapter 9 examines the concept of 'social marketing' and looks at some of the principles that have been in use in the health sector and other public arena for some time. Social marketing concerns itself with the application of the marketing mix, along with other concepts and strategies, in order to affect behaviour for a social or public good. There are many examples in the health sector (for example healthy eating, smoking cessation and exercise campaigns) as well as in policing and transport (seatbelt and tired driving campaigns). Case studies from a range of public sector agencies are used in the chapter to explain what social marketing aims to do and how it can be applied in housing. Social marketing can help to promote diversity and challenge behaviours that threaten cohesive communities, its application could help in particular cases of racial tension – for example in cases where there has been extreme hostility to proposed Gypsy and Traveller sites, positive campaigns about the culture of these recognised ethnic minority groups have helped to ease tension (Richardson, 2007). The application of social marketing techniques could also help to change behaviours in, say, the understanding of, and take-up, of welfare benefits. The chapter offers suggestions for adapting social marketing for use in the housing sector.

Chapter 10 looks at the importance of communication and information in empowering customers. There is an increasing body of work examining the collective power of social networking to create new services to quickly respond to a growing need. This new media has a big impact for the public sector generally but also the social housing sector. Following on from this contextual debate, this chapter focuses more on practical tools to reach a diverse customer audience. It looks at principles of good communications strategies and explores the different media needed to talk to internal and external customers of the organisation. It also reflects back on the importance of knowing the customer and being able to segment the audience so that messages can be targeted appropriately. It provides an overview of approaches to market segmentation from a housing sector perspective and discusses the increasing importance of ICT and electronic marketing media as part of an organisation's marketing mix.

The fundamental principles and models of advertising are examined in **chapter 11**, with examples and case studies of a range of campaigns from the housing sector. A number of different scenarios require advertising campaigns – from advertising single properties, through to advertising 'whole organisation' concepts such as stock transfer – and the range of possibilities is critically analysed here. Whilst the debate is grounded in principles and models, there is a greater focus on what works and what doesn't work in marketing and advertising campaigns in the social housing sector and the wider public sector.

In **chapter 12**, the book looks at how organisations can deal with the changing context for service delivery in the new performance management and regulatory frameworks, shifting needs and aspirations of existing tenants and a diverse range of potential customers? This chapter includes some change management models and tools so that executive and non-executive leaders can see how best to manage change and deal with issues as they arise. It provides a framework for organisations to understand the changing context around them, both as a result of policy and regulatory change, but also changes in local customer needs and aspirations.

The concluding **chapter 13** reviews the key messages on taking forward some of the principles discussed throughout the book. There is critical reflection on the appropriateness of using a marketing approach for social housing – on both a business and a social case – to involve service users, improve performance and increase customer satisfaction.

References and further reading

Beuret, K. and Hall, R. (1998) *Marketing in Local Government*. London: Financial Times Management.

Clarke, J., Newman, J., Smith, N., Vidler, E. and Westmarland, L. (2007) *Creating Citizen-Consumers, Changing Publics and Changing Public Services*. London: Sage.

Cole, I., Kane, S. and Robinson, D. (1999) *Changing Demand, Changing Neighbourhoods: The Response of Social Landlords*. Centre for Regional Economic and Social Research.

Cole, G.A. (1996) *Management Theory and Practice*. London: Continuum.

Cole, M. and Parston, G. (2006) *Unlocking Public Value, A New Model for Achieving High Performance in Public Service Organisations*. New Jersey: John Wiley & Sons.

Communities and Local Government (2008) *Communities in Control: Real People, Real Power*. White Paper, July. London: CLG www.communities.gov.uk

DETR (2000) *Quality and Choice: A Decent Home for All*. Housing Green Paper.

Durose, C. (2009) 'Front-Line Workers and 'Local Knowledge': neighbourhood stories in contemporary UK local governance', *Public Administration*, Vol. 87, No. 1, pp.35-49.

Feinstein, L., Lupton, R., Hammond, C., Mujtaba, T., Salter, E. and Dorhaindo, A. (2008) *The Public Value of Social Housing: A Longitudinal Analysis of the Relationship Between Housing and Life Chances*. London: The Smith Institute.

Flint, J. (2004) 'The Responsible Tenant: housing governance and the politics of behaviour', *Housing Studies*, Vol. 19, No. 6, pp.893-909.

Flynn, N. (2007) *Public Sector Management,* 5th ed. London: Sage.

Fung, A. (2004) *Empowered Participation, Reinventing Urban Democracy*. New Jersey: Princeton University Press.

Inside Housing (2010) 'Hyde sets its sights on £200m bond deal', *Inside Housing*, 5th February.

Le Grand, J. (2007) *The Other Invisible Hand, Delivering Public Services Through Choice and Competition*. New Jersey: Princeton University Press.

Lee, P. and Murie, A. (1999) 'Spatial and Social divisions within British Cities: beyond residualisation', *Housing Studies,* Vol. 14, No. 5.

Levine, R., Locke, C., Searls, D. and Weinberger, D. (2009) *The Cluetrain Manifesto*, 2nd ed. New York: Basic Books.

Mills, N. (2009) 'The Consumer and Social Housing' in Simmons, R., Powell, M. and Greener, I. (Eds.) (2009) *The Consumer in Public Services, Choice, Values and Difference*. Bristol: Policy Press.

Moore, M. (1995) *Creating Public Value: Strategic Management in Government*. Massachusetts: Harvard University Press.

Needham, C. (2006) 'Customer Care and the Public Service Ethos', *Public Administration*, Vol. 84, No. 4, pp.845-860.

Newman, J. and Clarke, J. (2009) *Publics, Politics & Power*. London: Sage.

Passmore, J. and Fergusson, S. (1994) *Customer Service in a Competitive Environment*. Coventry: Chartered Institute of Housing.

Pratchett, L. and Wingfield, M. (1996) 'Petty Bureaucracy and Woolly-Minded Liberalism? The Changing Ethos of Local Government Officers', *Public Administration*, Vol. 74, Winter, pp.639-656.

Sheaff, R. (2002) *Responsive Healthcare: Marketing for a public service*. Buckingham: OU Press.

Shelter (2008) *Homes for the future, a new analysis of housing need and demand in England*. London: Shelter.

Shelter (2009) *Ground Breaking, New Ideas on Housing Delivery*. London: Shelter.

Simmons, R., Powell, M. and Greener, I. (Eds.) (2009) *The Consumer in Public Services, Choice, Values and Difference*. Bristol: Policy Press.

Walker, R.M. (2000) 'The Changing Management of Social Housing: the impact of externalisation and managerialism', *Housing Studies,* Vol. 15, No. 2, pp.281-300.

CHAPTER 2:
Customer voice: the changing context for listening to and involving service users

Tim Brown, Joanna Richardson and Nicola Yates

Introduction

The aim of this chapter is to examine the changing framework for involving and listening to customers. The regulatory, policy-making and performance management frameworks have increasingly emphasised the importance of a customer orientation. But these are in a state of flux especially in England. For example, the Minister for Housing was quoted in summer 2010 saying the Tenant Services Authority (TSA), which was set up with the remit of being the 'tenants' champion', was 'toast'. In the government's (October 2010) review of social housing regulation, it was confirmed that the TSA would be abolished and that regulatory functions would be taken into the Homes and Communities Agency (HCA). The review aimed to ensure that regulatory and investment functions would retain their continued independence by legal separation of these functions through a statutory committee within the HCA. The review also suggests that 'co-regulation' principles should be further embedded – it puts the responsibility for effective service delivery with the landlord and makes clear that landlords are accountable to their tenants and not the regulator. The role of consumer regulation, says the review, '*...should be focused on setting clear service standards for social landlords and addressing serious failures against those standards.*'

This chapter aims to set out the issues. Specifically, we aim to set out the issues that will influence the direction of regulation, policy-making and performance management developments in relation to customers; clarify the relationship between service quality, user satisfaction and customer voice; and briefly summarise the relevance of broader debates on personalisation, choice, empowerment, co-production and localism. The chapter will also include lessons from other countries, principally the Netherlands, where there have been been considerable developments in involving and listening to customers; and it will draw attention to the emerging issues for housing organisations in engaging with customers and communities especially the need for collaboration and joined-up thinking between services and organisations.

Nevertheless, this chapter is part of the context setting agenda. More specific coverage of issues such as service quality and customer satisfaction can be found in chapter 6, while chapter 7 explores data on customers. It should also be noted that although the primary focus is on England, the principles apply equally to Scotland and Wales.

Policy-making, the regulatory framework and performance management

In England, customer voice and satisfaction are increasingly part of a wider debate on performance management, policy-making and regulation. The Cave Review argued strongly for a tenant-centred approach to regulation (Cave, 2007). This was taken forward with the creation of the TSA in the Housing and Regeneration Act 2008. But, the performance management, policy-making and regulatory frameworks underpinning public services have been changing and will continue to develop under the coalition government. It has been announced that both the Audit Commission and the Tenant Services Authority (TSA) will be abolished through the Localism and Decentralisation Bill in 2011. There is also a strong commitment to continue a 'bonfire' of targets and indicators. This can be seen in findings of the review of social housing regulation that 'co-regulation' should be enhanced, that regulation is for serious failings and that ultimately landlords are responsible to tenants, not top-down regulation and targets.

Policy-making: from command and control to localism?

'Localism' and the 'big society' (together with, of course, a reduction in public expenditure) are the key themes of the Communities and Local Government strategy. In some respects, this represents continuation rather than change from the previous government and its double devolution agenda. The role of councils as strategic enablers and place-shapers continues to be emphasised across the political spectrum. Until replaced, the key local policy document is still the sustainable community strategy that sets out priorities in terms of, for example, customer services and geographical areas. This is owned by a Local Strategic Partnership that comprises the council, other stakeholders and, in some cases, community/resident organisations.

Under the previous government, delivery at county and unitary levels was through Local Area Agreements (LAAs) that were signed off by the government and the Local Strategic Partnership (LSP). They comprised up to 35 from a national list of nearly 200 national policy indicators. LSPs could additionally select further indicators to reflect local circumstances. The national indicators included some limited measures of housing performance, e.g. percentage of non-decent council houses, net additional homes provided and the proportion of vulnerable people achieving independent living. There have been specific customer service indicators such as local authority tenants' satisfaction with landlord services and reducing avoidable contact between the citizen and the local authority. Analysis of LAAs has shown a mixed picture for housing and a customer orientation (Cooper, 2009). Only one out of 152 LAAs selected local authority tenants' satisfaction as a priority, while net additional homes was the third most selected indicator.

This raises interesting issues for the new localist agenda. Despite the reduction from over 1300 Best Value performance indicators for councils to less than 200 national indicators (NIs) and up to 35 priorities, the LAA system retained a command and control culture. Government departments emphasised in negotiations with councils and their LSPs that specific NIs should be identified as priorities. LAAs have been abandoned as part of the comprehensive spending review in October 2010, leaving the field open for local prioritisation. The 'government' announced in summer 2010 that it was culling the Comprehensive Area Assessments and also the Audit Commission itself – the assessments had monitored and evaluated the performance of public services in an area and the impact on quality of life. It remains to be seen whether the further development of a cluster of initiatives associated with 'big society' and localism will in reality represent a shift from command and control. Indeed, cutbacks in public expenditure could result in little room to manoeuvre at the local level in terms of priorities such as the design and delivery of customer-focused services. However, there are opportunities to radically rethink service provision. The previous government initiated a series of Total Place pilots that centred on bringing together the resources of public sector bodies to deliver better customer services more efficiently. This agenda is being taken forward in a more limited form by the Local Government Association through its place-based budgets concept and by the government (see, for example, the Local Government Association and *Municipal Journal*, 2010).

The regulatory framework: separating customer and economic regulation?

It is far still from clear exactly how the regulatory framework will operate by the middle of this decade. There are well-established principles that represent a continuation with the previous government. These include a more straightforward and simpler regulatory system. The Labour government's Better Regulation Task Force signalled the need for more effective working between independent regulators, the importance of a focused approach based on the themes of proportionality and transparency, an emphasis on assessing value for money and financial sustainability, and a strong customer orientation.

The Cave Review and the setting up of the TSA as a 'champion for social housing tenants' were impressive examples of this final point. The foreword to the regulatory framework for social housing (TSA, 2010a, p.3) states:

> *Our standards and approach to regulation are fundamental to us in:*
> - *Ensuring a fair deal for tenants – who cannot in most cases simply vote with their feet and move to another provider if services are poor.*

The link to the broader debate on exit, voice and loyalty are further strengthened through one of the six standards – tenant involvement and empowerment. This emphasises that social housing landlords should provide choices, information and communications in the delivery of all standards. There should also be a clear approach for dealing with complaints. There is a focus on co-regulation i.e. tenants should be

CUSTOMER VOICE: THE CHANGING CONTEXT

able to be involved and empowered. Finally, landlords need to take account of the diversity of their tenants.

A crucial aspect of the TSA approach was the development of local standards. This centred on the development between tenants and landlords of a 'local offer' by April 2011. It is noteworthy in the guidance that the TSA expected providers to pay particular attention to the neighbourhood and community standard in relation to local area co-operation, which requires dialogue with Local Strategic Partnerships. There has been considerable progress on local offers with 39 pilot projects underway (TSA, 2010b). The local dimension ties in with the localism agenda of the coalition government and could be part of the way forward for regulation. Whilst the shape of the regulatory apparatus for social landlords will now change, the review of regulation states that clear standards will still be needed for consumer protection.

The changing volume of customer voice

There has been an increasingly loud customer voice in recent years in the social housing sector. Some representative organisations have long been established such as TAROE[4] and TPAS[5] but newer collectives have been stopped in their tracks before they have been able to say a word. The National Tenant Voice (NTV) has had government funding and support withdrawn. The schism between the government rhetoric of asking communities to speak up and provide for themselves, whilst cutting funding to the very agencies who can help to support that, has sent a confused message to tenants on the commitment of government to listening to tenants. At a time when radical changes are being mooted, such as the removal of lifetime council tenancies as announced by the Prime Minister in August, the strength of tenant and customer voice is important and yet faces erosion.

The rapid and deep cuts brought in by the coalition government in the summer of 2010 have resulted in other community-led or -inspired organisations facing closure. Two examples just in the Gypsy and Traveller community illustrate the point. First, there is the Robert Barton Trust, which did brilliant work in Glastonbury, Somerset for New Travellers, and which had to close in September because the agencies that helped to fund them had had their budgets cut and could no longer provide financial support. Secondly, the Community Law Partnership in Birmingham which provided advocacy and legal representation for Gypsies and Travellers in the courts on a range of issues, but particularly planning and human rights cases, faced the end of their social contract which threatened their existence. These organisations, like the NTV, are the support for communities to provide for themselves, which is what the coalition government is calling for through community empowerment and its 'big society' initiative.[6]

→

4 Tenants and Residents Organisations of England.
5 Tenant Participation Advisory Service.
6 'Big society', which was a major feature of the Conservative government's election manifesto in 2010, emphasises social responsibility rather than state control in developing a progressive society. Detailed manifesto pledges included funding independent community organisers to help people establish and run neighbourhood groups – see respublica website at http://www.respublica.org.uk/blog/2010/04/big-society-or-big-societies

> Hopi Sen (2007) put this nicely in his blog about funding for a running track in London:
>
> *Yet take away that financial support, take away that coaching support, increase the cost of access to facilities (or forget to invest in them) and before long, these little platoons will begin to suffer desertions… So the next time you hear a politician wittering on about the little platoons, ask yourself who'll pay for their rations, their equipment and their resources. If that's the part that is met with vagueness and woolliness, then be sceptical about how serious they are about really making a difference.*

However, much of the debate in the social housing sector has tended to focus on a customer-orientated approach at the expense of other regulatory issues such as sound internal governance, financial probity and value for money. There has been little robust research on the relationship between these issues and customer satisfaction. Nevertheless, there is a consensus among national stakeholders that poor quality of services for customers goes hand in hand with weaknesses in organisational and financial management. Economic and customer-orientated regulation will, thus, continue. Economic regulation is to become the responsibility of the Homes and Communities Agency. Customer regulation will primarily centre on 'voice' (including complaints) and and will largely be the responsibility of the housing provider itself and, for unresolved complaints, the Housing Ombudsman.

Performance management and quality

Although the policy context and the external regulatory framework are in a state of flux, social housing organisations need to continue to focus on performance management and quality. There is a wealth of material on general principles that has been summarised by Van Dooren *et al.* (2010). They argue that there are four perspectives. These relate to different elements of quality and are:

i. Production of service/product
ii. Competence and capacity
iii. Outputs
iv. Long-term sustainable results or outcomes.

The authors suggest that performance management should focus increasingly on the latter and that there should be less emphasis on processes and outputs.

This has considerable resonance with the housing sector (as well as with other public sector services). Seddon (2008), for example, has argued that the Labour government adopted a top-down performance management system based on inappropriate targets. An illustration of this is a requirement that councils and their partners should be operating a CBL system by the end of 2010. Irrespective of the merits or otherwise of CBL, the target is, according to Seddon, 'dumb'. It requires the adoption of a process that has been increasingly prescribed by the government without any thought given to local circumstances. At the same time, it centres on a process rather than an output or an outcome. The emphasis from a performance management position should be on tackling the housing and related needs of households. The increasing focus on the outcomes of housing advice services and personalisation as well as on 'who gets housed and why' through the allocations system, are a helpful development.

A recurring message from the coalition government has been the abandonment of targets to drive performance management. For example, regional house building targets have been abolished. But the announced abolition of the TSA, while cutting back on external standards, leaves unanswered the question as to who regulates the performance of social housing landlords from a customer perspective (see above).

Service quality, user satisfaction and customer voice

Having set out the policy-making, regulatory and performance management contexts, this section centres on the principles of delivering quality services. The key themes that are explored are (i) the definition of quality, (ii) impact of public expenditure cuts, and (iii) a customer perspective. As Cole and Parston (2006) have emphasised, the crucial issue is 'delivering better services at less cost'.

Quality services and public expenditure cuts

Quality of service has three dimensions. These are:

1. 'Fit for purpose' i.e. a housing repair is completed so that it functions satisfactorily
2. The service is carried out in a customer-friendly way e.g. choice of appointment for a repair
3. The service is carried out in a way which leaves the customer with a favourable impression of the organisation, e.g. they were treated expeditiously and courteously.

These three dimensions are sometimes referred to as:

1. Product
2. Process
3. Perception.

A service can only be good or high quality if all three elements are achieved. There is, of course, an extensive array of techniques and toolkits to ensure quality. Quality control is associated with the detection of errors after the delivery of the service or product. Quality assurance systems centre on ensuring that services and products are to a consistent standard. Total quality management (TQM) represents a cultural approach in which there is an ethos across the organisation of putting the customer first and providing services and products to a high standard 'first time and every time'.

Current thinking on delivering high-class public services focuses on aligning TQM with systems thinking. Seddon (2008) and Middleton (2010) have illustrated the consequences of services not meeting the expectations of customers in areas such as allocations and lettings, repairs and housing benefits. There is, for example, high failure demand involving organisations having to deal with customer complaints and queries. Seddon (2008, p.33) in a case study of a local authority housing benefits department found that nearly 80% of contacts with the public by telephone were due to failure demand e.g. difficulties filling in forms, lack of progress on claims etc. Only just over 20% of contacts centred on value demand i.e. making a housing benefit claim or providing up-to-date information. Seddon (2008) argues that if policies and processes are designed around the needs of customers, greater efficiencies will be achieved as waste (i.e. failure demand) is driven out of the system. High-quality services are therefore provided at less cost, so achieving what is often regarded as two contradictory objectives that the public want – less taxation and better services (Cole and Parston, 2006).

This raises important issues for the future direction of public services including housing. These debates were highlighted in the headlines in the *Society Guardian* Public Services supplement on 7 July 2010:

> 'Better, cheaper: mission impossible?'
> 'How to do more with less?'
> 'The key change is that now we're putting the person at the centre of the service…this has been long neglected.'

The 2020 Public Services Trust (2010) argues that a fundamental reappraisal is required of the design and delivery of public services. The existing model based on service silos and top-down command and control is unsustainable. Although immediate fiscal austerity packages may drive the debate, there are equally if not more important long-term challenges. For example, it is estimated that addressing the issues of child poverty and an ageing society would require an extra 4-6% of GDP to be spent on public services over the next two decades. From a customer perspective, the 2020 Public Services Trust (2010) indicates that, although public services have improved over the last decade, outcomes are still disappointing – improving educational attainment has not necessarily equipped young people with the appropriate skills and fear of crime and anti-social behaviour remain high.

In an era of spending cuts and public expenditure constraints (see further Richardson, 2010) to what extent can high-quality, customer-orientated services help contribute to efficiency savings?

> **Portsmouth City Council**, for example, has re-engineered its allocation and lettings policies. Previously there were over 12,500 households on its housing register and this was increasing each year despite annual reviews. But unless a household was in urgent need the likelihood of being rehoused was low. As a result, much of the contact between customers and the council was 'failure demand' such as raised expectations of being rehoused and requests to have 'points' reassessed. The system has been redesigned so that customers on, or seeking to join, the housing register are made aware of their chances of being offered a property. Those with relatively little likelihood of being rehoused are provided with advice and support on other options such as shared ownership, private renting, disabled facilities grants and floating support. The housing register now comprises 2,500 households and the focus is on 'value demand' i.e. the offer stage of the allocations process. Customer satisfaction levels have risen significantly.

Nevertheless, it is important not to be complacent. Indeed the LGA (2010, p.1) Reputation Report said that *'...satisfaction with public sector organisations is at the lowest ever since tracking began'*. The precise scale of the impact of cuts on housing organisations will remain unclear until the outcome of the comprehensive spending review is digested and analysed for the medium- and long-term impact. Even so, the coalition government's review of spending for 2010/2011 and the June Budget in 2010 clearly indicated that housing unlike health was not a protected service. Capital spending through the Homes and Communities Agency faced total cuts of £450 million in 2010/2011. The Department for Work and Pensions has targeted the housing benefit budget with proposals to reduce expenditure in 2014/2015 by £2 billion. Even more radical re-engineering of housing services will be required to meet these challenges and improve customer satisfaction – in other words, better services at less cost.

Customer voice and satisfaction

Over the last four decades, there has been a shift from the traditional welfare model of the state and public sector which saw professionals designing and delivering services to passive and grateful clients, towards a greater customer-orientated approach. An example of this is the change in lettings processes from a system based on professional judgment on need and available properties to choice-based lettings (CBL). Evidence from evaluation indicates that customers prefer the customer-focused approach.

> A review of **Harborough Home Search**, the first district-wide CBL scheme, found that 80% of homeseekers who responded to a postal questionnaire and who could compare the previous points-based system with the new choice-based lettings service, preferred the latter (Brown *et al.*, 2002).

Le Grand (2003) in a thought-provoking study on the public sector summarised these changes by suggesting recipients had become 'queens rather than knaves' i.e. users want to be empowered to make choices rather than be grateful for what is provided. Choice, empowerment and personalisation are now embedded in the public sector. Simmons, Powell and Greener (2009) illustrate their central role in health, social housing, education and social care. In relation to the health sector, it includes choice of GP and appointment times. In social housing, the previous government set a target in 2002 that all local authority allocations systems should be using choice-based lettings by the end of 2010. In education, the focus has centred on choice and type of school. From a social care viewpoint, personalisation though individual budgets has become a mainstream policy. There is a political consensus. The three main parties in England support the principles of choice, empowerment and personalisation for users of public services. The previous Labour government pledged to protect frontline services during the recession (HM Government, 2009). Principles included guaranteeing high-quality public services, using technology to ensure personalisation of services and empowering people to take an active role in improving their own life chances. The Conservative Party in its 'vision for Britain' emphasised that people expect to be able to make more decisions for themselves. 'Advancing opportunity means shifting power from the state to individuals and civic institutions, in order to open up this new world of freedom to everyone' (Conservative Party, 2009). The Liberal Democrats in a policy paper set down the principles for a mandatory universal service code to ensure high-quality standards for both the public and private sectors (Policy Projects Team, 2009). It included a commitment to 'ensure that people are able to make informed choices'.

'Choice', 'empowerment' and 'personalisation' are, however, terms that are often used in an unsatisfactory, interchangeable way. For the purpose of clarity, we use 'choice' to refer to the opportunities for users to choose the content and level of service, the provider and form of access. 'Empowerment' relates to the provision of information so that the user has the knowledge of what is on offer, by whom and how? The state has a major role in performing this enabling function. 'Personalisation' refers to the ability of the user to actively make informed decisions i.e. operationalising the concept of choice.

Customer voice is, thus, closely associated with choice, empowerment and personalisation. The phrase was highlighted by Hirschman (1970) in a study of how customers respond to organisations where there is an actual or perceived decline in quality. They can exit by withdrawing from the relationship, or they can voice through a communication of the complaint, grievance or proposal for change. Hirschman (1970) further suggested that exit and voice are affected by loyalty. Customers may exhibit brand loyalty that may limit exit and voice. Reviewers and later writers have pointed out the challenges of applying these ideas to the public sector where there is differential ability to exit or inability to choose other providers. This is, of course, especially relevant to an increasingly residualised social housing sector. Households with the financial ability to exit may do so through a switch to shared ownership or owner-occupation. Other households may be able to exit from a provider or a neighbourhood by transfer or, less likely, mutual exchange. The remaining households have only the voice option that becomes critical in the relationship between the organisation and the customer. This can be enhanced by loyalty rewards.

> **Irwell Valley Housing Association** in Greater Manchester initiated in 1998 a gold service standard (Brown (Ed.), 1999). Membership criteria included paying rent on time and abiding by tenancy agreements. Benefits comprised a faster repairs service, access to education and training grants, and service guarantees. This was taken forward and adopted by a number of housing associations.

It is noteworthy that research on social housing estates in the Netherlands (see below) has found that where both exit from the area or voice are perceived by residents as unrealistic options, then households retreat inside their own private space i.e. the home, and do not maintain involvement in the community.

Housing providers thus need to ensure that quality is maintained and enhanced. Analysing the reasons why their customers are exiting provides an early warning of an actual or supposed decline in the product, process and perception of the organisation. Facilitating and responding to voice similarly is vital in influencing the development and delivery of services.

There is a relationship between customer satisfaction and management performance. But the former is also affected by other factors such as the profile of the stock and tenants. For example, landlords with a higher proportion of flats have lower satisfaction rates. They are also lower satisfaction rates in areas where there is a high level of deprivation and where there is a large proportion of black and minority ethnic tenants. There is, finally, an on-going debate on whether the credit crunch, the recession and public expenditure cuts will result in lower satisfaction ratings for public services. In April 2010, the TSA was planning a review of the approach on tenant satisfaction (Hardman, 2010). Concerns had included, first, that the information is out of date as the STATUS surveys only have to be carried out every three years and, secondly, that data is not available at a neighbourhood level. (As it now transpires, the government intends to end the STATUS survey completely.)

These are vital issues if customer voice is going to be effective as part of choice, empowerment and personalisation. Measuring customer (dis)satisfaction is, therefore, crucial but this is not straightforward. This is discussed in more detail in chapter 6 of this book, by Brown and Yates.

The new and emerging policy agenda

Reduced regulation and top-down performance management along with public expenditure cuts, localism and 'big society' provide a heady cocktail of policy drivers. But what are the implications and consequences for housing and the customer? Notwithstanding the start-up time for new initiatives, there are four overlapping and interrelated themes. These are joined-up thinking, choice and empowerment, co-production and two-tier services. These are briefly discussed below and more details can be found in later chapters. The 2020 Public Services Trust (2010) argues that these comprise a radical and necessary agenda for change. They will increase public sector productivity, create social value, unlock and build community capacity and enhance citizen choices.

Partnerships, collaboration and joined-up thinking continue to be part of the public services agenda. The health, housing and social care interface will become more significant with the reforms proposed by the Department of Health and the big issues such as the cost of care and an ageing society. Personalisation through individual budgets in health and social care will present challenges to housing organisations from customers who wish to negotiate over the type and nature of housing services. Similarly, households approaching councils and housing associations seeking social housing may have a wide range of other demands and requirements such as employment and training needs.

> **Home Connections** has rolled out an information communications and technology (ICT) solution that goes beyond CBL and housing options to incorporate employment options. The housing and employment connections service (HECS) aims to address a key finding from the Hills Review (2006) that highlighted the increasing level of worklessness among social housing tenants. HECS centres on providing links to services that improve skills, help to locate suitable jobs and provide volunteering and apprenticeship opportunities.
>
> Initiatives such as this require housing organisations to work with their customers and other providers to rethink the services that are offered.

The political consensus on taking forward the choice, empowerment and personalisation agenda has been frequently emphasised throughout this chapter. Customers expect that there will be increasing opportunities to make informed choices on services. But this is not an unproblematic issue. Le Grand (2007) noted that consumers in the private sector find excessive choice demotivating. He further pointed out that there is a widely held view that choice is a middle-class issue, even though there is considerable empirical evidence to the contrary. Finally, Le Grand suggested that there is an intellectual tradition associated with left-of-centre politics that is suspicious of choice. This, in part, stems from a belief that this programme has been engineered by rightwing politicians that have coupled it with competition and markets. Over the next decade, the challenge will be to respond positively to the customer voice for better services (including personalisation) at less cost. There is a danger with the localist agenda and public spending reductions of a postcode lottery with choice being available on a differential basis. Customers in deprived neighbourhoods may have little opportunity to exercise choice.

There is also much common ground between the main political parties on the promotion of co-production. Whilst the move towards social enterprises and voluntary partnerships running some public services needs critical reflection about the impact on communities and those working in the public sector, significant interest has been shown by politicians and the media in these concepts. There was considerable coverage of these concepts in the run up to the general election in 2010 including Boyle and Harris (2009) and Jowell (2009). It has also been highlighted by the coalition government through emerging initiatives such as local housing trusts and a community right to build. The focus is on governments supporting and creating organisations that give a greater degree of control to customers, communities and staff. Such organisations would work with providers through making use of their resources and skills to improve public services at less cost by designing out failure demand i.e. consumers contacting providers because of the inability to deliver 'a quality service first time and every time'. It is argued that employees and customers become 'more intolerant of waste and bureaucracy and significant savings can be made' (Stratton, 2010). Rewards for customers in getting involved in co-production might include council tax rebates. Nevertheless, it remains to be seen whether customers really wish to help design and deliver services or expect service providers to respond to 'voice'.

Co-production is frequently contrasted with an 'EasyBorough' approach based on the EasyJet or Ryanair philosophy. The latter espouses a basic low cost set of public services with an opportunity for the consumer to pay more for additional services. During 2009, there was extensive media coverage of developments in service provision in the Conservative-controlled London Boroughs of Barnet and Hammersmith and Fulham. The basic principle is that there are two levels of service. First, there is a minimum level to which the public is entitled. Secondly, there are areas where residents can opt for differing levels of service. Examples of the latter might include waste collection and the development control part of the planning service. It would involve working with customers to identify the value of additional services and the extent to which there would be opportunities to charge. It could also be linked to personal budgets for vulnerable households.

Learning from the Netherlands

Debates on social housing in the Netherlands have also centred on issues of voice and exit, customer choice, regulation and performance management. It is, however, vital to appreciate that there are significant variations between England and the Netherlands. Approximately 35% of Dutch households live in the social rented sector compared to less than 20% in England. All social housing is provided by housing associations, which are legally defined as private organisations with social responsibilities. Nevertheless, a review of Dutch issues provides useful 'shock therapy' i.e. a challenge to conventional thinking.

From the perspective of regulation and external performance management, local authorities (as strategic enablers) and housing associations set up a performance agreement that covers issues such as the scale and type of new development and regeneration, customer profile and services. These agreements are monitored and scrutinised by the municipality that has powers to report poor performance to the government. Housing associations, as private businesses with social duties, have in addition developed relatively sophisticated internal performance management systems compared to England (Koopman et al., 2008). For example, there is robust performance data collected for portfolio and asset management purposes so that income and expenditure profiles are available for each property. This is essential in an environment in which there are no government subsidies for development and housing associations have to borrow money against their stock or sell property and invest the receipts in new development or regeneration schemes.

Liveability has become an increasing issue over the last decade. It is defined as an assessment made by customers of the social and physical quality of their immediate surroundings. It developed in part because of customer dissatisfaction with social housing estates that were built in the 1950s to relatively low space standards with little investment in neighbourhood facilities. At the same time, socio-economic and demographic changes in recent decades have helped to create neighbourhoods that are perceived to have high levels of worklessness and tensions between different black and minority ethnic groups. Long-standing tenants have either opted for exit by moving to other estates or have retreated into their own personal space.

Customer voice has traditionally been conspicuous by its absence. Liveability information is regularly collected on resident neighbourhood satisfaction, community attachment and the willingness to stay in the area. These are all considered to be important measures and indicators of living conditions. It is recognised that much of the data is soft compared to the hard information on, say, property condition. There have, thus, been sophisticated attempts to create indices of neighbourhood quality. There are useful lessons here for housing organisations in England of bringing together customer data on neighbourhoods with performance management concepts.

Emerging issues

There is a consensus on the need for an even greater customer orientation in public services. Customer voice is increasingly significant for social housing landlords in developing and designing services. There are clearly tensions between developing better services and cutting public expenditure. Seddon's work on quality and lean services may help to tackle this issue. But there are three other interlinked issues that need to be addressed if customer satisfaction is to be taken forward.

First, there is the need to fully adopt a customer perspective. A focus on a specific service (such as housing benefits or allocations or repairs) remains organisation-centric. Instead, a shift in thinking is required that starts from the needs of the customer. As the Housing and Employment Connections Service (HECS) showed, the links between tackling worklessness and housing may be important for customers. This poses a challenging issue for service providers as there must be joined-up thinking between organisations.

Secondly, much of the debate on housing and the customer in England (and in the Netherlands) centres on social housing tenants. But there are equally significant issues for private sector tenants, low-income owner-occupiers and homeless households. The focus on council and housing association tenants should not be at their expense. For example, the coalition government has announced its intention to reduce the degree of regulation affecting private landlords. This poses significant challenges for councils as regulators of this sector and 'champions of the private tenant'.

Thirdly, there are long-term, socio-economic changes that could be marginalised because of the focus on public expenditure cuts. For instance, the demographic time-bomb of an ageing society has important implications for housing organisations. The customer profile will change with an increasing number of frail and very frail elderly single person households. It is clear that many will wish to remain independent as long as possible. It will require a radical rethink on the services that are offered and demanded including better co-ordination with organisations in the public, private and voluntary sector delivering health and social care.

Much of the focus of this chapter has been on the potential impact of the coalition government's policies for housing and the customer. The changes to the external regulatory and performance management systems have been highlighted as has the uncertainty caused by the demise of the TSA. At the same time, there are interesting ideas emerging as a result of localism, the 'big society' and co-production. On the one hand, these represent fundamental challenges. But there is also a window of opportunity at a local level to rethink the offer to customers.

References and further reading

2020 Public Services Trust (2010) *From Social Security to Social Productivity: A Vision for 2020 Public Services*. London: 2020 Public Services Trust.

Boyle, D. and Harris, M. (2009) *The Challenge of Co-production*. London: NESTA.

Brown, T. (Ed.) (1999) *Stakeholder Housing: A Third Way*. London: Pluto Press.

Brown, T., Dearling, A., Hunt, R., Richardson, J. and Yates, N. (2002) *Allocate or Let? Your Choice: Lessons from Harborough Home Search*. Coventry and York: Chartered Institute of Housing and Joseph Rowntree Foundation.

Cave, M. (2007) *Every Tenant Matters: A Review of Social Housing Regulation*. London: Communities and Local Government.

Cole, M. and Parston, G. (2006) *Unlocking Public Value*. New York: John Wiley & Sons.

Communities and Local Government (2010) *Review of Social Housing Regulation*. London: CLG.

Conservative Party (2009) *Advancing Opportunity*. London: Conservative Party http://www.conservatives.com/Policy/Opportunity_Agenda.aspx

Cooper, C. (2009) 'There are 150 Local Area Agreements – Why Does Just One Make Tenant Satisfaction a Priority', *Inside Housing*, 3rd April.

Hardman, I. (2010) 'TSA to Overhaul Satisfaction Data', *Inside Housing*, 16th April.

HM Government (2009) *Putting the Frontline First: Smarter Government*. London: The Stationery Office.

Hills, J. (2006) *Ends and Means: The Future Roles of Social Housing in England*. London: London School of Economics, CASE.

Hirschman, A. (1970) *Exit, Voice and Loyalty*. Cambridge MA: Harvard University Press.

Jowell, T. (2009) 'The Mutual Movement: How Progressives can capture the ownership agenda', *Speech to Autumn Lecture Series,* Progress and the Co-operative Party, 15 December.

Koopman, M., Van Mosel, H.J. and Straub, A. (2008) *Performance Measurement in the Dutch Social Rented Sector*. Amsterdam: IOS Press.

Le Grand, J. (2007) *The Other Invisible Hand*. Princeton: Princeton University Press.

Le Grand, J. (2003) *Motivation, Agency, and Public Policy*. Oxford: Oxford University Press.

Local Government Association (2010) *New Reputation Guide*. www.lga.gov.uk/reputation

Local Government Association and *Municipal Journal* (2010) *The Public Service Challenge*. London: LGA.

Middleton, P. (Ed.) (2010) *Delivering Public Services that Work. Vol. 1*. Axminster: Triarchy Press.

National Housing Federation (2010) *STATUS – The Standardised Tenants Satisfaction Survey*. London: NHF http://www.housing.org.uk/default.aspx?tabid=291&mid=1033&ctl=Details&ArticleID=717

Pawson, H., Sosenko, F. and Ipsos Mori (2009) *Assessing Resident Satisfaction*. London: London & Quadrant Housing Trust.

Policy Projects Team (2009) *Are We Being Served? Policies on Accessing Goods and Services*. London: Liberal Democrats.

Richardson, J. (Ed.) (2010) *From Recession to Renewal: the impact of the financial crisis on public services and local government*. Bristol: Policy Press.

Seddon, J. (2008) *System Thinking in the Public Sector*. Axminster: Triarchy Press.

Sen, H. (2007) *Little Platoons Need Rations Too*, 4th November. http://hopisen.wordpress.com

Simmons, R., Powell, M. and Greener, I. (Eds.) (2009) *The Consumer in Public Services*. Bristol: Policy Press.

Stratton, A. (2010) 'Labour's Plan for First 'John Lewis' Council', *The Guardian*, 18th February.

Tenant Services Authority (TSA) (2010a) *The Regulatory Framework for Social Housing in England from April 2010*. London: TSA.

Tenant Services Authority (TSA) (2010b) *Going Local*. London: TSA.

Van Dooren, W., Bouckaret, G. and Halligan, J. (2010) *Performance Management in the Public Sector*. London: Routledge.

CHAPTER 3:
Customer models and their application to social housing: a marketing approach

Tony Garry and Joanna Richardson

Introduction

This book explores the relationship between housing providers and the 'customer'. It suggests that there are business and social benefits to having a customer focus which can increase customer satisfaction and public service efficiency at a time when it is needed more than ever. Throughout the book a number of models are used to explain and explore concepts relating to the customer and the organisation in the delivery of social housing services. One such approach which is at the heart of this chapter is a marketing approach that can help to show the way to a truly customer-focused and efficient approach to the delivery of services.

Ambler (2004) suggests that marketing theory is a *'relatively new attempt to explain what business people have been doing for centuries'*. Indeed, the origins of marketing can be traced back hundreds of years to a time when function, market price (and economic benefit) and psychological benefits were used to determine the 'just price' of goods and services (Ambler, 2004). However, contemporary theories of marketing are more complex and draw on a plethora of disciplines including microeconomics, macroeconomics, psychology, sociology and even anthropology, reflecting increasing pressures from the macro and micro environment on organisations to adopt a marketing approach. The public sector and not-for-profit organisations have not been exempt from this process. However, in its purest transactional form, marketing is widely perceived as an *'overtly commercial concept'* in terms of its origins, relevance and indeed, its philosophical appropriateness to the public sector with a perceived onus on competition rather than collaboration by many public sector professionals (Laing, 2003). However, the introduction of quasi-market mechanisms such as outsourcing, competitive tendering and Best Value have instigated a re-evaluation of the contribution that marketing can make. Within such contexts, it is critical that organisations understand and appreciate the evolving complexity of their relationships with stakeholders and deliver effective and appropriately targeted service offerings to these stakeholders (Laing, 2003). This requires the identification and application of relevant marketing concepts and frameworks at both a strategic and operational level rather than a mere adoption of the *'trappings of marketing'* (Ames, 1970) frequently epitomised by advertising and selling.

To explore these issues in more detail, this chapter initially examines the background and definitions of marketing and their relevance to a public sector context. Subsequently, the concept of the exchange process is described with consideration given to value generation and consumption. Next, consumer and stakeholder behaviour, roles and decision processes are discussed before the relevance of segmentation, targeting and positioning processes are examined and applied to a public and social housing context.

Definitions of marketing

The concept of marketing has customers at its heart. Basically the marketing concept believes that the most important stakeholders in the company are the customers. This premise is key to the whole business. The marketing function is diffuse in the organisation and the customer is the main driver behind organisational decisions such as fixing prices, location, type of product and the type of promotion. Innovative and successful business will, in the most part, adopt a marketing concept.

The housing sector did pick up on the marketing concept. Indeed the National Housing Federation spent some time and money in 2002 and 2003 in trying to 're-brand' the sector and many housing organisations now work with the focus of their business on the housing customer.

Therefore, marketing is not just a case of advertising. It is the whole raison d'être for your business. Effective marketing is often described as *'making what you can sell, not selling what you can make'* (Ali, 2001). The Chartered Institute of Marketing's own definition is: *'Marketing is a management process of identifying, anticipating and satisfying customer requirements efficiently and profitably'*.

Proctor (2007) highlights that even within the public sector, much of the work organisations are involved in focuses on satisfying stakeholders within an exchange context and so defines marketing as:

> *The management process responsible for identifying, anticipating and satisfying stakeholder requirements and in doing so serves to facilitate the achievement of the organisation's objectives* (Proctor, 2007).

What these definitions highlight is that whilst some marketing concepts and frameworks may be applicable to a certain extent within a public sector context, their mere direct transposition is not appropriate as the public sector has a number of distinctive characteristics which need to be considered.

Marketing within the public sector

Laing (2003) suggests these characteristics fall into three main categories: the dominance of political rather than purely economic imperatives; the primacy of the citizen rather than the consumer and, finally, the need to serve many multi-dimensional 'consumers' or stakeholders. The consequences of each of these characteristics for a marketing perspective within the public sector are now explored in more detail.

- **The dominance of political objectives**
  Traditionally, the economic imperative has been subservient within public sector provision to other broader imperatives such as social justice, equity and legitimacy. The role of the state is to govern and not to produce or distribute services (Walsh, 1994). The government's main objective is to realise social effects in its policy portfolio. Given these imperatives, broader social indicators of achievement for society as a whole need to be considered as much as traditional economic-based performance measures that concentrate on the direct benefits to the user and which are increasingly being used at an operational level within the public sector. Related to this, such measurements are increasingly prone to 'metrification' in an attempt to increase accountability and transparency in relation to public sector funding. Inevitably this leads to an organisational culture dominated by target setting and measurement procedures and processes. This dynamic of governance over service delivery as a prime objective may shift following the global financial crisis of 2008 (see further Richardson, 2010) and the ideology of the Conservative-Liberal Democrat coalition government which came into power in May 2010.

- **Citizenship and consumerism**
  Increasingly, the relationship between public services and those who use them is being redefined within many public service contexts from that of 'citizen' to that of 'consumer' (Laing, 2003) whilst Clarke *et al.* (2007) argue we have gone beyond citizen-consumers. Whilst the concept of the 'citizen' is underpinned by the collective needs of society as a whole, this collective is not simply an aggregation of the preferences of all individual citizens. It is frequently the outcome of a political process that determines what and how a service will be supplied, perhaps against the wishes of a significant proportion of the citizenry. On the other hand, a focus on a 'consumer'-orientated approach suggests a need to focus more on the needs of the individual. This increasingly becomes a priority for many organisations as end users may be asked to make contributions or full payment for services. However, a consequence of this may be the tensions between the short-term wishes of the 'consumer', the professional judgment of the service provider and the collective good of society in general. A number of models are testing these

assumptions. The coalition government has highlighted its notion of 'big society' with citizen consumers co-producing their own services. On a more local level, councils like Barnet have been testing an 'EasyBorough' model[7] where in some services, provision above the basic may accrue an additional charge and in Lambeth where the 'John Lewis' model is based more on co-production of services with residents invited to get involved.

- **Multiple multi-dimensional customers**
  In many public services there may be multiple stakeholders. At one level, these will potentially include the individual recipient of the service, their family, their employer (e.g. education, health etc), the service providers and the purchasers and distributors of the service as well as indirect payers (e.g. taxpayers) and society as a whole as another level. In social housing we need to delve deeper into the multi-dimensions that make up our heterogeneous customer base, particularly the diversity of ethnicity, age, need and so on. This is examined in more detail by Bloxsom and Richardson in the next chapter (4).

Given these characteristics, it is important to consider which aspects of marketing are relevant and appropriate within a public service context. Public services are heterogeneous and part of the consideration process will need to take this into account. Critical to this is the balance between private and social benefit together with the balance between the judgments of the consumer and that of the producer. Laing (2003) suggests a continuum to aid in this identification process which is represented diagrammatically below (see Figure 3.1).

Figure 3.1: The spectrum of public services

Social benefits dominant					Private benefits dominant
Customs & Excise	Criminal Justice	Education	Healthcare	Public Transport	Public Housing
Professional judgment dominant					Consumer judgment dominant

Adapted from Laing, A. 2003: p.436.

A further consideration when deciding which and to what extent marketing concepts and frameworks are appropriate to the public sector context is the make-up of the exchange process between consumer and provider. This is considered in more detail in the next section.

---

7   So named after the no-frills airline 'EasyJet'.

The exchange process

At a basic economic level, the marketing philosophy focuses on achieving organisational goals (e.g. maximisation of profit) through satisfying (and exceeding) consumer *needs* and *wants* in an exchange situation through integrated organisational effort.

Needs are the basic forces that motivate individuals to take action. They often emerge from a state of felt deprivation, such as the physical need for clothing, food, shelter and security. *Wants* are the form that needs take as they are shaped and influenced by culture and individual experiences. Products may be tangible products, services or even ideas such as political ideologies that are offered by an organisation or individual in an attempt to satisfy a need or want. Within a commercial context, the motivation to supply is to maximise profit. *Exchange* takes place when a product required to satisfy an individual's need or want is offered in exchange for something in return such as money, other products or services (as in bartering) or something less tangible such as some kind of support, co-operation or even compliance to the rules and regulations of an organisation. Whatever the circumstances, the consumer normally has a *choice* among a number of competing suppliers and therefore exhibits a *personal preference* for the product or service.

Consider, for example, buying a ribbon on pink ribbon day. The money donated in exchange for the ribbon usually far exceeds the monetary value of the ribbon. The ribbon is however a tangible expression of much deeper and possible emotional support for Breast Cancer awareness. This then introduces the concept of *value*. As has been highlighted, what constitutes needs and wants and the costs to either party in providing and acquiring products that satisfy these through exchange may take many different forms in different contexts. *Value* in this context may be defined as the difference between the benefits a customer perceives in acquiring a product and the costs of obtaining those benefits whether it is financial, physical or emotional. However, drawing on the distinction of the 'citizen' and the 'consumer' discussed in the previous section, this interpretation of value relates to the individual's *private* interpretation of value (Alford, 2002) rather than any sense of publicly created value.

Value and satisfaction in the public sector

Private value is the perception the customer has of the product's benefits over the costs associated with acquiring that product. Costs may be financial, psychological or in terms of convenience. However, within a public sector context it is frequently the government through taxation that pays or subsidises public sector activity. Therefore individual taxpayers or citizenry do not necessarily endorse the private value they are paying for but may be legally obliged to pay against their will (Alford, 2002). However, some provision may be provided and consumed collectively (e.g.

defence or law and order) and in such contexts, the citizen receives *public* value. At this level there is an exchange between general taxation and the complete package of public facilities (Buurma, 2001). In effect, such an exchange has a redistributive nature. The government supplies public facilities, rules and other policy instruments that moderate the behaviour of its citizens. *Satisfaction* is the perception that the consumer or citizen has of the product's performance compared to their pre-conceived expectations. Pre-conceived expectations may be influenced by a number of factors including governmental or organisational communication, word-of-mouth discussion with friends and family and critically, the *price*. Expectations will therefore be influenced by the amount the consumer pays at the point of supply and consumption ranging from nothing to paying a significant proportion of the overall cost of the service. Customer satisfaction is examined in more detail by Brown and Yates in chapter 6.

It is important to understand consumer and citizen interpretations of value and how these may contribute towards the processes and behaviours they may adopt in a public sector context if appropriate strategies and tactics are to be adopted, and these are explored in the next section of the chapter.

Understanding consumer behaviour in the public sector

When purchasing any product for the first time, consumers will typically pass through a number of stages to reach a decision whether to purchase a product or not (see Figure 3.2).

Figure 3.2: The consumer decision-making process

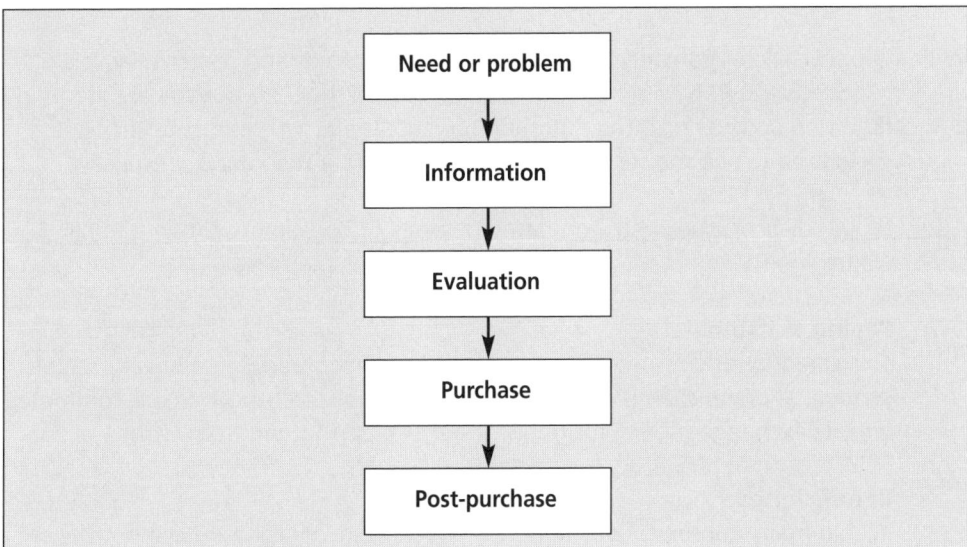

Based upon: Engel, J., Blackwell, R., Miniard, P. (1995).

There are myriad alternatives, preferences and individual circumstances affecting the decision to 'purchase' as well as a range of choices and constraints, particular to the public sector. Take, for example the letting of social housing through a choice-based lettings (CBL) system. In stage one, the customer recognises that their housing situation is due to change in the future and that they need a property to live in. They will search for information possibly in the private rented market, the private for sale market and also the social rented market, depending on their economic circumstances. In the social rented market, they will be asked to register and to look out for properties that meet their needs in the advertising process. However, there is not boundless choice and the customer will need to remember the constraints placed upon them and this can lead to stage three in evaluating alternatives (perhaps looking again at the private rental market or reappraising 'choices' to be more in tune with properties readily coming available – this may mean widening the geographical area of search). The fourth stage of 'purchase' involves bidding for a property – this does not equate to obtaining the property, so it is different to say purchasing a chocolate bar in a shop where one knows that once a decision to purchase has been made there is very little to prevent one actually obtaining the snack in return for money paid at the till. In the CBL system, the decision to purchase is more like a decision to bid for something in an auction – the success or not of the outcome depends on others in the room and their circumstances or ability to pay more than you can afford. The final stage of post-purchase evaluation is where the strengths of a CBL scheme can come into their own. Information from the bidding process for properties provides customers with a range of information which can then affect all of the preceding stages in the purchasing process, particularly in the case where a bid has been unsuccessful; there may be a reassessment by the individual of their own need, leading to a different – wider – information search and particularly an evaluation of alternatives.

Within a public sector context, the decision-making process and perceived levels of risk may be moderated by a number of factors. Indeed, how consumers are identified and categorised according to their attitude towards the service and supplier requirements to provide the service may be critical from a marketing perspective.

Alford (2002) distinguishes between different types of consumers within a public sector context:

- **Paying consumers**
  This category of consumer is similar to those encountered in a private sector context. A prime example of this category is public transport where commuters directly exchange money for public transportation to and from work.

- **Beneficiaries**
  Within many contexts, consumers do not pay directly for a service but benefit from the provision of such a service (e.g. health, social security benefits etc).

Within such contexts, supply is frequently determined by budgetary resources. The consequence of this is that organisations concentrate on rationing the service by applying eligibility rules that determine who are the most deserving. Frequently, this is accompanied by onerous obligations on the beneficiary to ensure they comply with such criteria. In many such situations, the consumer may use a particular service because of a personal emergency situation (such as being made homeless) and because there is not a choice of another provider. This is known as a 'distress purchase'.

- **Obligatees**
  The final category of consumer identified by Alford (2002) is obligatees. The concept of the obligatee focuses on the issue of when consumers do not have a preference for a service or are a *reluctant user* and may be coerced into consuming a service. Typically this may include law enforcement agencies, the Inland Revenue and prisons or even services linked to the receipt of benefits such as jobseeker's allowance.

When looking at categories of consumers, it is important to recognise that some will not only be proactive or inactive in terms of their search for and use of a service but many may also be reluctant users of a product or service. Similarly and as highlighted previously, many public sector organisations are compelled and/or constrained in the way they supply a service by legal restrictions and limited financial budgets and hence may be classified as active, inactive or reluctant/restricted providers of a service themselves. The table below (see Figure 3.3) illustrates the implications of these dimensions from a supplier-consumer relational perspective.

Figure 3.3: Categories of consumers-provider relationships in the public sector

		Provider perspective		
		Active	*Inactive*	*Reluctant/ restricted*
Consumer perspective	*Active*	**Private sector** Opt out of public sector	**Political demand** Lobby groups Social pressure	**Rights** As provider's duty As user's privilege
	Inactive	**Societal marketing** 'It's good for you'	**No exchange**	**Resignation** User must accept Provider attempts to minimise costs
	Reluctant/ restricted	**'We know best'** Legislation makes it work	**Distress purchase** Dire necessity	**Hostility** Mutual distrust

Adapted from Chapman and Cowdell 1998: p.42.

HOUSING AND THE CUSTOMER

Whilst the above section concentrates on individual buying decisions, many purchase decisions are made involving others. Within groups such as families or other types of households, there is often a combination of individuals and roles that make up a Decision-Making Unit (DMU).

From a public sector perspective, this DMU model may be extrapolated so as to include those that directly and indirectly influence the way in which a service is designed, delivered and consumed (see Figure 3.4 below).

Figure 3.4: Primary and secondary decision-makers within the public sector

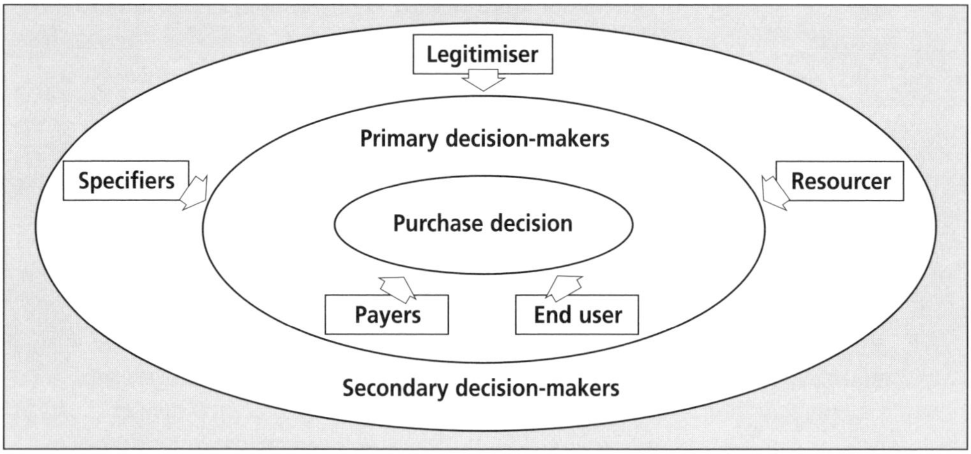

[Diagram showing concentric ovals: innermost contains "Purchase decision"; middle oval labeled "Primary decision-makers" contains "Payers" and "End user"; outer oval labeled "Secondary decision-makers" with external boxes "Legitimiser", "Specifiers", and "Resourcer" pointing inward.]

Primary decision-makers

This refers to those who are direct users and beneficiaries of the product and/or service or who are directly involved in paying for it. This will ultimately include the end user and payer.

Secondary decision-makers

Chapman and Cowdell (1998) suggest this may also be called the facilitator market and comprises of all those who may influence the primary decision-makers. There are three main elements to this:

- The *legitimiser* comprises of the systems and agencies who establish the regulations by which an organisation will deliver its service. This may be through governmental decree in many instances and provides power for appropriate bodies to ensure delivery of a service to, for example, obligates in the case of law enforcement.
- The *specifyer* will frequently determine the way or nature in which a service will be delivered through the establishment of minimum delivery standards and, more recently, targets.

- The *resourcer* provides the funding for the public service and at a macro level, is usually determined by central government through budgetary allocation. This is then allocated down the hierarchy until it reaches individual budget holders. The amount and nature of budget allocation will ultimately have a large impact on the way the service is delivered.

From an understanding of consumers and stakeholders and their needs and wants, organisations are able to blend a set of variables in such a way as they will communicate their product or service to customers (promotion), provide information about where it is available (place), how much it costs (price) and how the product or service will satisfy their needs and wants (product). At a basic level, this set of variables is collectively known as the four Ps of marketing. However, as resources are finite and different sets of consumers have different needs and wants, organisations will develop a mix of variables that will appeal to particular subsets of consumers. This process is known as segmentation, targeting and positioning.

Market segmentation and the identification of stakeholder groups

Market segmentation is the process of dividing a heterogeneous market of customers into distinct groups of customers or segments that have certain commonalities such as shared preferences, attitudes, or behaviours that distinguish them from the rest of the market. Within a public sector context, this may necessitate a slightly different approach requiring four key steps related to the identification of stakeholder characteristics rather than consumer characteristics (Proctor, 2007).

Instead of being used to identify consumer segments, this process may be employed to identify potential stakeholder groups. As highlighted earlier in the chapter, stakeholders will frequently include consumers, employees, families of consumers (e.g. for health and education services), pressure and lobby groups and the local community. Various stakeholder groups will have differing and often conflicting needs and wants. Related to this is the perception that each stakeholder group will have as to the importance attached to its needs or wants or its vested interest relative to those of other stakeholder groups. A numbers of variables may be used to segment the market or identify stakeholders. Within traditional markets these variables have included:

- demographics (age, gender etc)
- geographic (postcode, town, area of country etc)
- socio-economic grouping (A, B, C1, C2, D, E etc)
- ethnic origin
- values and lifestyle
- personality and attitude.

The issue of segmentation is discussed in more detail by Richardson in chapter 7 on customer relationship management and customer insight.

Once the various stakeholder groups and their interests have been identified, the next step is to identify which processes or programmes of service provision may add value for each of these stakeholder groups relative to their importance to the organisation, and to *target* these appropriately. Referring back to the section earlier in the chapter on value, at a general level this may be in terms of private or public value. From this, the exchange process required to provide this value may be established. Finally stakeholder expectations and contributions need to be established and communicated. This may be done using the set of variables known collectively within marketing as the 'marketing mix'. This marketing mix provides a framework that enables the organisation to develop the mix of variables for differing stakeholder groups and to deliver the optimum value to each of these groups.

The marketing mix

The marketing mix is a framework of variables for the tactical management of consumer and stakeholder targeting and comprises:

- *Products or services* that are identified that should be offered to the target group of stakeholders by the organisation and which will satisfy their needs and wants.
- *Price* incorporates decisions relating to the final selling price of the product or service to potential consumers of the service. This element of the marketing mix is particularly important in terms of its influence on the consumer's perceptions of service value. Within a public sector context, this may range from being free at point of supply to some form of contribution being made by the consumer.[8]
- *Promotion* relates to communication issues such as designing an appropriate message and selecting appropriate media to communicate that message. This may range from awareness-raising and setting expectations through to attempts at behaviour modification (e.g. issues surrounding drug abuse, drink-driving etc). It includes advertising, face-to-face communication, public relations, direct marketing and internet and online marketing activity.
- *Place* – concerns decisions related to the availability and accessibility (e.g. online) of the product and service including distribution channels, outlets, methods of inventory and transportation. In the social housing sector we also need to consider the geography of 'place' in relation to where housing is most needed and wanted.

Periodically, academics suggest additional elements or variables to the traditional marketing mix in an attempt to reflect the ever more complex nature of marketing interfaces. This is particularly relevant to the public sector which predominately

---

8   In social housing the issue of price can be particularly challenging and particularly so at a point with the new coalition government is reviewing security of tenure and the benefits system; and at a time when the recession is still having an effect on affordability and new house building is low.

provides services. It is widely recognised that services have a number of characteristics that distinguish them from tangible products or goods. These may be classified as follows:

- **Intangibility**
  Services are intangible. Consumers look for signs of service quality and sellers seek to provide surrogate measures of tangibility to reassure the buyer. As a result, many financial services are housed in buildings of solid appearance; airline signage (uniforms etc) is designed to instil a sense of security; lawyers and accountants are expected to dress in particular ways.

- **Inseparability**
  With many services, the service is inseparable from the provider of that service. A consumer must be present for the service to be administered. As a result provider-consumer interaction is especially important in services and sometimes is the distinct feature of the service sought by the customer.

- **Variability**
  Services are highly variable because they largely depend on human interaction. In large service organisations, standardising service across locations and employees is very difficult. Yet for many service organisations, reducing and controlling the amount of variability is a key part of successful service business growth.

- **Perishability**
  Services are perishable and cannot be inventoried or stored for later sale. This has major consequences for many service industries in terms of minimising over-capacity (e.g. empty seats in a theatre, or difficult-to-let properties in certain parts of the country).

- **Ownership**
  Across a range of services the issue of ownership is a challenge and particularly so in the public sector and in housing. A sense of ownership and investment is vital to the sustainability of communities, but in social rented properties this can be difficult, and perhaps especially so if security of tenure is under review.

As a result of these characteristics, the four Ps framework has been extended to incorporate three additional Ps that take these characteristics into consideration:

- **People**
  The organisation's employees occupy a key position in influencing customer perceptions of service quality. The importance of people has been repeatedly emphasised within services marketing literature because the service is

performed and the performers are employees. Indeed, Gummesson (1981; 1987) coined the phrase 'part-time marketers' to stress the critical marketing role performed by customer contact employees in terms of satisfying customers needs and wants.

- **Processes**
  The procedures, mechanisms and flow of activities by which a service is delivered to and acquired by the consumer. In the public sector, processes and procedures seem to be under constant review and there is criticism of some of the methods used to drive efficiency, such as targets and regulation. The coalition government has reviewed a number of elements of service delivery in the public sector and particularly within the social housing sector too (see further Richardson, 2010).

- **Physical evidence**
  The design of the environment in which the service is delivered and often consumed by the consumer. Physical evidence in social housing is, of course, the property itself, but there are other services provided such as advice either by phone, on the internet or in the office, ancillary care services, community services and so on that do need considering, as well as the physical bricks and mortar layout of the property and the estate.

Figure 3.5: The seven Ps of the housing marketing mix

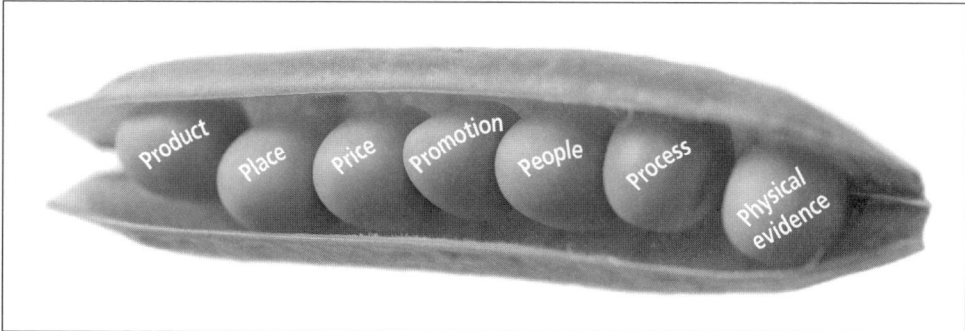

Once an appropriate mix has been designed, the organisation needs to ensure that it is positioned correctly using this mix.

Market positioning

Market positioning is the process of formulating competitive positioning for a product or service. The product's position is defined by how consumers perceive it based on its important attributes and relative to other deliverers. These may include price, quality or product range.

The marketing mix approach is typically appropriate within certain market contexts. Typically the features of these contexts include:

- wide target markets
- highly competitive distribution systems (e.g. supermarkets)
- target markets accessed through commercialised media channels.

A range of models such as Ansoff's (1984) Product/Market mix, Porter's (1985) Competitive Forces model and of course the Boston Consulting Group (1970) Product Portfolio model which looks at the cash cows, stars, dogs and problem children of the product and service offerings. Models and ideas related to brands and diversity of service offering are examined in more detail by James and Richardson in chapter 8 of this book. For now in the social housing sector though, it is sufficient to start to think about market positioning in terms of a PEST-type analysis where a housing organisation will examine the Political/Economic/Social and Technological external context which will have an effect on business, and within that should also be examining other public service agencies, private landlords, housing associations and other providers to establish their own position and any areas of gaps or duplications in the services offered.

Conclusion

In our experience, through talking to housing providers and teaching housing students, there is sometimes a resistance to marketing. Some argue that we are moving away from traditional notions of social welfare and moving towards a more commercial/capitalist model of provision. They might argue that tenants and prospective tenants are not customers; in reality they have little choice. It may be true that many customers do not have real choice in the property they are able to move into or over their service provider. No one is suggesting that the provision of housing is as simple as selling 'widgets'. However, a marketing concept is focused on examining what the customer wants and needs and on delivering products and services as efficiently as possible. As a moral and business case this has to make sense for housing organisations – why would we want to treat tenants as 'welfare recipients' rather than customers with choice? Why also would businesses want to ignore models of business efficiency – it is only going to benefit the customer in the long run as housing organisations do not make 'profit' in the traditional sense, but instead they make 'surpluses' which are ploughed back into improving properties and building new homes. Where marketing frameworks and concepts are applied to public sector contexts in an appropriate and sensitive manner, a marketing approach may offer huge potential for improving the stakeholder experience.

There is a need to exercise caution in extending marketing concepts and frameworks to the public sector. A direct transposition and application of narrow transaction-based marketing theory to a public sector context may be problematic. It should be recognised that different marketing concepts will have different degrees of relevance depending on the public service context. This chapter has highlighted some of the frameworks that may be used to determine which are the most relevant. There needs to be recognition of the existence of collective societal-based, as well as individual, objectives. The often conflicting and contradictory needs and wants of multi-dimensional stakeholder groups need to be identified and prioritised (Laing, 2003); and an appropriate mix of variables designed to satisfy individual stakeholder needs.

A marketing approach can help housing organisations identify who their customers are and what they want. In applying marketing concepts the customer is put at the heart of the service and that is what we are striving for – customer focus. We've already stated that we are unapologetic in our use of the term 'customer' and the same goes for 'marketing' too. Yes, there is a need to adapt rather than adopt – but it works and examples in the remainder of this book will show you how.

References and further reading

Alford, J. (2002) 'Defining the Client in the Public Sector: a social exchange perspective', *Public Administration Review*, May/June, Vol. 62, No. 3, pp.337-346.

Ali, M. (2001) *Marketing Effectively*. London: Dorling Kindersley.

Ambler, T. (2004) 'A long perspective of marketing', *European Business Forum,* 15 Dec 2005.

Ames, B.C. (1970) 'Trappings versus Substance in Industrial Marketing', *Harvard Business Review*, July/August, Vol. 48, pp.93-102.

Ansoff, H. (1984) *Implanting Strategic Management*. Englewood Cliffs, New Jersey: Prentice Hall.

Berry, L.L. (1983) 'Relationship Marketing' in *Emerging Perspectives on Services Marketing,* L. L. Berry, G. L. Shostack and G. D. Upah (Eds.). Chicago, IL: American Marketing Association, pp. 25-28.

Boston Consulting Group (1970) *The Product Portfolio*. www.bcg.com

Buurma, H. (2001) 'Public Policy Marketing: Marketing Exchange in the Public Sector', *European Journal of Marketing*, Vol. 35, No. 11/12, pp.1287-1300.

Chapman, D. and Cowdell, T. (1998) *New Public Sector Marketing*. Harlow UK: Pearson Education.

Clarke, J., Newman, J., Smith, N., Vidler, E. and Westmarland, L. (2007) *Creating Citizen-Consumers, Changing Publics and Changing Public Services*. London: Sage.

Dibb, S., Simkin L., Pride, W. and Ferrell, O. (1992) *Marketing: Concepts and Strategies* (3rd ed.). Boston: Houghton Mifflin.

Engel, J., Blackwell, R. and Miniard, P. (1995) *Consumer Behaviour*. New Jersey: The Dryden Press.

Howard, J. and Sheth, J. (1969) 'The Theory of Buyer Behaviour', Wiley in Jobber, D. (2001) *Principles and Practice of Marketing* (3rd ed.). New York: McGraw-Hill.

Gummesson, E. (1981) 'The Marketing of Professional Services – 25 Propositions' in J.H. Donnelly and W.R. George, *Marketing of Services*. Chicago: American Marketing Association, pp.108-112.

Gummesson, E. (1987) 'The New Marketing- Developing Long Term, Interactive Relationships', *Long Range Planning,* Vol. 20, No. 4, pp.10-20.

Hooley G,, Saunders, J. and Piercy, N. (1998) *Marketing strategy and competitive positioning*. New Jersey: Prentice Hall.

Jobber, D. (2009) *Principles and Practice of Marketing* , 6th ed. New York: McGraw-Hill.

Johnson, G. and Scholes, K. (2002) *Exploring Corporate Strategy.* Harlow, FT: Prentice Hall.

Laing, A. (2003) 'Marketing in the Public Sector: Towards a Typology of Public Services', *Marketing Theory*, Vol. 3, No. 4, pp.427-445.

Laurent, G. and Kapferer, J. (1985), 'Measuring Consumer Involvement Profiles', *Journal of Marketing Research*, 12th February.

Narver, J. and Slater, S. (1990) 'The effects of a market orientation on business profitability', *Journal of Marketing*, Vol. 54, No.4, pp.20-35.

Porter, M. (1985) *Competitive Advantage*. New York: Free Press.

Proctor, T. (2007) 'Public Sector Marketing', *Financial Times*. Harlow: Prentice Hall.

Richardson, J. (Ed.) (2010) *From Recession to Renewal: the impact of the financial crisis on public services and local government*. Bristol: Policy Press.

Walsh, K. (1994) 'Marketing and Public Management', *European Journal of Marketing*, Vol. 28, No. 3, pp.63-71.

PART TWO

POLICIES AND ISSUES

CHAPTER 4:
Who is the customer?

John Bloxsom and Joanna Richardson

Introduction

Housing organisations need to know their customers in order to fulfil their primary purposes in meeting housing need and making neighbourhoods and places sustainable. An understanding of the customer, their profile, needs, aspirations and location are essential to enable housing organisations to deliver against their purposes. This chapter looks at the diversity of tenants and the wider existing and future customer base. These patterns will be considered in the context of the equalities framework and the changing policy context for housing organisations. Diversity of ethnicity will be examined in this chapter, including the growth of what can be termed 'diversity within diversity' and the importance of social landlords knowing potential customers, for example refugees and new migrants. Customer focus allows housing organisations to develop and sustain demand for their core services, adapt and re-model those services, to offer additional services to those existing customers as well as attracting new customers through both new services and varied channels through which existing services can be accessed.

Customer focus does not mean the relentless promotion of standardised 'one size fits all' services but rather requires a process of differentiation with services aimed at particular market segments. Understanding market segments and targeting services appropriately and efficiently is vital after the Budget and the October Comprehensive Spending Review 2010 saw housing and other public sector budgets cut by at least 25%. This chapter will include consideration of the need to deliver services in appropriate ways for those customers who have additional support needs and may need the support and advice of public agencies. The argument will be developed that this approach should enable and empower people in a similar way to the position taken in health and social care services where users are now beginning to be provided with personalised services and the ability to utilise individual budgets. Finally, this chapter will address the need for diversity at the neighbourhood level if housing organisations are to reflect the spread of tenure types, income levels and ethnicities and avoid residualisation and polarisation within, and social exclusion of, some areas.

WHO IS THE CUSTOMER?

Who lives in social housing?

The majority of people (just under 70%) live in owner-occupied housing with 13% private renting and the remainder living in social rented housing, either with a local authority or a housing association for a landlord. It is important to understand the needs of the 17% of people who live in social housing in more detail so that appropriate homes and support services can be put in place as required. Further on in this chapter we will look at particular segments of the social housing population, such as by ethnicity, age, disability as well as other vulnerable groups such as Gypsies and Travellers. Broadly though, there are a range of reports which suggest the imperative to be alert to the needs of some of those living in social housing. There may be indicators of deprivation in terms of health, education and employment status as well as social exclusion, fear of crime, alcohol and drug dependency. It is important for social housing providers to be able to segment customer data along a range of different lines to examine the needs of different customers to see how services should be delivered.

For example, if social housing tenants are segmented on economic status; we can see that they are over-represented in the unemployed and the economically inactive groups as per Figure 4.1 below with 34% of social housing tenants in full- or part-time work and the remainder either unemployed or otherwise economically inactive. The review of housing benefit and jobseeker's allowance undertaken by the coalition government ahead of the emergency budget in June 2010 will have an impact on the lives of social housing tenants, and on the income stream for social landlords.

Figure 4.1: Economic status by tenure type for 2008-2009

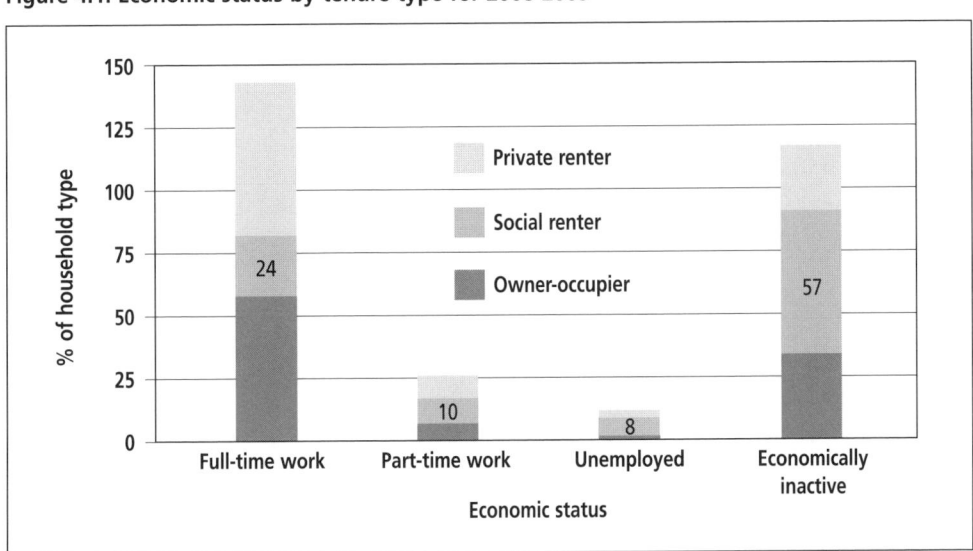

Source: *Housing and Planning Key Facts*, CLG, May 2010.

Understanding the customer base

In order to address a range of challenges, housing organisations must have an insight into their current and future customers. 'Customer Insight' is the collection and detailed analysis and use of data to develop a comprehensive understanding of customers in order to communicate with them and use this to develop and deliver the services that they need and expect. The process of insight involves both customer profiling (knowing who they are, their demographic characteristics and basic needs) and customer segmentation (focused on the aspirations, behaviours and lifestyles) of those that a provider may be able to offer services to. Past qualitative analysis of segmentation of the market for social housing by Beevers (1999) suggested that those most likely to be its consumers were *'generational renters'* raised on social housing estates and *'reluctant renters'* who would prefer to buy but do not have the means to do so. In contrast *'stepping stone renters'* were described as a segment that was happy to rent only in the short term and as such could be expected to exit the sector.

CIH/Housing Corporation (2008) concluded from research that residents of affordable housing could be segmented into four broad categories:

1. Young urbanites
2. Working families
3. Non-working poor
4. Older settled households.

Customer Insight involves, as a starting point, the collection of demographic information on the people that a housing provider seeks to serve in terms of age, ethnicity, income, health and support needs. This data can be drawn from internal sources, such as tenancy records, analysis of data collected at points of contact, and through STATUS[9] and other surveys together with CORE[10] data returns. External data can be added to give a richer and broader understanding of customers, using data in the public domain (such as crime statistics, hospital admissions, census, educational attainment). These sources can build knowledge of the market amongst existing customers, as well as those who are not currently customers and knowledge of opportunities to provide additional services, such as housing-related support to those already being providing with accommodation.

In the 1990s, when the focus of providers was on customer service standards and processes, it was argued that segmentation in social housing was led by

---

9   Standardised Tenant Satisfaction Survey commissioned to enable social landlords to consistently compare satisfaction data and produce performance indicators. The coalition government has announced the end of the STATUS survey at national level.

10 The COntinuous REcording System funded by the Tenant Services Authority and CLG that records information on the characteristics of both housing association and local authority new social housing tenants and the homes they rent and buy. The future of CORE is still unclear following the 2010 review of social housing regulation.

straightforward, largely demographic, distinctions and that what was missing was a correlation of household types to attitudes to services and how they should be delivered (Passmore and Ferguson 1994). The relevance of commercial classification systems such as ACORN and MOSAIC is considered further in chapter 7; however a number of housing providers are now making use of these to undertake market segmentation, provide an insight into preferred methods to access services and communicate with customers and indicate the types of services and products that they may be interested in. Housing organisations can use this type of customer relationship management tool to segment their customers into what can be described as 'value-based' profiles accordingly to their cost to the business, for example identifying those that tend to have a high level of arrears or be heavy users of repairs and maintenance services. This enables a provider to offer information, advice and support in particular ways that best suit particular groups, seek to adapt services in a way that meets those needs most efficiently or perhaps focusing some business development on services that are attractive to market segments that are less costly to the organisation.

Equalities and regulation framework

Housing organisations have to plan and deliver their services in compliance with equalities legislation and the regulatory framework. They will also wish to monitor and reflect needs in society which may not yet be reflected in the public policy framework. A pro-active approach to meeting community needs can result in the development of models of good practice for other housing organisations, more community cohesion in areas where appropriate provision is made and can result in better customer involvement and wider civic engagement. The Audit Commission's housing inspection regime regards an excellent organisation as being one that has a clear understanding of both its customer base and local demographics, knows the breakdown of residents (by age, ethnicity, disability, gender, sexual orientation and faith) and which prioritises resources and adapts services appropriately.

The Equality Act 2010 brought together previous legislation such as the Race Relations Act and the Disability Discrimination Act. Housing providers in all sectors are subject to the requirement that there be equal treatment in the provision of services, as well as in employment and training matters. Those who are designated as public bodies (such as local authorities) are in addition subject to duties to advance equality of opportunity and foster good race relations. The Equality Act 2010 now provides an additional duty on public bodies to have regard to inequalities of outcome which result from socio-economic disadvantage[11] and gives powers to the Secretary of State to impose equalities duties upon them in connection with the procurement of works, goods or services.[12] The Tenant Services Authority (TSA)

---

11 Equality Act 2010, s.1.
12 Equality Act 2010, s.155.

HOUSING AND THE CUSTOMER

regulates providers in relation to the seven strands covered by equalities legislation (age, disability, gender, gender identity, race and ethnicity, religion and belief and sexual orientation); although the regulatory body itself is now to be absorbed into the Homes and Communities Agency.

The national territories of the UK appear to be moving towards similar regulatory frameworks which cover all social housing providers and are led by a single co-ordinating agency. The Housing (Scotland) Bill 2010 introduced a Scottish Social Housing Charter defining the outcomes that social landlords should be achieving and providing a framework for an independent regulator charged with promoting equal opportunities. In Wales, the regulatory code for housing associations requires that they actively promote diversity, equality of opportunity, eliminate discrimination in all their activities and promote good race relations. In Northern Ireland, the Department for Social Development requires that associations have robust policy and procedural standards, offer equitable quality services, uphold and apply the principles of equality and diversity and are fair and open to all sections of the community.

Diversity within diversity

The impact of changing ethnic diversity on housing and neighbourhoods should not be underestimated. Neither should the importance of a safe home and a stable environment be forgotten in analysing the needs of all communities, including new migrants and refugees (Perry, 2008).

Figure 4.2: Diversity within diversity

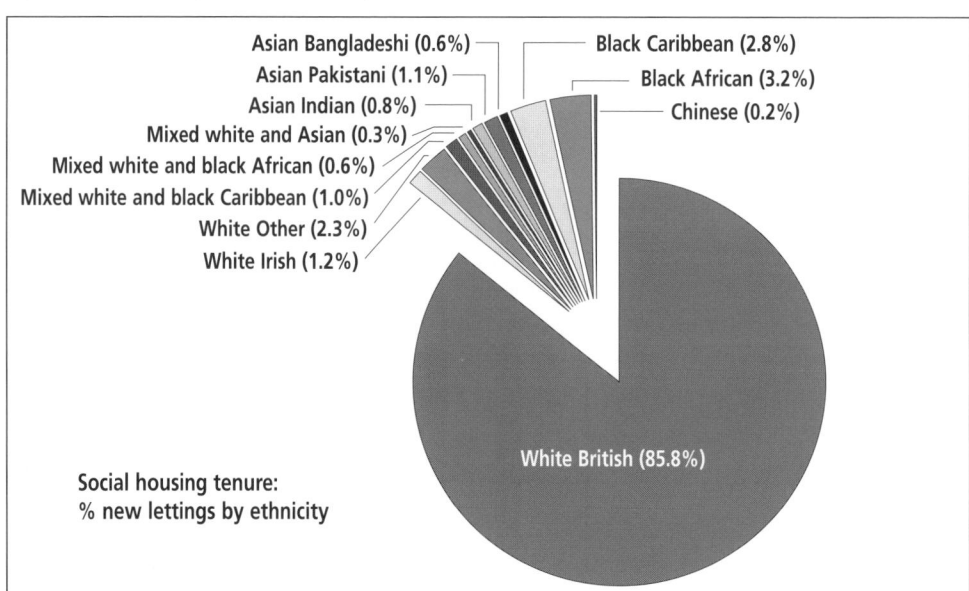

Source: Core data 2001-06 cited in CIH/HC (2008).

Upon examining the social housing sector according to its customer profile on ethnicity, it is immediately apparent that the vast majority of new social housing lettings were to 'White British', but the chart above at Figure 4.2 demonstrates the diversity within the black and minority ethnic communities in the sector. We can see that Indian and Chinese communities are under-represented in sector, but that Black Caribbean and Black African are over-represented with 2.8% Black Caribbean in social housing compared with 1.3% representation in all households and Black African households numbering 3.2% of the social housing sector's population compared with 0.9% representation in all households.

Patterns of disadvantage observed between different ethnic or racial groups reflect average positions within these communities and can mask the growing diversity of experiences and aspirations within and between BME communities. These can be referred to through the term 'diversity within diversity'. There is no homogeneous set of BME housing needs and aspirations and such customers have a diversity of needs related not just to ethnicity and religion but also to factors such as age, income, education and lifestyle. Tomlins et al. (2001) urged social housing providers to be cautious about stereotypes and to consult regularly. Housing providers need to understand these differences as they relate to the markets in which they operate and the communities that they serve and that diversity at the household or minority group level can be substantial (Harrison and Davis, 2001).

Changing family structures amongst communities where the extended family has been strong in the past is resulting in demands for new services to meet the needs of the older BME population, many of whom arrived in the UK as young migrants but are now of retirement age. Amongst second and third generations, and in particular amongst younger people, there is evidence of gradual out-migration from traditional 'reception areas' into adjacent areas and more prosperous areas further away. These aspirations are, however, more complex than classic models of urban development, such as the Burgess (1925) concentric zone, with affluence linked to progressively outward movement, would suggest. Younger and second and third generation households are seeking better quality housing and living environments whilst seeking to retain connections with, but not necessarily to live in, traditional BME community areas (Ecotec, 2005 and Harries et al., 2008).

Asylum seekers and refugees

Housing providers have been delivering services to asylum seekers and refugees through a variety of programmes and arrangements which have adapted as public policy towards these groups has shifted. The level of demand from asylum seekers and refugees has fluctuated according to international events that result in flight and migration. This has resulted in the profile of asylum seekers and refugees changing rapidly and a multiplicity of cultures and languages being represented in this population – which widens the complexity of the processes that providers need to go through when asking who the customer is?

The Opening Doors collaborative project operated through HACT (the housing action charity) and CIH in 2006-09 amongst eleven housing associations aimed to mainstream approaches to meeting the housing needs of refugees and other new migrant communities (Perry, 2009). With funding from the Housing Corporation and Communities and Local Government, projects included resettlement from refugee camps abroad (under the government's Gateway programme), housing allocated specifically to refugees, leasing of private sector accommodation, the provision of housing support and a range of strategic and organisational changes. The latter included examples of stronger strategic commitment, improved information on the customer base and migrants and refugees, better information on housing options, raised awareness amongst staff, capacity-building amongst refugee community organisations, provision of employment opportunities and inclusion of refugees and migrants in local community cohesion and black and minority housing strategies.

Opening Doors suggested that providers who were smaller associations with close links to communities find it easier to adapt their work to meet these new needs than do medium-sized or large associations. The main recommendations of Opening Doors to housing providers were first, that they should engage with diverse communities in their areas – in order to meet equality and diversity requirements and contribute to wider agendas around community cohesion, integration, worklessness and community empowerment; and secondly that they ensure staff are properly trained to deal with enquiries, they work with community organisations, consider how changes such as growth or mergers impact on their ability to work with these communities and that they integrate this work within their overall business plans.

Gypsies and Travellers

The predominant travelling communities in Britain are Romany English Gypsies and Irish Travellers; plus New Travellers, Welsh Gypsies and Scottish Gypsies, as well as new Roma migrants from the European accession countries. The size of Britain's Traveller and Gypsy population is also an estimate, with Council of Europe figures putting it at about 300,000, with approximately 200,000 in settled housing. However, government figures from bi-annual caravan counts show that just over 25% of the caravan-dwelling Gypsies and Travellers are on unauthorised sites, effectively homeless and often subject to move-on and eviction with reduced access to healthcare and education. Certainly, Gypsies and Travellers demonstrate many characteristics associated with marginalised and vulnerable people, and there should be a focus to protect this community from the multiple and compound effects of the financial crisis. Hills *et al.* (2010) in their report for the National Equality Panel referred to inequalities for Gypsies and Travellers in education, employment, health and employment issues. Gypsies and Travellers are already a vulnerable group in relation to health, literacy and other education issues. Distinguishable by their 'otherness' (see further Richardson 2006, 2007) they are marginalised and discriminated against in discourse which can lead to conflict.

The disjuncture between the number of sites currently provided and the estimated population numbers and the numbers of caravans on unauthorised sites demonstrates the continued lack of resources and sites for Gypsies and Travellers in Britain. Indeed, a variety of reports have suggested that 4000 more pitches are required (and some Gypsy and Traveller representatives say that this is an underestimation of need, indicating instead that there are at least 4,500 families with no official site to live on). It is important to note, however, that Gypsies and Travellers either on the road or on sites represent about only one third to one half of the total population in England. It has been suggested that approximately two thirds of Gypsies and Travellers live in bricks and mortar accommodation (Shelter, 2008).

Customer profiling information held by local authorities, housing associations, health and education agencies is patchy as the 2001 census did not record Roma, Gypsy or Traveller separately; but also because for a quieter life many Gypsies and Travellers in housing do not identify themselves as such. There are attempts to improve data collection amongst public agencies in order to understand the needs of travelling communities in social housing (whether in houses or on sites) better, and the Gypsy and Traveller Accommodation Assessments completed in recent years on a local authority or sub-regional basis are a good starting point.

Some public agencies have gone further and have applied Customer Insight principles to understanding Gypsies and Travellers.

West Sussex County Council hosted a Gypsy Roma Traveller (GRT) workshop in May 2010 to share insight and produce recommendations. Attendees highlighted some quick-win priorities such as:
- linking up outreach services into sites
- training staff on GRT culture
- ensuring partnership working between agencies.

The council also discussed data collected on GRT customers which showed in education at key stage two, attainments by GRT children at 28% compared with 73% for all West Sussex pupils, and at GCSE level, for 5+ A*-C grades, 8% of GRT children achieved compared with 68% of all West Sussex pupils. On accommodation issues, research by the Sussex Traveller Action Group for West Sussex Change Up showed that 43% of GRT had no permanent address and 35% travelled throughout the year.

Another Insight workshop on the issues related to GRT customers of the council was planned for the future, to share information with other interested agencies who had not been able to attend the first one.

HOUSING AND THE CUSTOMER

One of the principal causes of the sites shortage and growth in unauthorised encampments and numbers in housing has been a failure of policy in the past. More recent legislation and policy has sought to address the shortfall in accommodation for Roma, Gypsies and Travellers. The 2004 Housing Act created a statutory duty on local authorities to assess Gypsies' and Travellers' accommodation needs which had been used to set pitch targets through Regional Spatial Strategies; however the revocation of Regional Spatial Strategies by the new coalition government in July 2010 created huge uncertainty with many local authorities stopping or slowing their plans for new site development.

Young people and older people

Figure 4.3: Social tenants by age

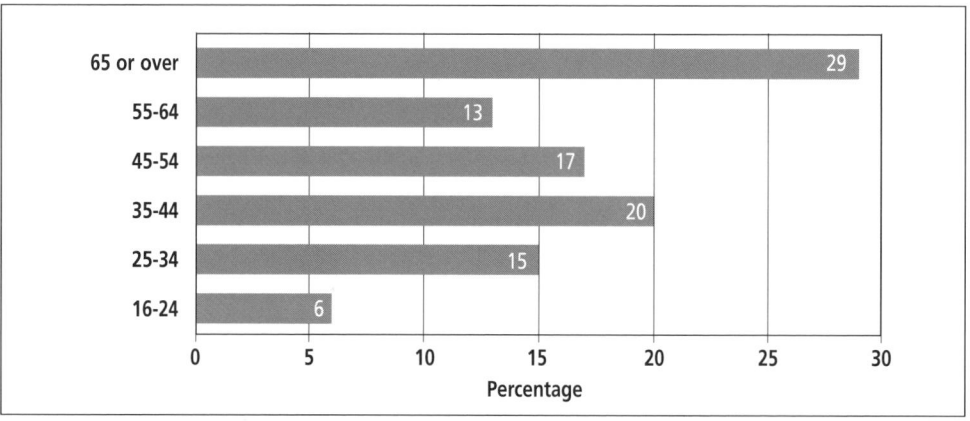

Source: English Housing Survey Headline Report 2008-09.

In line with broader demographic trends there is a growth in the number of people aged 65 and over in the social rented sector. The graph above at Figure 4.3 shows that just under 30% of social housing tenants are aged 65 or over and this has implications on a practical level on appropriateness of housing stock and the potential need for aids and adaptations, but also for social cohesion amongst the different age groups on estates.

Youth unemployment has risen from 2007 with disproportionate levels compared with the rest of the population. Shaheen (2009) reports this starkly: one in five people in the population are young, but they represent two in five of the total unemployment figures. The effect and indeed 'scarring' of youth unemployment can be severe and needs separate initiatives to deal with social and health consequences. There has already been a government response to try and stimulate more jobs or training for young people, and to encourage apprenticeship schemes. £1.2 billion was announced in the 2009 budget for the Future Jobs Fund for 2009-2011. National Indicator 117, which measures 16-18 year olds not in employment, education or training (NEET) has been prioritised by most Local Strategic Partnerships across the country; demonstrating the importance of this increasingly challenging area. The Public Service Agreement Target from the 2004 spending review was to reduce the percentage of NEETs by 2%, down to 8% by 2010. However data from the Department for Children, Schools and Families (DCSF, 2009) showed that at the end of 2008 the proportion of NEET 18 year olds had risen by 2.4% to 16.6%; which pushed the overall NEET statistic up by 0.7% to 10.3%. This will have an effect on the need for affordable housing for young people, but will also impact on aspirations for the future. Housing providers may be able to help with this issue of youth unemployment through targeted recruitment and training both in their own human resources management and through inclusion of appropriate clauses in procurement of goods and services.

> The **Can Do Toolkit** was launched in Wales for use by housing providers in their procurement processes to enable targeted recruitment and training for local people. CIH Cymru analysed the project and found that after one year (from September 2008) the housing providers who had used the toolkit had generated 487 employment and training opportunities through targeted social clauses in procurement contracts; this equates to 9.4 new opportunities per week.

Disabled people

As with other areas of customer profile, there is a dearth of published data analysis on the numbers of disabled people living in social housing. Hills (2007) reported that more than twice the proportion of social renting households comprised a member with a serious medical condition or disability than in the owner-occupied or private-rented sectors. Thornhill (2009) cites labour force survey figures to show that nearly one in five people of a working age has a disability. There are a range of needs within those figures, and a number of ways in which disabled people can be discriminated against in their application for, and consumption of, social housing.

Organisations such as Shelter and the (former) Disability Rights Commission have long recognised that there is an undersupply of appropriate affordable housing for disabled people, and new research by Habinteg Housing Association and London South Bank University further examine the housing need among, specifically, wheelchair users in England.

Digitally excluded customers

Consumer models for the delivery of public services have placed increasing emphasis upon the use of electronic channels such as the internet. Research has, however, identified that there is a digital divide with those who are socially excluded also being likely to be digitally excluded. Commentators argue that hardware and broadband access will not solve the digital exclusion problem on their own and suggest that home access, skills and internet content are significant factors (Winchester, 2009). As internet-based service channels become the norm there has been increased recognition of the need to promote increased internet access and enable and support usage amongst people who would otherwise be excluded. Official estimates are that 70% of people who live in social housing are not online (Royal Geographic Society, 2010) and that many social housing tenants form part of the estimated 6 million people who are both socially and digitally excluded. Lack of internet access is identified as an issue amongst low-income groups, older people, disabled people, people with learning difficulties, people lacking English language skills, offenders, people with mental health issues, those who are unemployed, early school leavers and those with literacy and numeracy skills needs (Digital Inclusion Taskforce, 2010).

The customer and personalisation: individuals should not be treated in isolation from communities

A major future challenge for the way in which housing providers relate to customers is the extension of the personalisation agenda, pursued most actively within health and social care services, into housing. Indeed it has been suggested that the real test of the personalisation agenda will come with social housing (Clark, 2008). The scale of that challenge will increase because demographic trends mean a projected increase of 1.7 million more people who need care and support in 2010-2030 (Chesseman 2010). Personalisation means starting with the person as an individual and giving them more choice and control over their living environment through new relationships between customers, providers and commissioners. This agenda has emerged from concerns about the inflexibility and lack of cost effectiveness of services (Wistow, 2009).

> The **Up2Us** project is a three-year programme in six pilot areas funded by the Departments of Health and Communities and Local Government to work with housing providers that are building and supporting groups of individual budget holders. It seeks solutions to concerns that individuals have very little influence on the quality of service provision, fears that service provision is unsustainable because of the fragmentation of the market and the pressure on providers to preserve existing services as they focus on economies of scale. These pilot projects involve social care users joining together to buy services, acting collectively to improve their negotiating position and, it is hoped, also benefiting service providers that will be able to negotiate with collective groups. This approach has similarities to the proposition that service users be asked to choose a package of core services, while being free to use personal budgets to buy services outside the core, in order to retain sustainable models of service that support people (Head, 2009) and overcome the risks of market fragmentation.
>
> www.hact.org.uk/up2us

The personalisation of social care allows housing providers to offer customers support services, personal assistant support, handyperson schemes, social support, administrative support with managing individual budgets and the planning of support (Taylor Knox, 2009) and this is discussed further in chapter 6 of this book. The real personalisation challenge, however, arises from matching action at the individual level, where customers choose a service or provider, with action at the collective and universal levels (Simpson, 2009). As social housing is rarely consumed individually and never in isolation from others (Clark, 2009) it is important to match offers of personal services to residents with collective choices about the nature of properties, the services delivered to them and the wider neighbourhood. This reality means that *'social housing and neighbourhood personalisation is always about more than just the person'* and must engage the resident as citizen as well as consumer (Clark, 2009). The contribution of housing and housing support to wider community goals to reduce isolation, maintain health and wellbeing and build social capital requires a view that these are collective as well as personal goods. This requires a dialogue with the citizen which enables collective action on the future of communities, avoids a fusion of the notions of the citizen and consumer (Clarke *et al.* 2007) and does not address and treat residents exclusively as consumers.

Customer choice

Choice-based lettings has been promoted as a means to achieve a shift from dependency to empowerment (Brown *et al.*, 2002) and a significant personalisation of housing (Audit Commission, 2006). This reflects higher bidding rates amongst those with internet access but also probably the use of intermediaries to gain internet access in order to bid. Access to information and the ability to bid for vacancies does not, however, transform the outcomes experienced by customers when they use such means to seek to exercise choice. Evaluation suggests that bidders remain confused about applicant ranking rules as many landlords explain bidding rules and procedures but play down their bidder prioritisation criteria (Pawson, 2009). In areas where the overwhelming majority of properties are let to customers with high-priority needs, CBL will not provide much in the way of real choice for most bidders, but it may well raise their expectations. The notion of the term 'customer' was examined in chapter 1 of this book, and the issues around choice and voice were discussed in chapter 2 with some further debate to come in chapter 6, but the point we want to make here is that CBL schemes can provide a wealth of information, not just to housing providers on who their customers are and what their needs and aspirations might be, but also back to the customer, so that realistic decisions can be made.

Customer aspirations

Tenants and users of other housing services are consuming services which are available to them within a constrained set of choices. They will often have aspirations both in terms of their current expectations and their future aspirations. The (former) Housing Corporation and CIH published a report (CIH/HC, 2008a) examining the housing aspirations linked to low cost homeownership (LCHO) and specifically shared ownership. Existing shared owners seemed to aspire to full home ownership, but for reasons of affordability saw LCHO as the next best thing. When compared to the private sector there has been a relative lack of developed segmentation analysis to support the building and marketing of homes and services aimed at specific consumer group studies and a reliance on problematic housing needs assessments (Bramley et al., 1999) and local authority-led housing market studies. The residual role ascribed to the social housing sector in the UK has mitigated against provision for middle-income households and has acted as a brake on the development of a highly marketised approach since bureaucratic determination of need has been the main determinant of housing policy (Pawson 2009). The adoption of customer-focused techniques for service delivery is perhaps more a reflection of broader social, political and cultural expectations than a specific response to changing demands and attempts to develop new markets.

The traditional relationship of social housing providers with their customers has been a paternalistic one in which tenants and other service users have been comparatively passive recipients of services allocated to them through rationing processes with little ability to exit that service and meet their needs and wishes in a wider market. Customer care practices introduced in the 1980s were a relatively limited and simple way of improving the offer aimed at the fallacious 'average customer'. Most responses were at that time limited to the piecemeal use of promotional aspects of marketing with little or no evidence of a systematic approach to marketing social housing (Beevers, 1999). Marketing and customer-focused approaches were discussed in chapter 3 of this book, but one can see that such an approach has been heightened by new regulatory requirements and standards to consult with tenants, adoption of strategic marketing techniques and their adaptation by social housing providers through Customer Insight techniques (Davis, 2008). Knowledge of housing customers (individuals and communities) their aspirations and the choices that they make, can inform the development of new products and services – and avoid making false assumptions.

The improvement in the condition of the social housing stock in 1997-2010 with the delivery of the Decent Homes Standard across most of the social housing stock has reflected contemporary aspirations of what a decent home should be. Whilst these programmes have improved social housing, the standards applied relate to the dwelling itself rather than the surrounding environment and wider neighbourhood. The concentration of socially excluded households within social housing estates relates in part to to their quality and condition but also the impact of the concentration effect of residualisation itself, characterised by high proportions of low-income households, low levels of sales, reputational damage and a lack of attractiveness to households with choice. In parallel therefore, to work to raise the standard of their existing stock-providers have to differing degrees re-modelled and redeveloped their stock and included within it some tenure diversification. This has formed part of the mix in neighbourhood and housing regeneration and renewal programmes since the 1970s and provides opportunities to offer new products including intermediate housing products, such as shared ownership, within formerly mono-tenure social rented estates. The restricted borrowing capacity, falling values and decreased sales following the financial crisis that started in 2008 (see further Richardson (Ed.), 2010) now require housing associations to explore alternative business models to develop, sustain and regenerate stock. Local authorities also continue to need a sustainable business planning framework as the basis to manage existing homes and, with their partners, deliver new homes.

Conclusion

Customer expectations of housing providers are similar to those expected of private providers of services – that they offer timely, efficient, quality services which provide benefits that represent value for money and which can be accessed in a way that is convenient. The regulatory framework sets the context in which housing providers must meet this challenge and reflects the fact that many of their customers find themselves in quasi-markets where choice is constrained.

Consumers can be profiled and segmented in order to better develop products and services and to market them towards target groups. Providers are, however, constrained by statute and their purposes in relation to the services that they deliver and the terms on which they do so, and may not be free to exit particular markets in the manner of a private provider. Both customer and provider therefore find themselves operating in quasi-markets. Consequently, mutual dialogue is required in which customers make personal choices at the individual level, participate in collective decision-making in neighbourhoods or through special interest and user groups and engage as citizens at civic and national level on public policy and regulatory matters which affect the services that they receive.

Each of these dimensions must be addressed if customers are to receive appropriate services which meet their needs to the best of the provider's ability. Where customers are offered only choice (often of a constrained type), without sufficient voice and with little, if any, ability to exit, then means to ensure their needs are meet must be through action as collective service users: tenants and residents and as citizens rather than as atomised individuals who are customers only. A framework for this balanced approach is offered by the localism agenda which offers the prospect of developing places through the engagement by and with people who can become participants in, if not masters of, their destinies rather than mere consumers.

References and further reading

Audit Commission (2006) *Choosing well: analysing the cost and benefits of choice in local public services*. London: Audit Commission.

Beevers, R. (1999) *The Challenge of Changing Housing Markets*. The Northern Consortium of Housing Authorities.

Beresford, P. (2009) 'Personalisation and housing: A Service User View', *Housing Care and Support*, Vol. 12, No. 4.

Blackaby, B. and Kusminder, C. (2000) *Black and Minority Ethnic Housing Strategies*. Coventry and London: Chartered Institute of Housing, Federation of Black Housing Organisations and the Housing Corporation.

Bradbrook, G. and Fisher, J. (2004) *Digital Equality: Reviewing digital inclusion activity and mapping the way forwards*. www.citizensonline.org

Bramley, G., Pawson, H., Satsangi, M. and Third, H. (1999) *Local Needs Assessment: A Review of Current Practice and the Need for Guidance*. Edinburgh: Heriot-Watt University.

Brown, T., Dearling, A., Hunt, R., Richardson, J. and Yates, N. (2002) *Allocate or Let? Your Choice, Lessons from the Harborough HomeSearch*. York: Joseph Rowntree Foundation.

Burgess, E., Park, R. and McKenzie, R. (1925) *The City*. Chicago: University of Chicago Press.

Cabinet Office (2005) *Government response to the PASC report – Voice, Choice and Public Services*. London: HM Government.

Chartered Institute of Housing and Housing Corporation (2008) *Housing Needs and Aspirations of Ethnic Minority Communities*. Coventry and London: Chartered Institute of Housing and Housing Corporation.

Chartered Institute of Housing and Housing Corporation (2008a) *Housing Aspirations and Shared Ownership*. Coventry and London: Chartered Institute of Housing and Housing Corporation.

Chartered Institute of Housing Cymru (2009) *How was it for you, the Can Do Toolkit one year on*. Cardiff: Chartered Institute of Housing Cymru.

Chesseman, M. (2009) 'Personalisation and housing: giving control', *Housing Care and Support*, Vol. 12, No. 4.

Clark, R. (2008) 'Getting the personal into social housing', *The Guardian*, 14th February.

Clarke, J., Newman, J., Smith, N., Vidler, E. and Westmarland, L. (2007) *Creating Citizen Consumers: Changing Publics and Changing Public Services*. London: Sage.

Cole, I., Kane, S. and Robinson, D. (1999) *Changing Demand, Changing Neighbourhoods: The Response of Social Landlords*. Sheffield: Centre for Regional Economic and Social Research.

Communities and Local Government (2008) *Allocation of Accommodation: Choice Based Lettings, Code of Guidance for Local Housing Authorities*. London: Communities and Local Government.

Communities and Local Government (2008) *Delivering Digital Inclusion: An Action Plan for Consultation*. London: HM Government.

Communities and Local Government (2008) *Delivering Digital Inclusion Annex: Public Sector Use of Information and Communications Technologies to support social equality*. London: HM Government.

Cooper, C. (2005) 'Involving users and carers in housing and social care planning – the rhetoric of "user empowerment"' in M. Foord and P. Simic (Eds.) *Housing, community care and supported housing*. Coventry: CIH and Housing Studies Association.

Department for Children, Schools and Families (2009) *16-18 year olds NEET*. www.dcsf.gov.uk

Department of Health (2005) *Independence, Well-being and Choice: Our Vision for the Future of Social Care for Adults in England*. London: Department of Health.

DETR (2000) *Quality and Choice: A Decent Home for All*. Housing Green Paper.

Dutton, W., Helsper, E., and Gerber, M. (2009) *The Internet in Britain 2009*. Oxford Internet Institute, University of Oxford.

Ecotec Research and Consulting Ltd (2005) *Black and Minority Ethnic Housing in the West Midlands*. Ecotec Research and Consulting Ltd for West Midlands Regional Assembly.

Eliot, J. and Hamilton, N. (2009) 'Supporting People and the future of housing-related support', *Housing Care and Support*, Vol. 12, No. 2.

Foord, M. and Simic, P. (Eds.) (2005) *Housing, community care and supported housing*. Coventry: Chartered Institute of Housing and Housing Studies Association.

Harries, B., Richardson, L. and Soteri-Proctor, A. (2008) *Housing Aspirations for a New Generation*. Coventry and York: Chartered Institute of Housing and Joseph Rowntree Foundation.

Harrison, M. (2005) 'Ethnicity, "race" and policy issues', in Somerville, P. and Sprigings, N. (Eds.), *Housing and Social Policy*. London: Routledge.

Harrison, M. and Phillips, D. (2003) *Housing and Black and Minority Ethnic Communities: Review of the evidence base*. ODPM.

Harrison, M., Phillips, D., Chanal. K., Hunt, L. and Perry, J. (2005) *Housing, 'race' and community cohesion*. Coventry: Chartered Institute of Housing and Housing Studies Association.

Harrison, M. and Davis, C. (2001) *Housing Need, Social Policy and Difference: Disability, Ethnicity, Gender and Housing*. Bristol: Policy Press.

Head, J. (2009) 'Personalisation and housing: connections, challenges and opportunities', *Housing Care and Support,* Vol. 12, No. 4.

Hills, J., Brewer, M., Jenkins, S., Lister, R., Lupton, R., Machin, S., Mills, C., Modood, T., Rees, T. and Riddell, S. (2010) *An anatomy of economic inequality in the UK: Report of the National Equality Panel*. London: Government Equalities Office.

HM Government (2010) *The Coalition: Our programme for Government*. London: HM Government.

Hunter, S. and Ritchie, P. (Eds.) (2007) *Co-production and Personalisation in Social Care: changing relationships in the provision of social care*. London: Jessica Kingsley Publishers.

Kent-Smith, J. (2008) *Customer Insight: Knowing Your Customer, Good Practice Briefing*. Coventry: Chartered Institute of Housing.

Leadbetter, C. (2004) *Personalisation through Participation: A New Script for Public Services*. London: Demos.

Lee, P. and Murie, A. (1999) 'Spatial and Social divisions within British Cities: Beyond Residualisation', *Housing Studies,* Vol. 14, No. 5.

Macadam, A., Gandhi, K., Granville, G., Bowers, H. and Vallelly, S. (2009) *Personal Budgets, Personalisation and Older People's Housing IGP Project – Fieldwork Phase: Final Report*. National Development Team for Inclusion and Housing 21.

McCann, S. and Haynes, M. (2009) 'Personalisation and Housing Support', *Housing Care and Support,* Vol. 12, No. 4.

Mullins, D. and Murie, A. (2006) *Housing Policy in the UK*. Basingstoke: Palgrave Macmillan.

Passmore, J. and Ferguson, S. (1994) *Customer Service in a Competitive Environment*. Coventry: Chartered Institute of Housing.

Pawson, H. (2009) 'Social Housing and Choice' in Fitzpatrick, S. and Stephens, M. (Eds.), *The Future of Social Housing*. London: Shelter.

Perry, J. (2005) *Housing and Support Services for Asylum Seekers and Refugees: A Good Practice Guide*. Coventry and York: CIH and Joseph Rowntree Foundation.

Perry, J. (2008) *The Housing and Neighbourhood Impact of Britain's Changing Ethnic Mix*. York: Joseph Rowntree Foundation.

Perry, J. (2009) *Opening Doors: Improving housing services for refugees and new migrants*. Coventry: Chartered Institute of Housing and HACT.

Pleace, N. and Quilgars, D. (2002) *housing.support.org.uk: social housing, social care and electronic service delivery*. York: Joseph Rowntree Foundation.

Public Administration Select Committee (2005) *Voice, Choice and Public Services*. London: House of Commons.

Richardson, J. (Ed.) (2010) *From Recession to Renewal: the impact of the financial crisis on public services and local government*. Bristol: Policy Press.

Richardson, J. (2007) *Contentious Spaces: The Gypsy/Traveller Site Issue*. Coventry and York: CIH and Joseph Rowntree Foundation.

Richardson, J. (2006) *The Gypsy Debate, can discourse control?* Exeter: Imprint Academic.

Royal Geographical Society (2010) *Fact and Figures of the Digital Divide*, May 2010 – http://www.21stcenturychallenges.org/60-seconds/what-is-the-digital-divide

Shaheen, F. (2009) *Sticking plaster or stepping stone? Tackling urban youth unemployment*. London: Centre for Cities.

Simpson, M. (2009) 'Personalisation: the implications for housing and communities' *Housing Care and Support,* Vol. 12, No. 4.

Social Care Institute (2009) *Personalisation briefing: implications for housing providers*. Social Care Institute for Excellence with the National Housing Federation.

Social Housing Providers and Digital Inclusion Strategy Group (2010) *2010 Action Plan*.

Taylor Knox, H. (2009) *Personalisation and Individual Budgets: challenge or opportunity*. Housing Quality Network Briefing.

Teedon, P., Bloxsom, J., Punja, A. and England, J. (2005) *Housing Needs of Refugees in the East of England*. East of England Regional Assembly.

Titman, L. (1995) *Marketing in the New Public Sector*. London: Pitman Publishing.

Thornhill, J. (2009) *Equality, Diversity and Good Relations in Housing*. Coventry: Chartered Institute of Housing.

Tomlins, R. et al. (2001) *A question of diversity: an evaluation of how RSLs meet the needs of black and minority ethnic communities*. London: Housing Corporation.

Turner, M., Brough, P. and Williams-Findlay, B. (2003) *Our voice in our future: service users debate the future of the welfare state*. York: Joseph Rowntree Foundation.

Vallelly, S. and Manthorpe, J. (2009) *Building Choices Part 2: 'Getting Personal' the impact of personalisation on older people's housing*. Beaconsfield: Housing 21.

Vallelly, S. and Manthorpe, J. (2009a) 'Choice and control in specialist housing: starting conversations between commissioners and providers', *Housing Care and Support,* Vol. 12, No. 2.

Walden, D. (2009) 'Personalisation – implications for housing providers: issues in supporting housing research, policy and practice', *Housing Care and Support,* Vol. 12, No. 2.

West Sussex County Council (2010) *Customer Insight Gypsy Roma Traveller Workshop Summary Report 2010*. WSCC Insight Team.

Winchester, N. (2009) *Digital Exclusion and Social Housing*. National Housing Federation.

Wistow, G. (2009) 'Universalism and personalisation: squaring the circle', *Housing Care and Support,* Vol. 12, No. 4.

CHAPTER 5:
What do customers want?

John Perry

Introduction

What do customers want and how do social housing providers respond? An IPSOS Mori poll for the 2020 Public Services Trust (2010) examined citizen engagement and tested policy ideas for public service reform. Their research found that there were three key things that people value in public services:

- *Security* – although there were aspirations for quality and flexibility, the aspect of public services as a reliable 'safety net' was key[13]
- *Fairness* – for example, providing uniform standards across the country and fairness in allocating resources to the most deserving
- *Responsiveness* – to specific citizen needs and to provide the best possible service.

In his (2006) report *What Tenants Want*, Mayo suggested that tenants had asked that their landlords should:

1. Get the basics right and 'go the extra mile'
2. Give us a choice
3. Make involvement personal
4. Be accountable.

Fairness, responsiveness, accountability, personalisation are therefore all part of a shifting pattern of public service delivery which focuses much more strongly on the citizen or service consumer as a 'customer'. In more and more service areas the premise of 'choice' has entered either explicitly or implicitly as a way of engineering a greater degree of transparency, fairness and accountability. Choice, then, is a very important aspect of what customers say they want and a part of the new landscape of public services; and it is something that the social housing sector in the UK has embraced.

This chapter explores this 'choice' agenda – how it has emerged and what it means in the UK context, followed by a comparison with the 'choice' agenda being pursued in a different social housing system. Aspects of this debate on choice have already been

---

[13] The coalition government in 2010 began a debate on security of tenure for social housing which may culminate in the end of the so-called 'lifetime tenancy' and this could undermine the very thing that people value in their public services.

discussed very briefly in relation to 'voice' in chapter 2, and are also debated again by Brown and Yates in chapter 6 on customer satisfaction.

The most fundamental choice for a housing customer is between owning and renting. First, we look at the cultural context for this choice, and argue that in the UK there is a bias towards owning which has to be borne in mind in considering customer attitudes towards the social sector and the choices they might seek within it. The second part of the chapter then examines, in more detail, the idea of choice in the social sector context – what 'choice' means to different advocates of it, and how the choice agenda relates to different views about the purpose and future of social housing.

Third, while sounding a cautionary note about international comparisons, we offer one about the treatment of choice in the Dutch social housing system, compared with the UK. We remind readers that ideas from abroad should be adapted to the context of the UK, not adopted uncritically. Finally, we suggest conclusions from the discussion, and offer a robust response to the choice agenda and the wider debate about social housing in the UK.

Cultural and political context for customer attitudes

Problems in asking housing customers what they want

Asking housing customers what they want is not as straightforward as it is in testing opinion about preferences in consuming other products. While many of the same considerations ostensibly apply as in (say) buying a car – cost, brand image, reliability, whether it maintains its value, etc – housing as a consumer-item is loaded with other characteristics that have to be tested, too. The most obvious is tenure – not many other consumer goods can as easily (or more easily) be rented as they can be purchased. Another is that housing can be an investment good (even expensive cars are not usually bought because of an expectation of appreciation in their value). And yet another is location – housing is almost uniquely tied to place and neighbourhood, the proximity of a good school, etc. While the brand image of a car is important, how much more significant is the 'brand image' of living in Chelsea, London or Morningside, Edinburgh!

These are not frivolous points to make in the context of consumer choice about social housing. These broader influences on housing choice are ones that have entered the culture, through a multiplicity of TV programmes, consumer-oriented housing magazines, property pages in the press, and so on. Even a homeless family with the most restricted choice as to where to live is much more likely to be aware of the housing opportunities unattainable to them than they are (with the possible exception of expensive holidays) of other unavailable consumer items. Social housing tenants' expectations might therefore be expected to be strongly influenced by the prevailing cultural expectations that support aspirations to homeownership.

HOUSING AND THE CUSTOMER

To illustrate the extent of such influence, an interesting comparison can be made with the United States, where attitudes towards the benefits of homeownership are particularly robust. For example, even after the recent recession (see further Richardson, 2010) which is known to have had as a principal cause the US sub-prime mortgage problem, more than 80% of people in the US think that it is 'important to the overall economy' that there is a high level of homeownership. Perhaps surprisingly, even three quarters of those who currently rent their homes believe this to be the case. Compared with pre-recession 2003, the proportion of people who believe that now is a good time to buy a house (64%) has barely changed. Only 12% of people believe that 'renting makes more sense' despite the US's well-publicised foreclosure problems (Fannie Mae, 2010).

Another point about the cultural context for housing choices is that McLuhan's old criticism that 'the medium is the message' applies equally in this area as it does in other areas of consumer culture. A recent example was provided by a survey of 1,700 potential housebuyers carried out for an online estate agency, Hooplahomes. Their press release, and hence the story reported in the media,[14] focused on the finding that 'one third of Brits admit they would avoid living near a council estate'. However, the actual findings were that 69% of respondents were unconcerned about living near council housing, while those who were concerned rated the issue the lowest of the ten items that would adversely affected their choice of where to live. Figure 5.1 sets out the results.

Figure 5.1: 'Top ten reasons that would prevent a homebuyer from settling on a house' from a survey of potential housebuyers

Reason	Percentage giving the reason (%)
1. High crime rate	93
2. Interior layout	91
3. Lack of garden/small garden	87
4. Close proximity to a main road	82
5. Lack of good schools	79
6. Close proximity to airport	78
7. Close proximity to bars and pubs	54
8. Known death in the house	42
9. Close proximity to a graveyard	39
10. Close proximity to council estate	31

Source: Hooplahomes, 20 May 2010.

---

14 See www.propertytalklive.co.uk, 20 May 2010.

The media message is therefore often a double one: not only does it strongly promote homeownership as an option, but it can contain prejudices against the alternative options, particularly social or council housing.

Of course, the point about customers who are asked what they think being influenced by what they are *expected* to think is not a new one. However, it might be expected to be particularly strong in housing as a factor – if not an obstacle – to be borne in mind every time the question 'what do customers want?' is posed.

Political attitudes towards housing tenure

The cultural context is reinforced by political attitudes, both towards homeownership and towards rented housing. The presumption is that UK consumers want to buy, and – if they need to rent – would choose social housing as a last resort. Thus, even in the current recession, the Labour Party's 2010 Manifesto said that 'owning your own home is the aspiration of most families' while the Conservatives promised to 'make it easier for everyone to get on the housing ladder' so that 'everyone has the chance to own a home'. The Conservatives additionally promised to make it easier for social tenants to own or part-own their house, while saying no more about those who choose to continue renting than that a Conservative government would 'respect' them.

Political attitudes may have been tempered slightly by the recession, but only insofar as the commitment to homeownership has retreated from fantasy levels to ones that are somewhat more realistic. It is only a couple of years since it was government policy to increase homeownership by one million by 2011, and by a *further* 1.5m by 2015, to achieve a target of 75% of households being owner-occupiers. This was despite the fact that since 2005 levels of homeownership had been level or had even fallen slightly, and the numbers buying with a mortgage had fallen more noticeably (Williams and Pannell, 2007).

Nevertheless, there have been small signs that political and social attitudes might be changing. John Healey, the previous housing minister, noted in December 2009 that homeownership was declining slightly and that this might not be such a bad thing. He set out a vision in which people would have broader options either to rent, or to part-own, part-rent.[15]

Healey could be said to be responding to the facts and to known market trends. For example, people in their twenties are considerably less likely to be homeowners now than they were in 1984, despite the overall growth of homeownership over that period. CIH noted survey findings in mid-2009, at the height of the 'credit crunch', suggesting that young people were moving away from wanting to own their own

---

15 Speech to Fabian Society, 9 December 2009.

home: within the previous 12 months the proportion of 25-34 year-olds who thought that ownership was 'the right tenure for them' had fallen from 83% to 69%.[16] In the latest British Social Attitudes survey, respondents were asked:

> *Suppose a newly married young couple, both with steady jobs, asked your advice about whether to buy or rent a home. If they had the choice, what would you advise them to do?*

While almost 45% said they would advise buying 'as soon as possible', an only slightly lower 40% would advise the couple to 'wait a bit' before buying, indicating a degree of caution.

However, despite the evidence of a shift in societal attitudes, and against the background of the roughest ride for would-be homeowners in a decade, the main political party manifestos in 2010 continued to assume the benefits of homeownership for all – or at least, for the great majority.

What about tenants' attitudes towards their tenure?

How does this dominant cultural context affect the attitudes of those who rent social housing? Perhaps surprisingly, social tenants in the UK (apparently unlike tenants in the US) have on the face of it defied cultural trends and have consistently shown a much greater proportionate commitment to social renting. This has been true both before and since the current recession. For example, in 2004 only 13% of housing association tenants expressed a preference for homeownership in the long term (Housing Corporation, 2005). In 2008, the overall proportion was almost the same (14%).[17] This later survey was extended to include local authority and ALMO tenants, and LA tenants showed a higher proportion (17%) aspiring to homeownership in the long term compared with tenants of ALMOs and housing associations (12% each).

How can the low desire for homeownership among social tenants be explained? Important factors emerge if the data are disaggregated according to employment and age. In the 2008 survey, almost all those with an aspiration to own were households in employment. The desire to own among households with at least one person in full-time work was 72%. Among households where the tenant was aged 25-39 it was also relatively high: 36%. In other words, a large proportion of the desire for homeownership among social tenants comes from those who could afford it or are of an age where they might expect to make the transition, as they start to have a family or their family grows. In contrast, desire for homeownership declines sharply in higher age cohorts.

---

16 See www.cih.org/news/view.php?id=1070
17 Tenant Services Authority (2009) *Existing Tenants Survey 2008: Tenant mobility and aspirations*. London: TSA. The 2008 survey was similar to the Housing Corporation's previous survey, but was extended to include local authority tenants.

Researchers for the Housing Corporation's 2004 survey (writing in 2005) also suggest that the difference between the results from the surveys carried out by the Housing Corporation (more recently the TSA) and those obtained in broader studies such as the British Social Attitudes (BSA) survey might be explained by the nature of the questions. The BSA survey in 2004 showed that for 82% of respondents homeownership was their preferred tenure: and this aspiration had increased steadily over time. It is borne out by similar figures from Council of Mortgage Lenders' surveys. However, such questions are framed to find out general aspirations, unfettered by time or considerations like affordability. The Housing Corporation/TSA questions are part of a series about tenants' specific plans: they are therefore more likely to be tempered by practical considerations.

For social landlords there are lessons to be drawn from the data about tenant aspirations. First, it would be wrong to be complacent about the stability of the sector: although the proportions wanting to leave social housing appear low, the tenants who *do* want to leave tend to be younger, more affluent and those who are planning families – precisely the groups that landlords want to attract to stay in their stock if the sector is to be sustainable.

Second, even though higher proportions of tenants in these groups want to be homeowners, their reasons for doing so tend to be more related to their housing or neighbourhood circumstances, rather than to their aspirations to make an investment. Both in 2004 and in 2008, the main positive reasons for moving were factors such as size of house or wanting to be able to choose the location of their house. The negative reasons are evident in the fact that tenants who are dissatisfied with their landlord or the service they receive are also markedly more likely to want to be homeowners.

Third, the evidence therefore offers the possibility that social landlords could have an influence on attracting better-off tenants to remain within the sector. In the first place, the quality of service which tenants receive is clearly of vital importance – the higher the proportion of satisfied tenants there are, the lower will be the likely proportion who want to buy out of the sector. Another, much less significant factor, might be addressed by devising financial incentives for tenants who remain in the sector in the long term and who also meet tenancy conditions. (A number of such schemes have been devised, all of which aim to offer tenants some of the benefits currently available only to homeowners.[18])

The response on which we concentrate in the remainder of this chapter is about offering tenants more choice. As the authors of the 2004 study put it:

---

18 For example, Terry, R., Simpson, M. and Regan, S. (2005) *HomeSave – Increasing choices for tenants to own assets*. Coventry: CIH and Shelter and also Conservative Party (2009) *Strong Foundations: building homes and communities*.

...some tenants' aspirations could be met by increasing choice, both in terms of location and individual properties, and the ability to exercise more control over these, as well improvements to the neighbourhoods in which housing association homes are located. It is possible that policies that addressed these issues could improve the sustainability of the sector by encouraging tenants with higher incomes to continue renting from a housing association.

What kinds of choice?

We conclude that social tenants are not immune from the cultural pressures towards homeownership, including the associated consumerism and the attractions of investing in an appreciating asset. But they are considerably tempered by tenants' experience in the sector and also by their realism about their prospects of buying, taking account of factors such their income and their age. Many younger, more affluent tenants show almost the same levels of aspiration to own as the general population. However, their motives are mixed – and in many cases could be addressed *within* the social sector – if tenants were able to exercise more *choice* of the kinds that they might aspire to as homeowners.

What does 'choice' mean?

Advocating greater choice within the social housing sector is hardly a new concept. Individual choice to buy rather than rent, for example, has long been an option offered by some social landlords and was put in statute in 1980 as the right to buy (for local authority tenants) and in 1996 as the right to acquire (for certain housing association tenants). Collective choice to change landlords within the sector was offered by the ill-fated 'Tenants' Choice' legislation in 1988 and (although not at tenants' instigation) by the large-scale voluntary transfers which actually began in the same year – although there had been antecedents such as the Stockbridge Village Trust (1983) and the transfers of individual estates in Glasgow to community-based HAs. Later came the right to manage, which had more impact than Tenants' Choice, with some 84,000 properties moving into management by Tenants' Management Organisations by 2002.

Of the various measures, by far the biggest impact on tenure across the UK came from the right to buy (2.5m homes sold into owner-occupation) followed by stock transfer (1.4m homes transferred from local authorities to housing associations). The big shifts in tenure in the UK in the last three decades – the growth in homeownership from only just over 50% to almost 70%, the doubling in size of the HA sector, and the dramatic fall by almost two thirds in the size of the council sector – have resulted in large part from these two policy measures alone.

Yet only the right to buy can be said to have transformed choice for individual tenants, and this has been by taking them out of the sector. Choice within the social sector has been more limited and has developed more incrementally. Also, unlike the right to buy, choice within the sector has until recently been mainly collective rather than individual choice. For example, the growth of tenant participation (often associated with area management initiatives) in the 1980s was largely about the role of tenant associations. When the Labour government introduced 'Best Value' to replace the previous compulsory competitive tendering regime in 1997, one of its precepts (called 'the four Cs') was consultation with service users. This was followed by the Audit Commission's newly established Housing Inspectorate developing its 'Key Lines of Enquiry' (KLOEs), which included expectations that social landlords would respond to customer views in shaping their services overall (but not by providing choice at individual customer level).

Such developments were initially aimed at achieving uniform changes in customer services – the assumption that 'one size fits all' still prevailed. The emergence of individual customer choice as a goal came later as the previous government's 'modernisation' agenda for public services began to develop. What has been called the 'consumerisation' of public services was exemplified by the 2006 white paper on local government saying that:

> *People want to be treated as individuals, and to receive a service that is tailored to their personal situation* (CLG, 2006).

Consumer choice in public services came to be seen as operating at two levels: individuals choosing the level and type of service they want, and customers either individually or collectively choosing *between* service providers, including having the option of the service being provided by the community itself.

Early development of the individual 'choice' agenda – choice-based lettings

The initial focus of efforts to provide more choice for individuals in housing was of course the experiments with and then wider introduction of choice-based lettings (CBL) schemes. CBL was based on experience in the Netherlands (in what became known in the UK as the 'Delft model', Brown *et al.*, 2000) and by 2006 was already starting to be used by a variety of landlords. The idea of choice at the allocations stage had been supported by government as early as 2000. The housing green paper of that year said that:[19]

> *Applicants for social housing who are more involved in decisions about their new homes are more likely to have a longer-term commitment to the locality. This will promote more sustainable communities… It will increase personal well-being, and help to reduce anti-social behaviour, crime, stress and educational underachievement.*

---

19 DETR/DSS (2000) *Quality and Choice: A decent home for all*, para. 9.7.

Following largely favourable reviews of the CBL pilots, government placed an expectation on all social landlords to operate CBL schemes by 2010.

CBL as an instrument of individual choice has been reviewed by Hal Pawson (2009) who had also been the main author of the government's official review. He concludes that CBL has had some impact in making tenancies more sustainable, although the impact on tenants' mobility (within the sector) is more mixed. He sees them as part of the intended transformation of social housing from a 'command system' ('you take what you are given') to a 'social market' model, akin to how it operates in the Netherlands and elsewhere in Northern Europe. But as he points out, there are limitations on this as even CBL schemes operate within allocations rules and homelessness legislation which prioritise need rather than choice. Particularly for applicants considered to have low-priority in terms of housing need, CBL might be more frustrating than empowering unless providers find ways to offer guidance to applicants on how realistic their expectations of CBL schemes are.[20]

Pawson describes CBL schemes as the previous government's 'flagship' housing policy in pursuing its modernisation agenda for local services. Yet as a flagship the schemes have hardly been transformational. There are considerable constraints on choice, resulting in part from the statutory allocations criteria and in part from the declining supply of social lettings (lettings fell by 40% in the decade up to 2006-7). CBL schemes still therefore only provide an initial choice of properties from what in practice is likely to be the rather narrow range for which any one applicant can make successful bids. As schemes become wider in their coverage, the range may be extended to include properties owned by different landlords or in wider geographical areas. But once a property has been chosen and the tenancy starts, individual choice largely comes to an end.

More radical individual choices in lettings?

In the run-up to the 2010 election there was a plethora of critiques of social housing, many of which focused on allocations and lettings policies, calling for more fundamental reforms. Not all of these proposals were intended to provide more individual choice, but within them were several that would have done so, if only for some categories of applicants. Many would, for example, give less priority (and less choice) to the most vulnerable groups, favouring instead categories like working households who would then have more access and therefore potentially more choice.

Here are some changes that have recently been promoted:

- *Put more emphasis on waiting time and on transfers between existing tenancies* – this would allow non-priority need applicants to have more choice,

---

[20] Hal Pawson cites the example of a private sector tenant in Edinburgh, officially in low housing need, who wanted to move to the social sector: she made 370 unsuccessful bids for council tenancies over a three-year period up to 2007.

while providing fewer opportunities to homeless and other priority need applicants (Conservative Party, 2009).
- *Have a two-stream allocation system, separating homeless applicants from waiting-list applicants* – again to provide more choice to waiting-list applicants, probably from slightly higher socio-economic groups (Blunkett, 2007).
- *Allow greater weighting (more 'points') for certain categories* – which might allow more choice to people in work, people contributing to the community, etc.[21]
- *Relax or remove rules about numbers of properties an applicant can refuse* – to extend choice (but at the cost of a greater administrative burden) (Cole *et al.*, 2001).
- *Access allocations schemes through 'housing options' services* – which would be aimed at encouraging applicants to choose more widely, including within the private rented sector.[22]
- *End central rules about allocations and allow social landlords to establish their own rules* – which would involve the abolition of 'reasonable preference' categories and might well result in people with strong 'local connections' having more choice – but could severely limit options for homeless applicants (Greenhalgh and Moss, 2009).

A cautionary note – the dangers of the 'choice' agenda

Looking at these examples raises a question of whether their proponents really want social housing to be a 'tenure of choice' for a broader cross-section of the population, or whether they believe that its role should be limited only to meeting 'genuine need'[23] – with the aim of having a smaller sector. There is therefore no underlying consensus in the 'choice' debate about what the aims of social housing should be.

Since the seminal official review of English social housing by John Hills in 2007 identified a range of issues about the tenure and who it houses, there have been a variety of reform packages claiming to address the problems which the report is said to pose. Many of the proposals above form part of these packages. Ian Cole has reviewed a range of these reform proposals (Cole, 2007). He suggests that they fall into four categories. At opposite extremes are the 'market idealists' and the 'preservationists'. The preservationists largely want social housing to be kept as it is but with more investment, while the market idealists want to encourage tenants to move out of social housing, so that it can be wound down and eventually disappears.

---

21 Proposed in different forms by various commentators. See, for example, CIH (2008) *Rethinking Housing*. Coventry: CIH.
22 *Ibid.*
23 The pre-election Conservative Party paper on housing policy called for social housing allocations to cater for those 'genuinely in need'. See Conservative Party (2009), *op.cit.* p.32.

Cole argues that in the debate there are two middle groups: 'revisionists' and 'reformists', who currently have more influence than the two extremes. Both of these tend to favour social sector customers having more choice, and have made proposals along the lines summarised above. However, the revisionists interpret the Hills Report as showing that social housing has failed. While it is therefore still needed, it should have a much reduced role, becoming a short-term expedient for people who need help in a crisis. Choice would essentially be about ways of leaving the sector as quickly as possible (see authors such as Dwelly and Cowans, 2006).

The reformists, on the other hand, who include Cole and Hills (and the present authors), favour a sector which offers options to a broader client group, including those on middle incomes, taking the sector towards the 'wider affordability' role found elsewhere in Northern Europe. The sector would aim to be a 'tenure of choice', and would be one that would offer this choice not only at the start of a tenancy, but during it.

Choice during a tenancy

In the last few years there has been growing interest in ways of providing choice *during* a tenancy. These have taken various forms, and again some come from different viewpoints within the debate on the purpose of social housing. For example, some want forms of 'choice' that would fundamentally *change the nature of social housing tenure* (for example Greenhalgh and Moss, 2009); these might be limited to single reforms such as ending security of tenure or making tenancies subject to periodic review, or they might be more sweeping changes such as having market rents or new forms of tenancy, more like private sector tenancies. It is questionable, however, whether these changes would provide genuine choice for current tenants. Many tenants value security of tenure so removing this would take away a feature of social housing which is generally regarded as one of its important advantages over private renting. Similarly, market-level rents (and greater dependency on housing benefit) might well be seen by working tenants in low-paid jobs as a severe constraint, perhaps making it difficult for them to continue working.

A second set of reforms on which there is more common ground has been about making it easier to make a *change of property*. CBL schemes have been widened in many cases to operate across several local authority areas and to include low cost homeownership and even private rented properties. The coalition government has promised a resuscitated national mobility scheme to make it easier for existing tenants to move. More radical proposals to allow more choice of property have included the suggestion that tenants could have the power to trigger the sale of the property they occupy, with the proceeds being used to buy an alternative property that they would continue to rent from the same landlord.[24]

---

24 Made both in Conservative Party (2009), *op.cit.* and in Leunig, T (2008) 'An equal footing', *Inside Housing*, 13 June.

A third set of reforms has been about making *change of tenure* easier, which might be about providing more opportunities for tenants to buy a share in their home, or might be a more radical move towards 'flexible tenure', in which a householder can staircase both into and out of an ownership share in the property. These measures do represent an extension of individual choice but involve a change of tenure. Furthermore, genuine flexibility is so far limited to a few experimental schemes benefiting only a tiny proportion of tenants. Nevertheless, wider adoption of 'flexible tenure' could be a radical move towards increasing choice, albeit choice about tenure rather than about services received *as a tenant*. It could also be an element in delivering genuinely mixed-income and mixed-tenure communities (on which there is a much broader literature).[25]

A fourth set of reforms has been about the ability to *change landlord or choose the provider of services*. This might be the sanction of a negative change if the current landlord is judged to be poor, or a positive change to a preferred provider.

Finally, there are reforms aimed at providing a greater *choice of services from the same provider*. At one extreme, this might mean choosing between different levels of rent relating to different standards of service. Or it might be limited to choices about service delivery, such as choosing the time of day when a repair will be done or choosing different styles of kitchen in a new property.

The latter two sets of reforms, about changing the service provider or choosing different services from the same provider, were suggested in two recent reports, such as Lupton *et al.* (2008). Exercising collective forms of choice is also of course one of the main aims of various methods of tenant involvement or empowerment, progress towards which has been recently reviewed (in the UK context) elsewhere.[26] In practice, providers seem to be moving to combine these more longstanding, collective involvement methods with the more recent, individualised approaches.

Having explored what 'choice' means in social housing, the next section of the chapter looks at experience outside the UK. It takes as the comparator the social housing system in the Netherlands, which was the inspiration for UK choice-based lettings schemes and which is itself subject to pressures to provide more individual choice. Does it have lessons to offer in the domestic debate about choice?

---

25 Summarised in Bailey, N et al (2006) *Creating and Sustaining Mixed Income Communities*. Coventry: CIH for the Joseph Rowntree Foundation.
26 In the context of the evolution of the new regulatory framework in England, practice in tenant participation was recently reviewed in Lupton, M et al. (2010) *Making Voices Count: Reviewing practice in tenant involvement and empowerment*. Coventry: HouseMark.

Tenant attitudes and tenant choices – experience in the Netherlands

Another cautionary note – about international comparisons

What caveats apply to learning from the experience in other countries? While there is a heavy traffic in social policy ideas from abroad – perhaps especially from North America – it is worth entering a note of caution. As commentators such as Mark Stephens (2009) have pointed out, the aims of social housing in other countries are often very different, sometimes mirroring aspects of the debate in the UK following the Hills Report. Stephens suggests a contrast between the 'ambulance service' function of social housing in the USA, Canada and Australia (where it is a small sector in each case) compared with its 'wider affordability' role in Northern European countries (with their generally larger social sectors). The four administrations in the UK fall somewhere in between these models – having moved away from a wider affordability objective to having what Stephens describes as a 'safety net' role. Examples of tenants' expectations, and of landlords' ways of addressing them, therefore need to be seen in the context of the overall aim of the national system in which they are located.

In considering the Netherlands, we are therefore making an explicit decision to review experience in a country where the social sector already has many features of a 'tenure of choice' in order to see what lessons it has for a wider choice agenda in the UK. Before doing so, it was worth summarising the differences about the sector in the Netherlands that justify this description of it.

Differences and similarities in the Dutch social sector

The most obvious difference about the Dutch sector is its size and importance: it constitutes 33% of the housing stock, compared with the UK's 20%. It therefore caters for a wider range of tenants, in a social context in which there is a smaller gap between rich and poor. So that although the Dutch sector is oriented towards meeting need, it is an example of a sector having the 'broader affordability' role which Stephens describes: for example, some 47% of tenants have jobs (Ditch *et al.*, 2001).

Another characteristic is that the sector is largely run by housing associations, and these have moved to a position where they have a good deal more autonomy than those in the UK. However, lettings systems remain the responsibility of local authorities and housing allowances (the equivalent of housing benefit) are part of the national welfare system as they are in the UK (although they are structured so that those receiving the maximum allowances still pay a proportion of their rents).

Dutch social and private tenants have similar security of tenure to social tenants in the UK. There is no right to buy.

In the different context of Dutch social housing, it is to be expected that any 'choice' agenda will also be different, and this is to some extent true although there are also similarities and worthwhile points of comparison. We now consider how the choice agenda has developed either in practice or in debate within the Dutch social housing sector.

Choice of tenure – new tenants

How polarised is the choice between tenures for new residents? How many of those who choose to rent also have an option to buy? This is a more difficult issue to tackle than choice for existing tenants, but it has been suggested that one measure of this choice is whether there is a big or small gap between median incomes in different tenures, the hypothesis being that the smaller the gap the more effective choice is likely to be.

Marja Elsinga (2007) and others have compared the UK and Dutch housing markets in this respect, as well as the balance between working and non-working residents/tenants. They show that the median incomes of social tenants are some €3,000 higher in the Netherlands, and those of owners are over €5,000 lower. A similar picture emerges from looking at the differences in terms of proportions in work or dependent on benefits. The gap between tenants and owners is therefore much smaller in the Netherlands and they conclude that more social tenants are likely to have an *effective choice* between owning and renting.

Interestingly, while as a result there does seem greater social mix in Dutch social housing, this has not prevented concentrated poverty in particular areas, which has led to similar debates about how to promote more mixed neighbourhoods as those in the UK. This has led to policies that have parallels with some of the untested proposals for UK social housing mentioned earlier – for example, measures that limit the scope for new, low-income tenants to choose certain inner city neighbourhoods of Rotterdam. (Unfortunately, in the Dutch context, the debate has become racialised as a high proportion of those affected by these measures, and denied the choice to move to certain areas, have been immigrants.)

To what extent do Dutch landlords offer low cost homeownership (LCHO) options? In the UK, 170,000 LCHO units have been provided in the last thirty years. In the Netherlands, LCHO is much less developed. However, the Dutch Government adopted a target to achieve 65% homeownership by this year (2010), and although this has not been achieved it put pressure on housing associations to develop schemes. One is outright sales of existing vacant units to new residents. While discounts of up to 30% are available to sitting tenants, there are only much smaller ones (10%) for new purchasers. Another model is shared ownership, but configured slightly differently from the UK in that the owner buys the interior of the dwelling (a flat) while the HA remains the owner of the external structure. More than 150 Dutch associations are now engaged in low cost homeownership schemes.

Choice of tenure – existing tenants

Can Dutch social tenants more easily move out of the sector if they are dissatisfied with it? The evidence above suggests that a higher proportion of existing tenants are likely to be able to buy out of the sector, if they wish to. And indeed, Elsinga and colleagues show that movement *out of* social housing into ownership is more than four times as great in the Netherlands. Interestingly, moves *back into* social housing are also nearly four times as common. Dutch social tenants have less propensity to move to private renting, however, than those in the UK.

This level of movement occurs despite the fact that, while municipal tenants in the UK have had the right to buy since 1980 (and later, for many housing association tenants, the right to acquire), Dutch social housing tenants have never had this right. However, partly because of the government policy change mentioned above, associations are now starting to offer properties to buy to their sitting tenants.

> One example comes from the association **Woonbron**, which wanted to create more choice in their contracts with residents, such as renting, buying or variants of renting/buying. Woonbron is doing this through its 'For Living' scheme, under which residents decide for themselves whether they wish to buy or continue renting their house. So far, the scheme has been offered to just under half of Woonbron's 50,000 residents and about one in eight have chosen an option other than their original rental contract.

Choice of landlord and property – new tenants

The Netherlands is of course the home of choice-based lettings (CBL) schemes, which have now been the norm in Dutch social housing for twenty years. As in the CBL schemes in the UK, the aim has been to give applicants more choice about their landlord and their rented property, as opposed to being 'allocated' a home under earlier systems. The Dutch CBL schemes appear to be a durable feature of their social housing system, but they are not without critics or attempts to alter the schemes. Van Daalen and Van Der Land (2008) have summarised recent developments. One in Nijmegen has been an attempt to offer more choice, by abolishing income criteria attached to qualification to enter the CBL scheme. Another variant in Rotterdam is a lottery to find the 'winners' of a rented property between those bidding for it. Two schemes have attempted social engineering of poorer neighbourhoods, by asking 'lifestyle' questions of applicants and using these to select groups eligible to bid for lettings. The changes have been variable in their effects, but a common outcome has been either no improvement or a worsening of the choices for the lowest-income applicants – none of the reforms have improved the choices of those on low incomes.

Choice of landlord and property – existing tenants

Can Dutch social tenants more easily 'vote with their feet' if dissatisfied with their social rented property or their landlord? Elsinga and colleagues looked at choice of *landlord* in the Dutch and English contexts. However, their conclusion was that much depends on locality. Some social tenants in both countries are in places where they have an effective choice between different social landlords, but many are not. In general, there is more choice in the Netherlands but this is by no means universal.

Movement between *properties* within the social sector is however much more common in the Netherlands. Interestingly, a study of Eindhoven showed that such movements may be of poorer tenants in receipt of housing allowance moving to better properties, and better off tenants 'downsizing' to save on rental payments, echoing some of the conclusions just mentioned about developments in CBL schemes (Dogge and Smeets, 2007).

> One recent development in the Netherlands has been a move towards self-regulation. Associations with more than 60% of the social rented stock have created the 'KWH rented housing label' which is a kitemark scheme, with performance tests not unlike Audit Commission KLOEs (Perry and Lupton, 2009). These include measures of tenant satisfaction and 'mystery shopping' and other tests to assess how a landlord treats customers. The label and the published rankings against it create a strong element of competition and an objective test for tenants of how their landlord compares with others.

Choice of services in the social sector

As noted earlier, a recent aspect of the 'modernisation' agenda in the UK has been that of creating greater consumer choice. To some extent this has built on a longer-standing drive towards greater collective participation by tenants, but recently it has also considered whether tenants could make individual service choices, possibly reflected in their rents.

The Dutch social housing sector appears to be starting to behave in the entrepreneurial way foreseen in the UK's 'modernisation' agenda. It has for several years been independent of government grant, and is much more lightly regulated than the UK sector. Although it has a remit to help low-income groups, it also has one to promote 'liveability' and in any case (as we have seen) caters for a wider range of incomes.

> This has led to some Dutch associations offering different 'packages' in terms of living arrangements. For example, Woonbron offers a range of options from a choice of types of kitchen to enhanced management packages such as extra security, personal alarms and insurance protection. The packages are offered through 'home outlets' where they can be seen or explained.

Conclusions

Although there are obvious differences between the UK's social housing systems and those of the Netherlands, many of the debates about the future role of social housing are similar: how best to cater for low-income groups, how to promote mixed neighbourhoods, and how to promote homeownership. In particular, it is noteworthy that the Dutch Government wants to encourage owner-occupation, in a situation where owners still get mortgage tax relief and yet social housing is free of subsidy except for housing allowances for lower-income tenants.

By implication, the Dutch Government seeks a smaller social sector, but from a much larger base than the sector in the UK (where, as we have seen, there are similar calls for a reduced sector). The response of Dutch associations appears to be a robust one – attempting to promote homeownership (but finding that most tenants do not want it) and yet finding other ways to promote choice within their services – for example having arrangements for easier moves within the sector.

Part one of this chapter looked at the factors affecting long-term housing aspirations, concluding that although UK social tenants appear to have surprising little aspiration towards ownership, the detailed figures reveal a number of factors which might cause this to change. It was suggested that an important factor in maintaining the attractiveness of social renting is to provide more choice – in various different senses – when entering the sector and while living as a social tenant. Evidence from the Netherlands – accepting crucial differences such as the size of the sector – does support this view. Many Dutch social tenants, given the chance to buy, turn it down, and this includes those on higher incomes. People are more easily able to move within the sector, and do so. Although mobility is greater between sectors in the Netherlands, the numbers leaving social housing are almost balanced by those returning – and most of these are former owners.

The Dutch social housing sector has a very important scale advantage. The UK social sector is unlikely to have the potential to expand in the next few years and indeed may be subject to further pressure to sell stock. However, there are other lessons from the Netherlands that might have application in the UK: the benefits (now perhaps outweighing the costs) of freedom from direct subsidy, and the looser regulatory regime which has been partly filled by sector-led self-regulation. Although addressing the 'choice' agenda in different ways, Dutch social housing seems at least as well equipped to survive a period of cuts in public budgets and reduced welfare benefits for low-income customers, as does the social housing sector in the UK.

References and further reading

2020 Public Services Trust (2010) *Citizen engagement: testing policy ideas for public service reform*. Ipsos Mori. London: 2020 Public Services Trust.

Blunkett, D. (2007) Reported in *The Guardian*, 22nd April.

Brown, T. *et al*. (2000) *Lettings: A Question of Choice*. Coventry and York: Chartered Institute of Housing and Joseph Rowntree Foundation.

CIH (2008) *Rethinking Housing*. Coventry: Chartered Institute of Housing.

CLG (2006) *Strong and Prosperous Communities*. Local Government White Paper.

Cole, *et al*. (2001) *Social Engineering or Consumer Choice? Rethinking housing allocations*. Coventry: CIH for the Joseph Rowntree Foundation.

Cole, I (2007) 'What future for social housing in England?' in *People, Place and Policy Online*, Vol. 1, No. 1.

Conservative Party (2009) *Strong Foundations: building homes and communities*. London: Conservative Party.

DETR/DSS (2000) *Quality and Choice: A decent home for all*. London: DETR.

Ditch, J. *et al*. (2001) *Social Housing, Tenure and Housing Allowance: An international review*. London: DWP.

Dogge, P. and Smeets, J. (2007) *Freedom of Choice in the Housing Market: The case of Eindhoven*. European Network of Housing Research.

Dwelly, T. and Cowans, J. (2006) *Rethinking Social Housing*. London: The Smith Institute.

Elsinga, M. *et al*. (2007) *How Competitive is Social Rented Housing in England and the Netherlands?* European Network of Housing Research.

Fannie Mae (2010) *National Housing Survey* www.fanniemae.com/about/housing-survey.html

Greenhalgh, S. and Moss, J. (2009) *Principles for social housing reform*. London: Localis.

Hills, J. (2007) *Ends and Means: The future roles of social housing in England*. London: LSE.

Housing Corporation (2005) *Aspirations to ownership*. London: Housing Corporation.

Leunig, T. (2008) 'An equal footing' in *Inside Housing*, 13th June.

Lupton, M. *et al*. (2008) *A Real Choice for Tenants?* London: Tribal.

Lupton, M., Lomax, A. and Duggan, G. (2009) *Choosing Choice*. London: Tribal.

Lupton, M. *et al*. (2010) *Making Voices Count: Reviewing practice in tenant involvement and empowerment*. Coventry: HouseMark.

Mayo, E. (2006) *What Tenants Want*, report of the Tenant Involvement Commission. www.housing.org

Pawson, H. 'Social Housing and Choice' in S. Fitzpatrick and M. Stephens (Eds.) (2009) *The Future of Social Housing*. London: Shelter.

Perry, J. and Lupton, M. (2009) *What Tenants Want – Globally!* Coventry: Chartered Institute of Housing.

Richardson, J. (Ed.) (2010) *From Recession to Renewal: the impact of the financial crisis on public services and local government*. Bristol: Policy Press.

Stephens, M. (2009) 'The Role of the Social Rented Sector' in S. Fitzpatrick and M. Stephens (Eds.) (2009) *The Future of Social Housing.* London: Shelter.

Tenant Services Authority (2009) *Existing Tenants Survey 2008: Tenant mobility and aspirations.* London: Tenant Services Authority.

Van Daalen, G. and Van Der Land, M. (2008) 'Next Steps in Choice-based Letting in the Dutch Social Housing Sector' in *European Journal of Housing Policy,* Vol. 8, No. 3.

Williams, P. and Pannell, R. (2007) *Home Ownership at the Crossroads?* London: CML.

CHAPTER 6:
The revolting customer? – the meaning of customer satisfaction

Tim Brown and Nicola Yates

Introduction

There has been a coalescence of factors that have driven forward the customer satisfaction agenda in recent decades. They include, first, the need to demonstrate to governments the effective performance of social housing landlords. Secondly, there is the focus on competition between organisations. Thirdly, there is the emphasis on greater accountability over the use of public finance. Fourthly, and most importantly, putting the customer first has become central in the design and delivery of services. As was pointed out in chapter 2, there has been a shift from the traditional welfare model of the state with professionals designing and delivering services to passive and grateful clients towards a greater customer-orientated approach. This has paved the way for a refocusing of the concept of quality from 'conformance to specification' to 'fitness for purpose' involving a judgment by the person using the service and product. Ideas such as customer voice and exit (as originally developed by Hirschman, 1970) have therefore become commonplace in debates on housing and other public services. At the same time, there is strong evidence that customers want better services at less cost (Cole and Parston, 2006). Indeed it could be said that customers are revolting against poor service provision and low satisfaction through increasing numbers of complaints.

- The Housing Ombudsman service has seen a 72% increase in the number of complaints from housing association tenants in the last three years from 3,206 in 2007/08 to 5,519 in 2009/10 (Hardman, 2010a).
- The Local Government Ombudsman consistently finds that housing is one of the largest sources of complaints at approximately 20% of all complaints (Local Government Ombudsman, 2010).
- The Citizens Advice Bureau dealt with a 10% increase in housing enquiries in the first quarter of 2010/11 compared with the first quarter of 2009/10 (Citizens Advice Bureau, 2010).

> - At a local scale, for example, Homes for Haringey (an arms length management organisation) found that in 2007 it investigated 1,200 stage one complaints and 100 stage two complaints. The organisation spent approximately £340,000 dealing with these issues and it involved 14,000 hours of officer time.

An example of the shift in customer expectation of the cost and quality of service delivery is the lettings process that has moved from an approach based on professional judgment determined by need and available properties to a choice-based lettings (CBL) system where households on the housing register make informed decisions as to whether to respond to specific advertised properties. This system was first developed in the Netherlands in the late 1980s in response to concerns that social housing organisations were not responding to developments in other public policy areas on choice, empowerment and personalisation.

The focus on customer and tenant satisfaction is, therefore, not a new phenomenon of the 21st century. It has developed over many decades. Pollitt (2003, p.35) provides a revealing quote from Dimock in 1936:

> *The customer satisfaction criterion applies with as much force to government as to business. In the past, the failure of public enterprises generally to pay sufficient attention to customer attitudes and citizen relations has been the aspect of public administration, which is most inefficient and subject to criticism...*

Among housing practitioners, policy-makers and academics in the 1980s and 1990s, there were extensive debates and discussions. A study on allocations and lettings covering the period from 1986-1992 found that over 60% of local authority housing departments had undertaken tenant surveys that included satisfaction issues (Prescott-Clarke et al., 1993). The Best Value initiative in the late 1990s generated a further surge in interest. As Wisniewski (2001) pointed out, in Scotland this resulted in the piloting and testing of generic models developed by Parasuraman et al. (1985) derived from an analysis of service quality gaps in organisations.

Nevertheless, there is now a heightened interest in customer satisfaction. The three main political parties in England as well as the coalition government have espoused a localist agenda encompassing a greater say for households in decisions affecting their neighbourhoods and services. At the same time, housing organisations are rethinking their offer to customers in the light of public expenditure cuts. Radical suggestions such as co-production (i.e. the design and/or delivery of services by users and providers) and individual budgets in health and social care are influencing thinking on housing and related services. In addressing this heightened focus, measuring and responding to customer satisfaction is crucial.

The aim of this chapter is to build on the material in chapter 2 by exploring in depth the issues surrounding customer satisfaction in housing and public services. More specifically, the four objectives are to: set out current policy and practice on measuring customer satisfaction; analyse key trends – for example, customer satisfaction levels do not necessarily equate with improved organisational performance (see, for instance, Flynn, 2007, chapter 5); indicate how measuring customer satisfaction can be taken forward as part of a broader agenda for improving public services including housing; and finally to consider the implications of the findings on customer satisfaction for the design and delivery of services i.e. should and how can housing organisations effectively utilise information for rethinking their offer to tenants?

The next section, therefore, summarises the national policy agenda on measuring customer satisfaction. This is followed by a review of national and local approaches. The key and often contradictory findings as well as emerging issues on customer satisfaction are considered in the fourth section. The penultimate section considers how the weaknesses with customer satisfaction techniques and principles could be addressed. The concluding part of the chapter centres on how customer satisfaction information can make a crucial contribution to the redesign of services.

Measuring customer satisfaction – the national perspective

A useful starting point is a statement from the middle of the last decade by the Cabinet Secretary:

> We must be relentlessly customer-focused. Many people want a single point of contact for a range of services. The public are not interested in whether their needs are met by Department X or Agency Y, they just want a good, joined up service where X and Y talk to each other and share the information the public have provided. We should strive to meet this demand (O'Donnell, 2006, front page).

Understanding customer satisfaction and its measurement is central to achieving this aim. Nevertheless, as chapters 2 and 4 have highlighted, this is not straightforward. Unlike the private sector, customers have until recently had relatively few choices. Voice (e.g. complaints) rather than exit has been central. In addition, people want both their individual needs met and those of the whole population. Good quality hospitals and schools are demanded by citizens rather than just by patients and parents. Similarly, public sector organisations, unlike the private sector cannot indulge in cream-skimming i.e. providing services to only high value or low cost customers. For many services (including social housing), the focus is on those in greatest need that are often difficult to identify. Measuring customer satisfaction in the public sector must, then, be robust and sophisticated.

HOUSING AND THE CUSTOMER

There has been a well-established policy framework supporting a customer satisfaction agenda in housing including its measurement. The Audit Commission through its key lines of enquiry (KLOE) methodology has placed considerable emphasis on this issue. For example, the access and customer care in housing service KLOE states that an organisation delivering an excellent service:

> *Monitors customer satisfaction with complaints and has customers who are satisfied with the way complaints are handled...(H)as high levels of satisfaction with opportunities to inform management and affect decision-making and service delivery* (Audit Commission, 2007, pp.6-7).

More generally, the Audit Commission (2008) has emphasised that poor decision-making often stems from inadequate data including the lack of robust material on customer satisfaction. Similar views were expressed in an independent review for Communities and Local Government (2009) on 'Getting it Right and Righting the Wrongs'. This study took forward the recommendations on individual redress and customer satisfaction in the government White Paper on 'Communities in Control' (Communities and Local Government, 2008).

National and local approaches to measuring customer satisfaction

Collecting and analysing information on customer satisfaction may appear superficially to be straightforward. There is a long-term consensus in support of a customer-orientated approach and this necessitates measuring customer satisfaction. At the same time there are many useful sources of guidance, good practice and toolkits on how to undertake such work. However, the reality is more complex. Organisations need to carefully consider which are the most effective techniques to capture information that is robust and relevant.

National surveys

A useful national starting point is a decision made by the coalition government in summer 2010. It decided to scrap the national Place Survey.[27] This was only introduced in 2008. It involved a postal survey in every local authority area every two years. It included questions about satisfaction with the local area, local public services, information, local decision-making, getting involved, respect and consideration and community safety. One of its functions was to populate up to 18 national performance indicators linked to Local Area Agreements. A number of these have relevance for housing organisations:

---

27 For more details, see http://www.audit-commission.gov.uk/localgov/audit/nis/Pages/placesurvey.aspx and http://www.communities.gov.uk/publications/corporate/statistics/placesurvey2008update

- NI 17 Perceptions of anti-social behaviour
- NI 138 Satisfaction of people over 65 with both home and neighbourhood
- NI 139 The extent to which older people receive the support they need to live independently at home.

The 2008 Place Survey reports include tabulated findings for every local authority in England. Although concerns have been raised about the statistical reliability of the results for some questions and areas because of small sample sizes, it represents a useful source of information. The decision to abandon the Place Survey was because of 'intrusive and personal questions' and that its abandonment would free up councils to focus on delivery. Similar points could, of course, be made about other nationally led surveys (see below). Most significantly if organisations do not collect and analyse comparable information on customer satisfaction, how would they know whether the services were improving in relation to other providers? It is, therefore, not surprising that Local Government Improvement and Development (formerly the Improvement and Development Agency) and Ipsos Mori are set to pilot a new resident feedback questionnaire. Both parties have acknowledged the weaknesses of the Place Survey but have argued that councils need this type of data for benchmarking purposes and, more importantly, for customer feedback (Illman, 2010).

There are, thus, a number of surveys co-ordinated and organised at a national level that generate information on customer satisfaction that are relevant for housing organisations. There is the British Crime Survey that includes information on resident perceptions of anti-social behaviour. There is also the British Social Attitudes Survey and the Citizenship Survey. The latter has been commissioned every two years since 2001 and now involves a rolling survey of 15,000 households. The findings have been hailed by the coalition government as supporting the 'big society' agenda as it shows a high level of resident satisfaction with progress on community cohesion. This marks an interesting contrast with the abolition of the Place Survey. A weakness of some of these national surveys is, however, that the sample size is small and thus results are not generally available at a neighbourhood scale and, even in some cases, a local authority level.

Housing organisations are most familiar with STATUS (standardised tenant satisfaction survey). It has been overseen and managed by the National Housing Federation (2008) and has been approved by the Tenant Services Authority (TSA), formerly by the Housing Corporation, as well as more recently by Communities and Local Government. It was endorsed by the TSA as important for individual housing organisations in assessing performance on customer satisfaction as well as enabling tenants to compare different social landlords. The findings are also used as part of the regulatory system. The TSA is, however, to be abolished and there are clear implications for the future of STATUS and other surveys. More importantly, hidden within the announcement of the abandonment of the Place Survey was the statement that stock-holding local authorities would no longer be expected to report on national indicator 160 (local authority tenants' satisfaction with landlord services. As a result, the requirement for councils to use STATUS is to be removed. But, of course, this statement does not apply to housing associations.[28]

STATUS has nevertheless been the key customer satisfaction survey for housing organisations (National Housing Federation, 2008). It was introduced over ten years ago and has been mandatory for councils and housing associations with over 1,000 properties. It has been estimated that the cost of carrying out STATUS for landlords is over £2 million per year (Pawson *et al.*, 2009). The guidance has differed with councils being required to carry out STATUS every two years since 2008/2009. Housing associations have been required to undertake a survey every three years. These include different versions of STATUS for general needs tenants, those in supported housing and sheltered housing, and homeowners. There is detailed guidance covering issues such as:

- survey methods – postal survey with up to three mailings
- statistical reliability
- weighting of results to reflect, for example, property types
- sampling
- presentation of results
- use of additional questions to reflect local requirements.

The general needs survey form comprises over 40 questions. It is disaggregated into a number of parts including information about the household, background information, future plans and an open section for additional comments as well as five sections that focus on customer satisfaction and these are:

- housing and services
- contact with the landlord
- repairs and maintenance
- communication and information
- anti-social behaviour.

Apart from the open section, the survey comprises closed questions with a selection of pre-determined responses. For instance, there are three questions on repairs and maintenance – the first of which asks how satisfied or dissatisfied the respondent is on the way the landlord deals with repairs and maintenance. Responses are by tick box and the respondent can select from very satisfied, fairly satisfied, neither, fairly dissatisfied, very dissatisfied and no opinion/don't know. Overall, STATUS incorporates a number of key elements that underpin satisfaction e.g. profiling data, customer priorities, a focus on homes and neighbourhoods as well as services, and benchmarking possibilities because of universality.

---

28 It is worth noting that with the demise of the TSA, there is uncertainty over the future of other national data collection exercises such as the regulatory statistical returns (RSR), CORE and the national register of social housing (NROSH) as well as STATUS.

There are, nevertheless, both opportunities and challenges using national surveys. They are usually aligned with regulatory requirements. There is a well-established methodology as well as guidance and there are often economies of scale in using established approaches. Benchmarking is frequently hailed as a further advantage in that it enables regulators, providers and customers to compare satisfaction levels between organisations. Nevertheless, there are dangers especially if benchmarking degenerates into merely league tables of performance and satisfaction. Selecting relevant comparators is essential to ensure that organisations and customers are able to make sound judgments. More importantly, it should be remembered that benchmarking is only the beginning of the process of exploring satisfaction issues – it is a 'can opener' rather than an end in itself. In-depth analysis is required on why, for example, similar organisations may have quite different satisfaction ratings. However, national surveys may have had their day! The coalition government viewed the Place Survey and STATUS as part of the command and control approach that they inherited from the previous government. Like the TSA, they have become 'toast'.

Local approach

Local rather than national approaches on customer satisfaction are in the ascendancy. The Minister for Housing, Grant Shapps, in his announcement on the abolition of the Place Survey and STATUS for councils is alleged to have commented that *'as a good landlord I know that you will do whatever is necessary to ensure that your tenants are satisfied through your own measures'*. In fact, housing organisations in Britain, Western Europe and North America have a lengthy track record of measuring customer satisfaction. Varady and Carrozza (2000) illustrate how a large North American city developed a long-term sophisticated strategy for measuring changes in tenant satisfaction. This adequately addressed many of the issues on methodology that are raised in later sections of this chapter. However, the key issue is whether this is an appropriate direction of travel in a period of public expenditure cuts? Nevertheless, it could be argued that without detailed and local robust customer satisfaction data, social housing landlords will not be able to design and deliver appropriate services.

In England, for example, Leicester City Council has for many years focused on this issue. On day-to-day repairs, personal visits are made to check a random sample of jobs that have been completed. In addition, a random 10% postal survey is undertaken of households who have had work carried out. In relation to housing management, questionnaires and mystery shopping exercises are extensively used in relation to allocation and lettings and managing tenancies. More recently, a tenants' inspectorate was established. Its activities include regular quarterly audits of estates and reception areas in local housing offices.

There are a number of sources of information on local customer satisfaction techniques. The Audit Commission, for instance, compiles and updates good practice from its inspection programme. It currently has over 70 examples in relation to the access and customer care KLOE. These include using customer complaints (Victory Housing Association), 'you said, we did' (Places for People), using technology to monitor customer satisfaction (Aspire Housing) and effectively making use of customer surveys to drive service improvements (Ashfield Homes).

> 'You Said, We Did' is an initiative by **Places for People** to demonstrate to customers that feedback through 'voice' (including complaints) is taken extremely seriously and is an important component of service improvement. This helps to ensure that high levels of customer satisfaction are achieved.
>
> Notices and information on 'you said, we did' are prominently displayed in specific schemes and in newsletters and annual performance review reports.

In relation to utilising customer complaints, Homes for Haringey make use of this information as one of a number of sources for producing twice-yearly learning reports that involve a collection and analysis of issues leading to a focus on continuous improvement to services. Hull City Council, in its quarterly corporate health performance measures, includes the number of compliments and complaints as part of the improvement stream on implementing customer feedback. A ratio of compliments divided by complaints is calculated for each service area and function.

The Chartered Institute of Housing good practice guides frequently contain sections of a customer orientation. For example, Thomas (2008) has a specific chapter on a customer focus for improving repairs and maintenance services. This incorporates a wide range of information on the principles and practice of customer satisfaction. It notes that there is no one best method. Instead it points out that there are strengths and weaknesses with continuous customer monitoring, service delivery checks, one-off satisfaction surveys, mystery shopping, tenant auditors and dealing with complaints.

Increasingly, customer satisfaction is being incorporated into a Customer Insight approach. This is defined as combining 'a knowledge of demographic factors with information about customers' behaviour, needs and aspirations' (Chartered Institute of Housing, 2008, p.3). The Improvement and Development Agency (2008) comment that in practical terms Customer Insight is not new as councils routinely make use of the tools and techniques. These include hard and soft data (i.e. quantitative and qualitative material) from, for instance, surveys, feedback exercises and mystery shopping. The step change centres on two aspects. These are, first, a focus on a customer rather than a service-centric approach and, secondly, a greater user role in the design and delivery of services. More details can be found in the next chapter.

Interpreting customer satisfaction results

Despite the focus on customer satisfaction, there has been relatively little robust and critical coverage of the overall findings and implications on national and local approaches. Books on public sector management, apart from Flynn (2007), barely mention the topic. Coverage in government reports has ebbed and flowed, although the Office of Public Sector Reform (2004) produced useful material. Regular analysis of national data and surveys is highlighted for a short period of time by the media at the launch of annual reports on, for example, the British Crime Survey and the British Social Attitudes Survey. Organisations, such as HouseMark and Housing Quality Network, produce summary reports on performance and satisfaction, but these are only accessible to subscribers. Apart from a study by Pawson *et al.* (2009), there have been few if any publications that have critically reviewed the topic in recent years. This is surprising as there are three important interrelated issues. These are:

- the factors that affect customer satisfaction and their implications for quality/ 'fit for purpose' services
- public satisfaction with services and the relationship to performance
- the methodology of measuring customer satisfaction.

These are now discussed in turn.

Factors affecting customer satisfaction

Chapter 2 identified three components that influence the quality of a service – product, process and perception. Studies on customer satisfaction have reinforced and added to this framework. The Office of Public Sector Reform (2004) found that there were five factors. First, there is delivery i.e. the product or service meets specifications. Secondly, there is speed of response and avoidance of delay and repeated contacts; this ties in with the work of Seddon (2008) on the reduction of failure demand and a focus on value demand. Thirdly, information should be readily available about the service and in particular the status of a specific request. Fourthly, there is the competence and knowledge among staff. Fifth and last, there is the manner in which staff deal with customers. The research highlighted principles of fairness, equity and politeness. Organisations that address each of these five factors are likely to receive high customer satisfaction ratings. Similarly Gaster and Squires (2003) point out that the recurring messages from studies by organisations such as the National Consumer Council in the 1980s and 1990s highlight that customers value reliability, good and relevant information, timeliness of performance, access and helpfulness.

From a housing perspective, studies on specific services have yielded similar findings. For example, the Chartered Institute of Housing (2005) carried out a project on how housing associations could improve their responsive repairs service. It found that tenants considered the service to be of high quality where work was completed to a good standard, the process of organising the repair was straightforward and did not require repeated contacts with the landlord (i.e. failure demand) and that there was a choice of appointments. The report concluded that tenants expected their social housing landlord to provide realistic choices on services and their delivery, give opportunities for involvement in decision-making and meet their expectations. Again, this highlights the factors that tenants feel are important in achieving high levels of customer satisfaction. It is also noteworthy in the light of the growing debate on co-production that tenants did not want to be involved in the design and delivery of the repairs service. Instead, what they wanted was a good service.

Levels of satisfaction and performance

A useful starting point is that there has been a growing tendency to equate customer satisfaction scores with performance. Flynn (2007) summarised the relationship between performance management targets and public satisfaction in three services – tackling crime, health and education. He found that there was little relationship between the actual level of crime and satisfaction with the police service. The former declined as did the latter! In relation to secondary education, he found that performance measured by pupil attainment increased but that public satisfaction decreased. For health, performance data shows improvements in service standards, outcomes and value for money. But public satisfaction has risen and then fallen over the same time period.

Although housing was not covered in Flynn's study, Pawson *et al.* (2009) provide an in-depth analysis and review of STATUS. Their 'headline' findings centre on comparisons. For instance, they report from a survey in 2008 that 72% of housing association tenants were satisfied with landlord services compared with under 60% for their local authority overall. They also note that there were satisfaction scores of 85% and 86% for services provided by telephone companies and banks respectively! Other findings include a narrowing of the gap between councils and housing associations on customer satisfaction ratings. Stock transfer landlords tend to score higher than longstanding, traditional, general needs associations. Finally, associations with over 10,000 units fare less well than those with less stock.

In relation to satisfaction and performance, a complex picture emerges. Pawson *et al.* (2009) point out that the relationship between performance and satisfaction is positive for the housing associations that formed part of the research. More detailed analysis by Pawson (2010) on local authority housing management performance and by Hall (2010) for housing associations highlights a mixed picture:

- local authority tenant satisfaction has bottomed-out after a period of significant improvement in the middle part of the last decade

- council performance measures improved on issues such as void management and rent arrears but fell slightly for the proportion of repairs completed on time
- for housing associations, overall tenant satisfaction remains high and has slightly increased over the last twelve months
- tenant satisfaction with participation opportunities is much lower than for repairs and overall
- housing association performance on void management and rent collection has declined.

Clearly, there is a complex picture between performance and satisfaction in housing and public services. The evidence from the housing sector suggests that for those services that directly impact on tenants, there is a strong correlation. For example, repairs and opportunities for consultation and participation are likely to be of more relevance than void management, rent collection and managing rent arrears; this ties in with the views of Flynn (2007, p.144) who argues that 'matters that generate satisfaction are not those that are measured in performance management systems'. He also notes there are a range of other related considerations including:

- Satisfaction varies between service users and non-service users – satisfaction ratings are often as much about the manner in which the customer is treated as for the service/product provided (see above).
- Satisfaction with a service is a function of the satisfaction with the organisation or, in the case of local and central governments, with the relevant political party.
- Satisfaction is a function of the relationship between perception and expectation. Flynn (2007) also points out that expectations may be relatively low because of adverse media coverage of a service or an organisation. Customers may be pleasantly surprised when they access a specific service.
- Expectations are rising as highlighted by Cole and Parston (2006) in their comment on customers wanting 'better services at less cost'.

Methodological issues

So far we have assumed that the methodology for customer satisfaction techniques is unproblematic. Pawson *et al.* (2009) and Hall (2010) highlight a number of important issues. The latter identifies a series of 'health warnings' such as the regular redefining of performance indicators and tenant satisfaction measures that makes it difficult if not impossible to compare long-term trends. He also notes that there can be difficulties where there is a group structure and data collection is organised centrally. This can lead to situations where the reliability of data may be problematic if properties are owned and managed by different group members.

Pawson *et al.* (2009) provide a more detailed critique indicating a range of technical and methodological weaknesses with STATUS such as:

- *Guidance:* Although there is detailed guidance from the National Housing Federation, it would appear that this is not always adhered to by social housing landlords. For instance, avoiding significant changes to the questionnaires and carrying out surveys by telephone rather than postal self-completion by tenants.
- *Response rates and re-weighting data:* There is approximately a 40% response rate for general needs STATUS. But only 50% of respondents to the study by Pawson *et al.* (2009) re-weight the data to take account of differential non-response.
- *Reporting of results:* A minority of housing associations did not follow the guidance by excluding 'no opinion/don't know' responses. This results in higher satisfaction scores.

However, the most significant problem centred on the interpretation, commentary and presentation of results. This is a point that is also commented on by Flynn (2007) in relation to public services more generally. Much analysis fails to acknowledge that satisfaction ratings are influenced by factors outside the control of the organisation. They include the stock profile, as a high proportion of flats is likely to lead to lower scores. Similar points apply to the geographical pattern of property. Over-representation in areas with low levels of deprivation are likely to led to lower levels of customer satisfaction as more affluent households tend to be more demanding of service providers. Demographic differences can also be important – lower levels of satisfaction are likely if there is a younger household profile. Localities with relatively high black and minority ethnic populations tend to have poorer satisfaction scores. Finally, there is a likelihood that the impact of the credit crunch, the recession and public expenditure cuts might negatively influence the views of customers. It is even more disappointing that the effect of external factors is marginalised as this has been highlighted for many years. For example in the early 1990s, Satsangi and Kearns (1992) commented that tenant satisfaction was dependent on many factors that were unconnected to landlord performance. Gaster and Squires (2003) in a review of satisfaction noted that some sections of the population were consistently intolerant of poor service – higher socio-economic groups, carers, younger users and those who were refused a service. On the other hand, there were other groups that are generally more likely to be satisfied and these include older people and lower socio-economic groups.

Overall, there is a real danger of, first, comparing 'apples with pears' because of the different approaches adopted by organisations in using STATUS. More importantly, the level of customer satisfaction scores may be mistakenly attributed to actions by social housing landlords when the reality is that it is external factors that are significant. Clearly customer satisfaction reports should have a 'health warning'.

Improving the measurement of customer satisfaction

As has been pointed out frequently throughout this book, systems of performance management and regulation are under review. The Place Survey has been abandoned, the Audit Commission's comprehensive area assessment has been discarded and the organisation is to be closed, and the TSA is to be culled. The future of STATUS is unclear. This presents opportunities and challenges for customer satisfaction. There is a view that national and local approaches could become more significant if performance management is linked with customer satisfaction. Flynn (2007 p.146) refers to this 'as aligning managerial targets with those matters that generate satisfaction'. The difficulty with this approach is that it focuses exclusively on users of services rather than non-users and the wider society. Flynn (2007) utilises the example in health of doctors spending more time with fewer patients. User satisfaction rises, but non-users and overall health outcomes would be less positive.

Even if more emphasis is placed on nationally co-ordinated customer satisfaction surveys, the methodological and technical weakness would have to be addressed. There is a need to engage with the literature on research methods and surveys. The concept of 'satisfaction' needs to be dissected and debated. It has many interpretations and what might be satisfactory to one person may be unsatisfactory for someone else. The design and operationalisation of questionnaires is crucial (see, for example, Robertson, 2008, chapter 10). Consideration, for instance, has to be given to:

- questionnaire method – postal, telephone, computer-based or face-to-face
- wording of questions – for example, asking whether a service is satisfactory is meaningless without an explicit clarification of 'satisfactory'
- open-ended or closed questions
- single or multiple response options
- use of the Likert scale that tests respondents' strength of attitude to statements.

Overall, there are advantages (focus on efficiency and standardisation) and disadvantages (superficial and descriptive) with questionnaires. They lack the ability to explore the reasons for responses to customer satisfaction. One reaction to this situation is to make greater use of qualitative methods such as customer journey mapping. Researchers highlight that such methods provide a rich and in-depth set of data but they lack statistical robustness. It also is challenging to present the findings so that comparisons can be made between organisations, which is often a key requirement for regulatory agencies.

From a quantitative perspective, the TSA announced that it was intending to review STATUS. But the proposed culling of the organisation has left this re-appraisal on hold especially with its abandonment for councils with stock (Hardman, 2010b).

Pawson *et al.* (2009) suggest a number of ways forward with STATUS. They call for a standardised and more robust way of measuring tenant satisfaction in order to generate accurate and relevant performance information. Detailed recommendations centre on opting for a centralised approach to overcome the tendency for social housing landlords to ignore the guidance produced by the National Housing Federation (2008). Reference is made, for example, to kitemarking and accreditation schemes. One way in which this could be achieved is through the UK Statistics Authority, which promotes and safeguards the production and publication of official statistics. Its functions include ensuring the quality and comprehensiveness of official statistics and good practice. It is, however, debateable whether the current political climate would be conducive to a centralisation of STATUS by an independent government watchdog. The experience of the abandoned Place Survey suggests that this would not be the case.

An alternative strategy would be to encourage social housing landlords to develop their own approach to reflect local circumstances. This might incorporate a mixed research methodology involving both quantitative and qualitative approaches. The impact of the cost issue could be reduced by social housing landlords sharing the development and implementation. This would have the advantage of the potential for a much more robust approach to benchmarking. It would overcome some of the weaknesses of STATUS such as the duplication with internal customer profiling by individual organisations and the reliance in the case of housing associations on a survey only once every three years. Continuous assessment of customer satisfaction is essential.

Lastly, public sector agencies, including housing organisations, frequently suffer from 'DRIP' (data rich information poor). They hold vast amounts of disaggregated 'bits' of data on different administrative ICT systems, but fail to aggregate and process it into information. Much of the data relates to customers and includes basic socio-demographic characteristics, complaints, requests for information and methods of communication. It is directly relevant to customer satisfaction. There is, thus, a strong case for organisations to make more effective use of existing data before proceeding with new questionnaires. There are a wide range of techniques based around business intelligence systems including data warehousing, data mining, data visualisation (e.g. geographical information systems – GIS) and online analytical processes (including statistical techniques). Although these are increasingly used by public sector agencies, there has been little impact so far on the housing sector (see Brown and Healey, 2009).

Designing and delivering services

The emphasis on customer satisfaction is likely to increase. It is driven by the focus on 'putting the customer first'. However, measuring satisfaction is a means to an end rather than an end in itself. The focus should be service improvement, utilising data and information from customers in the decision-making process.

We have seen, however, that defining and measuring satisfaction is not straightforward. There are many different approaches ranging from analysing complaints by 'revolting customers' through to questionnaires. The centre of attention is users. Frequently, non-users and society at large are marginalised. From a customer perspective, users may be satisfied not by the product or service but because they are treated with respect (i.e. process). Alternatively, they may be content because of the brand and image of the organisation (see further James and Richardson in chapter 8 of this book). These pose challenges in using customer satisfaction as the core basis for designing and delivering services. Gaster and Squires (2003, p 21) summarise this as *'my satisfaction is not necessarily your satisfaction'*.

It has also been highlighted that there is no necessarily strong correlation between performance management and customer satisfaction. This is illustrated in the matrix below:

Figure 6.1: Customer satisfaction and performance

		Customer perception of satisfaction	
		Low	*High*
Performance management	*Low*	Low objective performance and poor customer feedback. Intervention likely by regulator	Low objective performance but high customer satisfaction. This may be because of low customer expectations
	High	High objective performance but customer expectations are more demanding i.e. better services at less cost	Alignment of high performance and high satisfaction

Organisations should be achieving high performance management scores and high satisfaction ratings i.e. the bottom right cell of the matrix. But many organisations are in the top right and bottom left cells. Actions that may be required include:

- aligning performance management indicators with customer satisfaction measures (see Flynn, 2007)
- ensuring that an appropriately broad definition of customers is adopted i.e. users, non-users and citizens
- raising the aspirations of customers that may have a culture of low expectations of the quality of services
- challenging customers with high expectations over the balance between improved services and the costs.

This raises questions about designing and delivering services based on a private sector organisation-consumer model. It has been argued by Needham among others (in Jones and Needham, 2008) that this approach assumes a passive customer and this is inappropriate for a government-citizen relationship with values based on democracy, accountability and the needs of communities. Rather interestingly and topically, she argues for co-production of services and voluntarism. These, in some respects, tie in with the coalition government's support for localism and the 'big society'. From a housing perspective, initiatives such as tenant management co-operatives, social enterprises and community land trusts take centre stage. Yet, as has already been pointed out, studies have shown that tenants want a good service and do not necessarily wish to get involved in its management (Chartered Institute of Housing, 2005).

An alternative perspective is service differentiation. The basic principle is that there are two levels of service. First, there is a minimum level to which the customer is entitled. Secondly, there are areas where they are higher or quicker levels of service. Analysis of customer expectations and aspirations can be used to identify the relevant service levels. It may be based on rewards as developed by Irwell Valley Housing Association in Greater Manchester in the late 1990s through its gold service standard. Alternatively it might involve additional payments by the customer. This ties in with some of the ideas associated with right-of-centre political thinking such as the London Boroughs of Barnet and Hammersmith and Fulham (see Richardson, 2010). It is already in operation in parts of the public sector. One example is the offer from the Identity and Passport Office of a one-week turnaround and a same-day service for passport renewal instead of a standard service (Brindle, 2010). The respective charges as of summer 2010 were £122.50, £129.50 and £77.50. Could this approach be applied to parts of the social housing service without detrimentally affecting the principles of equity and social justice?

Overall, the design and delivery of public services including housing is undergoing a rapid process of change. The impact of public expenditure cuts is a key driver. Radical changes are being proposed such as co-production and two-tier services. Comprehensive and broadly based customer satisfaction information is a vital consideration in future developments.

References and further reading

Audit Commission (2008) *In the Know: Using Information to Make Better Decisions*. London: Audit Commission.

Audit Commission (2007) *Cross Cutting Themes: Access and Customer Care in Housing Services*. London: Audit Commission, Housing Inspectorate Key Lines of Enquiry.

Brindle, D. (2010) 'Better Cheaper: Mission Impossible', *The Guardian Public Services Supplement*, 7th July.

Brown, T. and Healey, L. (2010) *Using Data and Information to Improve Decision Making and Performance*. York: Housing Quality Network.

Chartered Institute of Housing (2008) *Customer Insight: Knowing Your Customers*. CIH Good Practice Briefing 32.

Chartered Institute of Housing (2005) *Right First Time: How Housing Associations are Improving their Responsive Repairs*. Coventry: Chartered Instutute of Housing.

Citizens Advice Bureau (2010) *'CAB Enquiries Still Increasing'*, CAB Press Release, 1st September.

Cole, M. and Parston, G. (2006) *Unlocking Public Value*. New York: John Wiley & Sons.

Communities and Local Government (2009) *Getting it Right and Righting the Wrongs*. London: CLG.

Communities and Local Government (2008) *Communities in Control, Real Power, Real People*. London: Communities and Local Government.

Flynn, N. (2007) *Public Sector Management*, 5th ed. London: Sage.

Gaster, L. and Squires, A. (2003) *Providing Quality in the Public Sector*, Buckingham: Open University Press.

Hall, C. (2010) *Analysis of 2008/09 TSA Performance Indicators for Housing Associations in England*. York: Housing Quality Network.

Hardman, I. (2010a) 'Complaints Soar 42%', *Inside Housing*, 16th July.

Hardman, I. (2010b) 'TSA to Overhaul Satisfaction Data', *Inside Housing*, 16th April.

Illman, J. (2010) 'Place Survey Replacement on Blocks', *Local Government Chronicle*, 11th August.

Improvement and Development Agency (2008) *Customer Insight: Through a Total Place Lens*. London: IdeA.

Jones, G. and Needham, C. (2008) 'Consumerism in Public Services – For and Against', *Public Money and Management*, April, pp.70-76.

Local Government Ombudsman (2010) *Annual Report 09/10 – Delivering Public Value*. London: LGO.

National Housing Federation (2008) *Running STATUS: A guide to undertaking the standardised tenant satisfaction survey*, 2nd Edition. London: NHF.

O'Donnell, G. (2006) as quoted in Delivery and Transformation Group (2006) *Customer Insight in Public Services*. London: Cabinet Office.

Office of Public Sector Reform (2004) *Customer Satisfaction with Key Public Services*. London: Cabinet Office.

Parasuraman, A., Zeithaml, V. and Berry, L. (1985) 'A Conceptual Model of Service Quality and its Implications for Future Research', *Journal of Marketing*, Vol. 49, pp.41-50.

Pawson, H. (2010) *Analysis of English Local Authority Housing Management Performance 2008/09*. York: Housing Quality Network.

Pawson, H., Sosenko, F. and Ipsos Mori (2009) *Assessing Resident Satisfaction*. London: London & Quadrant Housing Trust.

Pollitt, C. (2003) *The Essential Public Manager*. Buckingham: Open University Press.

Prescott-Clarke, P., Askins, J., and Clemens, S. (1993) *Tenant Feedback: A Step-by-Step Guide to Tenant Satisfaction Surveys*. London: HMSO.

Richardson, J. (ed) (2010) *From Recession to Renewal: the impact of the financial crisis on public services and local government*. Bristol: Policy Press.

Robertson, D. (2008) *Looking into Housing: A Practical Guide to Housing Research*. Coventry: Chartered Institute of Housing.

Satsangi, M. and Kearns, A. (1992) 'The Use and Interpretation of Tenant Satisfaction Surveys in British Social Housing', *Environment and Planning C*, Vol. 10, No. 3, pp.317-331.

Seddon, J. (2008) *System Thinking in The Public Sector*. Axminster: Triarchy Press.

Thomas, A. (2008) *Improving Repairs and Maintenance Services: A Good Practice Guide*. Coventry: Chartered Instutute of Housing.

Varady, D. and Carrozza, M. (2000) 'Toward a Better Way to Measure Customer Satisfaction Levels in Public Housing: A Report from Cincinnati', *Housing Studies*, Vol. 15, No. 6, pp.797-825.

Wisniewski, M. (2001) 'Using SERVQUAL to Assess Customer Satisfaction with Public Services', *Managing Service Quality*, Vol. 11, No. 6, pp.380-388.

CHAPTER 7:
Customer Relationship Management and Customer Insight: knowing and satisfying the customer

Joanna Richardson

Introduction

The bottom line is this: the US Government had sufficient information to have uncovered this plot and potentially disrupt the Christmas Day attack, but our intelligence community failed to connect those dots, which would have placed the suspect on the no-fly list (President Obama, 5 Jan 2010).

The 'failure to connect the dots' as highlighted by President Obama after the attempted Christmas Day attack in the US is one example of many across the globe where data is collected routinely, but its importance is not understood and information is not analysed and utilised to achieve desired outcomes. We have our own examples in the public sector in England with the Baby P case just one tragic example of a failure to connect dots between public service agencies. To achieve our goals and ideals of public service delivery and to provide the services that are needed, it is essential that we understand who exactly our customers are, and what they need and want from us. Customer Insight then, is not just a whizzy off-shoot of a marketing approach, it is not the application of the label 'customer' just for the sake of it, it is a vital part of service delivery in the public sector and the social housing sector that can have a very real impact on life outcomes for tenants, and on efficient use of resources for public agencies.

Knowing who your customers are and what services they want from you is key to social housing organisations. Customer Relationship Management (CRM) and, more latterly Customer Insight (CI) have found prominence in public sector and housing sector notions of delivering services efficiently to people in most need. Customers of housing organisations are, of course, numerous and varied. In this chapter the focus is on the external customer – the end user of the service; however it must be remembered that there are customers within the quasi-markets of public service and social housing delivery.

This chapter aims to look behind the labels and the marketing speak to demonstrate why knowing who your customers are, and satisfying their housing needs, is supported not just by a social imperative to do right by those in need, but by a business case to target resources more efficiently in a period of financial constraint.

Customer Relationship Management (CRM)

So what is CRM? Stone *et al.* (2000) describe it as:

> The use of a wide range of marketing, sales, communication, service and customer care approaches to:
> - identify a company's named individual customers;
> - create a relationship between the company and its customers that stretches over many transactions;
> - manage that relationship to the benefit of the customers and the company

They go on to say that if customers asked a company what CRM meant, the company could say:

> *It is how we:*
> - *find you;*
> - *get to know you;*
> - *keep in touch with you;*
> - *try to ensure that you get what you want from us in every aspect of our dealings with you;*
> - *check that you are getting what we promised you*
>
> (Stone *et al.*, 2000, p.2).

Customer Relationship Management is really quite straightforward. It is about keeping a good and lasting relationship with your customer. Ideally you want your customer to enjoy your service so much that s/he is someone who wants to buy from you (and will advocate your services to others) rather than someone who you have to sell to.

In the public sector, and particularly housing, we have been guilty of taking advantage of a long and dependent relationship. Quite often our customers have little choice other than our product, but that does not mean to say we can ignore their needs or forget that they are there; we must not take the customer for granted.

Who is the customer?

Here, we start by looking at customers in a generic marketing way. Organisations have future, present and past customers. These can be segmented more specifically:

- *Advocate* – if very happy the customer tells all their colleagues and friends about the excellent product/service they received.

- *Client* – if happy the customer will continue to buy products and services.
- *Customer* – new customer makes a one-off purchase.
- *Prospect* – a prospective customer is weighing up the options of buying from you or buying from a competitor.
- *Target* – someone who receives information from you on your product or service.
- *Unknown* – is not familiar with your product or service.

There are many other ways to categorise existing and potential customers too. For instance a fairly general model is the 'adopter categories'. One can think about these 'adopters' in relation to innovative technology, e.g. the iPod:

- *Innovators* (about 2.5% of the total customer base) – will be the very first to buy a new product, initial high prices will not be prohibitive.
- *Early adopters* (about 13.5%) – they take fewer risks than the innovators but are still keen to be seen to garner respect by having the latest 'cool' gadgets.
- *Early majority* (34%) – these people have thought about purchasing this product for a little while and they may have waited for the price to come down a little bit.
- *Late majority* (34%) – have less disposable income and fewer qualifications, will buy the product out of necessity or social pressure.
- *Laggards* (16%) – older and less well educated according to the Chartered Institute of Marketing, but perhaps they are just bargain hunters and have waited for a significant price drop and for thorough market testing of the product?

(CIM, 2001: pp.180-181)

One can examine and categorise the personality traits and buying habits of a range of customers; and cutting edge companies with risky products and services will have to do this. As social housing providers there is not so much risk – however we do need to conduct housing needs analyses to understand who our customers and potential customers are, and what their needs are now and in the future. One needs to know whether the product and service you are providing now will be of use to older/vulnerable people in five years' time and further into the future. If it is an unpopular type of property now then one has to do some sort of market analysis with customers and examine the options for the stock, e.g. renovating to make it more appealing, withdrawing barriers to accessing the property for particular groups, or removing it from the stock portfolio altogether where appropriate.

Collecting data and analysing customers' needs

As housing organisations, this is a fundamental part of our business – local authorities are obliged to undertake housing needs analyses and then a local strategy will be developed to meet those needs; increasingly through housing associations and some councils building new schemes. However, there are different ways of analysing needs. One of the traditional frameworks used in many different industries, is Maslow's hierarchy of needs, this is based on a pyramid of five levels. The lower levels are labelled 'deficiency needs' and these are basic physiological requirements of human beings. The remaining two groupings of levels are related to 'growth needs' and then 'being needs' which are more psychological and more to do with aspirations than physical needs.

Housing organisations already collect a range of data, so there is not necessarily a need to collect more data, but instead to analyse it in order to turn data into useable information. As noted in the introduction in this chapter, it is possible for organisations to be data rich, but information poor.[29]

Figure 7.1: Don't be a DRIP

Victoria Climbié and Baby P in London and the Pilkington family in Leicestershire are three high-profile examples of the fatal consequences that can occur from data not being analysed and turned into information, and from agencies not talking to one another and viewing the range of services delivered from the customer's point of view. Whilst systems have been introduced such as 'Notify' in the Laming report following the Climbié Inquiry, there is still not universal use of such facilities and there are still gaps in information which affect vulnerable families. Sometimes the blame for lack of sharing information is put at the door of data protection legislation (this is discussed a little more by James, Richardson and Winn in chapter 10). Perri 6 et al. (2010) argue that the barrier to information-sharing is not so much to do with regulation as with a lack of confidence and skills. Trust needs to be brought back into the system – both in terms of collecting private data on individual customers, and with regard to trust between agencies to share pertinent information.

In most areas of the population that local authorities and housing associations serve, there is collection of core data to better inform service delivery.

---

29 Thanks to Bob Line who I think coined this phrase.

However, there are some segments of the population that have very little information collected on them – for example Roma, Gypsies and Travellers. In recent years English sub-regions have commissioned Gypsy and Traveller Accommodation Needs Assessments (GTAAs) to try to find out about accommodation and other needs. More comprehensive studies include findings on health and education issues too. Whilst the future of new site building is more uncertain following the changes brought in by the coalition government in May 2010, and there are concerns that expectations have been raised in travelling communities without the insight being turned into outcomes, there is at least a better knowledge of these communities and their needs. On a wider European level the findings are more damning with McDonald and Negrin (2010) asking in their report *No Data – No Progress*: 'With gaps and unknowns like this, how can policy-makers devise effective policies and responsibly allocate resources?'. They refer to the European countries involved in the *Decade of Roma Inclusion* and their mid-term analysis shows *'gaping holes, lack of disaggregated data according to ethnicity'* and so on. They say that *'Without comprehensive data...the situation of Roma – a group already on the margins of Europe – is likely to remain dire'*. The act of purposefully not collecting data on Roma, or any other vulnerable or so-called 'hard-to-reach' group is an act of disempowerment and can further reduce life chances and negate the responsibility of governments in their duty to provide support for those who cannot otherwise do so.

Decision-making processes

With the increasing use of choice-based lettings systems, there is more commonality with other commercial businesses in that there is a decision-making process which is much more transparent (this was touched upon in chapter 3 and is examined in a little more detail here).

A simple decision-making process can include the elements as shown in Figure 7.2 on pages 110-111.

Increasingly, customers in the social housing sector do have choices and decisions to make – they are less passive in the process than before; although this choice is of course constrained by limited supply. Increased choice can have strange effects on buyers' decision-making processes and purchasing behaviour. Muthiah (2010) examined the issues faced by Home Connections at the outset of choice-based lettings in London in 2001. One of the things he noted at the start was customers' 'wacky' expectations – those at the top of the list (e.g. the equivalent to those with most points under the old allocations system) became pickier about the sort of property they felt was right for them – they had more opportunity to select than accept and so there was increased deliberation in making the 'purchase decision'. This observation accords with famous social experiments, such as the 'Jam Study' (Iyengar, 2010) where a larger array of jams attracted a big audience but longer deliberation and fewer sales; whereas a display with fewer jams resulted in quicker purchasing decisions and higher sales; or put succinctly: more = less.

Figure 7.2: Decision-making process

Element	Comment
Need/problem recognition	Leads to motivation. There are degrees of complexity here, in some processes the trigger may be psychological, physiological and/or social factors and this can often lead to a 'need versus want' debate about a particular product or service in the public sector. Marketers can identify needs/problems for the consumer, through product positioning. In the commercial sector entire industries can be developed on aspirations and wants for a product that an individual does not need. In the social and public sector there is an element of rationing increasingly scarce resources and funding and there is a responsibility on service providers not to trigger a demand that will be impossible to satisfy; and yet we should still meet growing aspirations for healthy, happy lives in communities and neighbourhoods.
Pre-purchase/information search	A range of information needs to be available in a variety of different ways, for example on websites, local newspaper adverts for properties, at the offices of the organisation for people who need face-to-face meetings and so on. In a more complex model of demand trigger, the purchaser would be affected by sources, attitudes, perceptions. So for example a footwear company targeting young 'cool' kids might not use standard television or magazine marketing, for fear of being perceived as too conventional. Instead a campaign of 'viral' marketing might be used, where a 'cool kid' is seen wearing a pair of trainers and others want to follow. This has been used in a wider sense with celebrity endorsements; but this can backfire if a particular celebrity loses their star appeal. Marketers can provide product information, tailored to the differing information needs of a range of customer profiles.
Evaluation of alternatives	Marketers can make products available for evaluation and provide comparative information about competing products: the important thing, though, is to get the product onto the short-list of options. In social housing and the wider public sector there are some options that, taken in the short term, can help the customer and save public money in the long term. →

Evaluation of alternatives *(contd.)*	For example by publicising mortgage rescue schemes during the recession, local authorities and housing associations could help people remain in their home (customer satisfaction) and save the money it would cost for the mortgage company and the courts to evict, the local authority to process a homelessness application, and the housing provider to assess and process an application for a socially rented property. If all the alternatives are presented to the customer, then the most appropriate and efficient choice can be made.
The purchase decision	Traditionally in the social housing sector, there was little customer input into the purchase 'decision'. Properties were allocated according to need. Now, with many organisations having established choice-based lettings, there is more input from the customer, but often this can lead to an alternative 'purchase' decision where a bid is unsuccessful – either a wider and more realistic search area, different property type, or indeed a different tenure where this is a possibility. In more complex models, the decision would be affected by situational factors: intention is not everything – this is particularly true for the social housing sector.
Post-purchase evaluation	Experience 'feeds back' to the beginning of the process, providing positive or negative reinforcement of the purchase decision. If the consumer is dissatisfied, s/he will be back at the problem recognition stage again. If the consumer is satisfied, the next decision process for the product may be cut short and skip straight to the decision, on the basis of loyalty (or in a more complex model, expectations and learning constructs). This links to strength of brand (see further James and Richardson in chapter 8 of this book). Tesco, for example, now sell insurance, mobile phone services and many other products on top of their supermarket offering. Housing associations are following suit with some (for example Places for People) offering nursery childcare provision, outright sale, support services and so on. If a customer is satisfied following post-purchase evaluation of a core product (a rented property) then they may cut short their pre-purchase information search and go to the same provider for different but related products and services because they perceive the quality to be good. It is in these services that added value can be created for the customer, and for the wider community.

Adapted from CIM, 2001, p.176.

There is also a challenge with increased choice and the assumption that choice and free markets benefit everyone. There is a dichotomy at work here in the assumption that choice = empowerment, when studies show that too much choice can have the opposite effect. Choice can also result in more individual and selfish purchasing decisions which at best have no positive impact on the wider community and at worst have a negative impact on the more vulnerable and on community cohesion in general. Salecl (2010) warns of this tyranny of choice being an individual matter which can prevent wider social change.

In this chapter, I examine increased stratification according to a growing variety of customer profiles and this may lead one to think that more choice is the only option to meet this range of needs and aspirations. It will serve the social housing sector well to heed the Iyengar Jam study and to understand the psychological as well as the practical limitations to choice.

Customer Insight

Customer Insight is a process of collecting data and then using and processing that information to understand the customer much better and to demonstrate real customer focus – or insight. There are some key strands to Customer Insight (CI):

Figure 7.3: Key strands of Customer Insight

- **Setting clear aims and objectives** – What will the information be used for? Knowing this will affect the questions asked, the target audience, the method of collection and monitoring and the type of feedback given to the customer and the organisation.

- **Research** – Appropriate mechanisms of data collection will enhance response rates – e.g. organisations need to tailor surveys to the needs of their intended audience. Questions should not just be about process of service delivery, but also about needs and aspirations both now and in the future for existing customers and their families. It is only in widening the net to capture information on future needs and from people who are not customers yet, that an organisation can properly plan for the future and be responsive to the changing environment.

- **Turning data into insight** – This is all about analysing the evidence and making sensible assumptions based on the data. The process of making assumptions about types of customers, and broad trends of needs, is often referred to as *customer profiling* and this has been used as a method in the commercial sector for some time. An organisation making widgets, say, might collect a range of data which provides evidence of key characteristics about customers purchasing widgets. The company can then group together some of these characteristics and assume a typical consumer personality who they then imagine as the target for advertising and information on the product. They can combine information from surveys, or information from purchase interaction (supermarkets have their loyalty cards which tells the company exactly what they are buying in each purchase; housing organisations can collect information each time someone 'bids' for a property, orders a repair, applies for housing benefit and so on).

→

Organisations can then group together individuals who may have similar values, needs, wants and behaviours etc in a particular profile in order to better target service delivery.

- **Translating the insight into outcomes** – In the commercial sector, a company selling widgets would increase supply or increase the price of purchase in the face of growing demand. For housing organisations, if 200 people bid for a two-bed bungalow in the centre of town, they cannot immediately build an additional 199 bungalows to satisfy demand. Housing is a special kind of good which defies many of the supply and demand rules, plus it takes a long time to plan and build, and there is reduced supply of capital from banks to support new building, and a slowing of government grant in this area. Whilst there are innovative financial products being used in the social housing sector to boost supply of housing (see further Richardson 2010), turning insight from data in the bidding process for a property into new outcomes for existing and aspiring customers is difficult in the area of housing supply. There are however areas of service delivery, particularly to existing customers, that quickly demonstrate new outcomes in response to Customer Insight. Improved repairs, better feedback information, easier to navigate websites, new methods of payment, different opening hours etc are all areas of activity that can be changed to meet changing customer demand and can demonstrate to the customer that you are listening and acting quickly and appropriately to insight gained.

- **Monitoring and evaluating effectiveness** – As with any data-collection exercise it is important to monitor the process of the research as well as the evidence gained. Did as many people respond as you hoped. If not, what could be done differently next time to boost response? Has a particular segment not responded, if so could the survey be done online, or perhaps publicised on social networking sites? Has anything been done with the data you have collected, if not should a different question be asked next time, which will lead to insight that can be turned into outcomes? It is important to think about Customer Insight as an evolving conversation with your customer base. It should not just be a snapshot survey that is left in a file to gather dust, but a genuine attempt to engage the customer so that appropriate and good quality services can be produced, and perhaps even co-produced with them.

Your organisation will be collecting customer data in a number of different ways, such as:

- transactional data (information from existing customers through your day-to-day business with them – think of this in relation to information held on supermarket club cards, information on your buying behaviour is stored at each transaction)
- survey data (how do you consult your customers)
- purchased data (e.g. ACORN or MOSAIC – see below)
- mystery shopper findings
- focus groups or reference groups
- complaints!

However, CI is more than data collection – it is important to use it wisely and effectively. The LGA (2006) report, *Putting the Customer First: lessons from business*, suggests that the difference between data collection and Customer Insight is in the analysis of data:

1. Trends – performance indicators such as customer satisfaction are difficult to interpret without knowing previous performance
2. Targets – a useful way of interpreting performance is whether it is better or worse than expected
3. Combining data sources to provide a deeper understanding – no one piece of data can completely describe the performance of an organisation.
(LGA, 2006, p.14)

In their 2009 report the LGA refers to the phenomenon of 'too much data, too little information' which can result from poor-quality data arising out of duplication and inconsistency, lack of basic data, poor system design and inefficiency and confusion. This chapter highlights the importance of knowing what the information will be used for – to design a better data system that will produce better customer outcomes. LGA (2009) amongst others highlight a rationale for improved systems so that data = information = insight.

CIH along with HouseMark and the TSA published a report (2010) called *Tenant Insight* which provided a practical toolkit on some of the elements of insight needed to better understand tenants' needs. They suggested that this could lead to greater satisfaction, value for money, more cohesive communities, more focused services and greater efficiency.

HouseMark (2008) undertook research on the local data that should be collected under the new regulatory regime (see further chapter 2 of this book). They suggested that for data to provide insight it was necessary to keep performance reporting simple and allow a mix of local and 'whole organisation' data collection where appropriate; options for surveying customer satisfaction were also examined. The Housing Quality Network (2010) also offered explanations for the collection and use of customer data, suggesting that customer-profiling data should be used to improve and develop housing, allow better accessibility to customers, tailor services to need and engage customers. The Improvement and Development Agency (2010, p.6) reported that *'Customer Insight provides the basis for a strategic approach that enables local authorities to re-design services in ways that improve customer satisfaction while saving money'*. Whether the focus is on method or rationale, it is clear from key housing and government organisations that Customer Insight is vital to housing businesses.

There are a range of data sources that can inform CI; two of the most popular tools that local authorities and housing associations can purchase are:

CUSTOMER RELATIONSHIP MANAGEMENT AND CUSTOMER INSIGHT

1. Mosaic Public Sector: www.experian.co.uk – this service classifies all UK citizens into 69 types and profiles according to 15 key groups using 440 different data elements. This product is used increasingly in the housing and local authority sector. A wider commercial package is also on offer and is utilised by companies like Ford.
2. ACORN (a classification of residential neighbourhoods) developed by CACI: www.caci.co.uk. This package produces geo-demographic segmentation of the UK's population which segments small neighbourhoods, postcodes, or consumer households into 5 categories, 17 groups and 56 types.

Free sources of government information have also been available, such as the indices of multiple deprivation published by the government, as well as the census; however organisations need to be aware of how quickly this evidence can date and that it represents a snapshot at one particular time. This type of information does not replace the need for continuous data collection from housing providers' existing and future customers.

Some areas will have their own observatories which host a range of data across a variety of subjects such as health, education and so on. Finally, of course there is the Office for National Statistics which looks at data across a number of government department areas: www.neighbourhood.statistics.gov.uk

But we have seen the importance and rationale for moving beyond data collection to analysis and then insight. In a report to cabinet (April 2010), Hull City Council illustrated the different stages in the process:

Figure 7.4: Framework for improving research and intelligence management

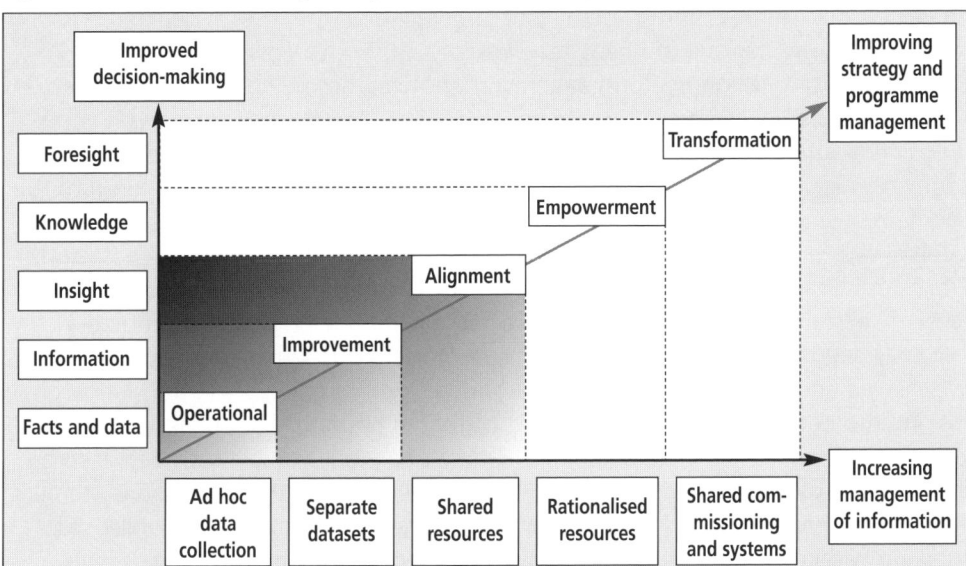

Hull City Council, Report to Cabinet, April 2010: Improving the Collection and Use of Research and Intelligence.

The collection and analysis of data are vital to delivering targeted services to the customer to best meet need, as well as allowing the organisation to manage resources and to change in the context of the economic and social climate around them.

Customer segmentation – profiling

Segmentation is basically a method of profiling customers according to key common needs or characteristics. This process, linked to Customer Insight, is explained well by Dr Foster and Tetlow Associates Ltd (2007, p.9) who cite the benefits as including the ability to:

- use resources more efficiently by targeting service delivery to relevant community segments
- achieve higher public satisfaction through better targeting and understanding of local need
- obtain greater value from existing research by combining and re-using survey data, including data from partner organisations
- conduct survey research efficiently by identifying the minimum sample sizes necessary to understand key segments.

The report by Dr Foster *et al.* (2007) analysed data in three different scenarios with differing levels of homogeneity of customer base. For example they examined Somerset according to Census (2001) Output Area Classification (OAC) types in each of the district areas – so this included so-called blue collar communities, city living, countryside, prospering suburbs, constrained by circumstances and typical traits. The characteristics can be mapped locally and depending on the level of supplementary local data, a varied range of needs can be analysed. The Dr Foster example in Somerset looked at how the population was stratified according to OAC type and then analysed each segment's responses on priorities for improvement locally (housing featured prominently), key differences between the districts and the segments on priorities, social capital (the perception of community cohesion that the segment has), voice (segment perception of their own influence) and then overall general satisfaction. Some findings can seem to be a discrepancy, for example, in the Dr Foster research, the segment 'constrained by circumstances' had an unusually high level of satisfaction for this profile. Further examination, along with anecdotal evidence suggested that this may be a result of the group being disproportionately well served and engaged by the local authority. Thinking back to the translation of insight into outcomes and the challenges of that in housing – it is possible to see that even in segments of the population where one would expect satisfaction to be low because of constrained circumstances, it is still possible through good customer focus and service processes and delivery to increase overall satisfaction whilst still working within constrained physical supply and reduced financial resources with which to provide public services.

> The **East Thames Group** has proactively used customer profiling for some time in a number of areas to ensure equality of access to the various groups in their customer base. By comparing the customer profile with the users of a particular service they can ensure fair and equitable access and quickly address any issues that come out of the customer profile expectations. This approach has recently been used in the areas of repairs, complaints, gas safety, lettings and resident involvement. Details are reviewed every six months to monitor changes.

In addition to using free public information (e.g. census and other sources) some local authorities and housing providers have been purchasing Customer Insight technology from organisations such as Experian who bring together a range of data points and analyse them according to 15 customer profile groups and 69 types of customer. They look at information on demographics, property value, socio-economic information, consumption, property characteristics, geographic location and financial measures (e.g. benefit claims, credit behaviour etc).

Figure 7.5: Mosaic public sector 15 groups and types[30]

Group	Description of key characteristics
A	Residents in isolated communities – living in small villages with farming and tourism as key industries. Access to public services is difficult, they are increasingly enthusiastic users of the internet even where broadband is limited.
B	Residents of small and mid-sized towns with strong local roots – there is relatively little change in the population from year to year and there are strong roots in the community.
C	Wealthy people living in the most sought-after neighbourhoods – people in positions of power with a high degree of influence; concentrated in fashionable inner suburbs of London.
D	Successful professionals living in suburban or semi-rural homes – people in executive or managerial positions; reliance on public services is limited, but use will be made of museums, libraries etc.
E	Middle-income families living in moderate suburban semis – mostly married and in middle age, mostly employed and valuing independence, not necessarily involved in the wider community.
F	Couples with young children in comfortable modern housing – influenced by value for money as well as ethical and environmental considerations; users of technology.

→

---

30 This is a summary of the 15 group profiles – more information is included in the Experian brochure on the website.

G	Young well-educated city dwellers – professional people with liberal views and diverse tastes; they demand a high degree of ethical responsibility from the public bodies with which they do engage.
H	Couples and young singles in small modern starter homes – typically living in new build; expectations of a 24/7 online service.
I	Lower income workers in urban terraces in often diverse areas – tend to work in routine occupations and are poorly educated; living in densely packed neighbourhoods of older housing traditionally built for factory and mill workers which offers a cheap entry point onto the housing market.
J	Owner-occupiers in older style housing in ex-industrial areas – traditional and conservative people, socially responsible and consider themselves from a working-class background.
K	Residents with sufficient incomes in right-to-buy council houses – mix of incomes and occupations, high degree of respect for one another and low levels of ASB; they value self-reliance and responsibility.
L	Active elderly people living in pleasant retirement locations – have moved to downsize and make a new start but some may struggle to maintain homes in face of ill health and rising utility bills.
M	Elderly people reliant on state support – no longer physically active and living in a mix of accommodation types including those with a resident warden. They have a lack of familiarity with ICT and so a range of service delivery and communication methods are necessary.
N	Young people renting flats in high-density social housing – on limited incomes and living in communities with high levels of disadvantage and vulnerability; often in neighbourhoods of less desirable and 'difficult-to-let' properties. Reliant on state benefits and susceptible to dubious money lenders. Limited access to a computer.
O	Families in low-rise council housing with high levels of benefit need – brought up in families with a history of dependence on the state, high levels of unemployment, social deprivation and ASB. Unfamiliar with ICT.

Adapted from Experian, nd: pp.10-15.

CIH (2008) looked at traditional profiling along the lines of demographic characteristics, as well as on behaviour (e.g. preferred payment method of rent), but they also referred to the increasing use of value-based profiling. Mixing values with other types of profiling data can help an organisation understand where best to target support – for example at a tenancy sign-up there may be more of a need for intensive support at that stage for certain people to ensure rent payments are made and other conditions of tenancy are understood and adhered to.

CUSTOMER RELATIONSHIP MANAGEMENT AND CUSTOMER INSIGHT

In an example from the private sector:

Ford Retail segments its customers by the type of vehicle they purchased, whether or not they purchased a service plan, the delivery date for new and used cars and the age of the vehicle. After-sales service customers are also segmented by MOT or service date and all customers are segmented by postcode so that staff can recommend a local Ford service operator for those buying a vehicle out of their area. This segmentation allows Ford Retail to target appropriate marketing materials to its different customer segments.

Ford Retail runs a scheme called Moments of Truth, a major training programme where everybody in the network is trained to the same level to offer a consistent approach to customer service. A 'moment of truth' occurs every time a member of staff comes into contact with a customer. Moments of Truth 24 is an independent contact centre service set up to measure customer satisfaction by asking simple questions relating to satisfaction and loyalty.

This example was provided by Customer Plus, for more information on the case study and other work in this area visit www.customerplus.co.uk

---

A public sector example from **Experian**:

The challenge related to a peak in levels of anti-social behaviour during Halloween and Bonfire Night, making them the busiest nights of the year. Focusing on the Home Office target of public confidence and National Indicator 21, Surrey Police used Experian's Mosaic Public Sector people classification to help with targeted interventions and reassurance measures for the public. This resulted in a mix of operational and communications activity (including posters and postcards mailed to vulnerable groups and Bluetooth messages to young people in youth clubs and local parks) known externally as 'The Pumpkin Patrol'.

www.experian.co.uk/publicsector

A more in-depth qualitative approach has been undertaken by The Hyde Group (2010) in a research project undertaken for them by DEMOS. Forty interviews were undertaken with Hyde residents to find out more about their lives in the round – their stories about how they came to be in social housing – and broad themes such as 'the journey', 'quality of life', 'life challenges', 'life choices' and 'looking ahead'. The research identified a number of shifting trends as well as identifying some very deep-rooted personal characteristics, such as levels of personal agency (ability to make choices and influence decisions), alongside indicators such as length of tenancy. From this, the research identified four key resident group profiles.

Figure 7.6: Profile of resident groups based on personal agency and length of residency

Future planners	'Heartlanders'
This group are newer residents with high levels of personal agency. They see home as a springboard and whilst they may have problems they are not defined by them or feel they are moving on from them. These residents have wider social support networks beyond neighbourhood and although there is a high investment in home, they are aware of limitations.	This group of residents have been with the organisation for a longer period, but they also have high levels of personal agency. They are at the heart of their community and positive about the area and home. They have strong family/community/regional identity but are at risk of becoming isolated as communities change.
Security seekers	**Disconnected**
These residents are new but have low levels of personal agency. They are in the midst of, or recovering from, personal crisis. Home is seen as a refuge and there is an uneasy relationship with the local area. They are relieved to have been able to access social housing.	Residents in this segment have been in their tenancies for a long time and they have low levels of personal agency. They are dissatisfied with their home and their local area. They feel disengaged from support services and they face challenges in health and employment.

Adapted from The Hyde Group, 2010, p.19.

This smaller scale, qualitative approach to profiling the customer base can tell housing organisations so much – not just about the core housing product or the associated ancillary services – but also about the role of social housing providers in community cohesion and empowerment/enablement of individuals and groups who are vulnerable.

The word 'journey' in the Hyde approach to customer profiling is also key. Increasingly in the public sector, a process of 'customer journey mapping' is used particularly for local government to better understand service provision from a customer's point of view. A report by HM Government (nd) on this process provides a rationale again on two levels (1) better customer experience and (2) greater efficiency. On the former they suggest that journey mapping allows organisations to see things from the customer's point of view, identify points of confusion, meet expectations and deliver information. On the level of greater efficiency, journey mapping is supposed to cut across silos, reduce duplication, minimise costs and identify 'baton change' points where services or communications break down. From a customer focus point of view then, journey mapping by public agencies is vital to have a customer's-eye view rather than an organisational perspective. It is also important in service delivery areas that involve a number of different agencies to always retain the customer journey as the focal point – the tragic outcome of the breakdown in 'baton change' points in the Baby P case highlights the importance of such an approach.

It is important to listen to the views from customers' own mouths, as well as to analyse data collected around the customer. Feedback, either as part of a regular exercise, or an ongoing conversation with tenants in everyday transactions with them, is vital to good Customer Insight.

Some examples in the social housing sector:

> **Affinity Sutton** reported in their Summer 2010 newsletter that following feedback from tenants they have introduced new ways of working. Tenants said they wanted longer opening hours for the contact centre and the organisation noted that staff would be available until 7pm to answer queries, in response to this feedback. The organisation also reported that they were trialling netbooks with some staff so that they could access systems whilst in customers' homes and respond to issues and queries there and then.

> **Solihull Community Housing (SCH)** has an innovative and holistic approach to listening to the customer; these are just some examples:
> - If a tenant has dyslexia, SCH ask which colour they prefer to read documents on, the preferred colour acetate is then sent out for the customer to put over the top of any letters and other correspondence.
> - For tenants in some high-rise blocks who are waiting to move out to a different property, SCH aim to make customers' lives a little better by offering homework clubs for the kids, access to broadband and laptops and advice on jobs and training. They thus provide a holistic service to those waiting on the list to move to a more suitable property for their needs.
> - SCH does not limit staff to call length as a measure of good service – one call may take four minutes instead of three, but in that time an advisor might have solved multiple issues, offering a better service and greater efficiency in the long term for the organisation.
> - Advisors at the contact centre are taught to listen properly. One example was a customer who rang in for a repair because her heating had broken whilst she was away. Because the advisor listened they were able to find out that the customer had actually been in hospital and now needed aids such as grab rails to deal with her increasing disability and to maintain the length of time she could remain in her current home.
>
> The contact centre at SCH also runs scripting which helps provide a consistent response to customers across the organisation. Scripting may bring to mind the cold-calling telephone conversations with insurance companies that occur at the most inconvenient times of day; however the SCH approach is different.
>
> →

> This is a learning organisation with an evolving script which saves time on the part of the advisors, resources for SCH, and anxiety on the part of the customer. Whenever doubts arise in my mind on scripting and contact centres, I think of how SCH learnt to interpret 'green goo', reported by a customer, into a repair order which was understandable by the staff. This saved time in possible repeated misunderstandings from future different customer calls on the same issue, because the scripting system learnt from one experience and shared that information across the organisation.

Managing customer expectations

It is important throughout any CRM/CI processes that communications are clear, and this means to all stakeholders, including staff. An organisation might have the best system of external communications, through its website, glossy brochures, advertising etc; but unless that information is shared with all of the staff in the organisation then the message will get lost; this is discussed in more detail by James, Richardson and Winn in chapter 10 of this book.

Quite often in the social housing sector the delivery of the message is as important to levels of customer satisfaction as the answer. Remember the Dr Foster (2007) research referred to earlier in the chapter with the Somerset example of unusually high levels of satisfaction amongst the 'constrained by circumstances' segment? In many cases the answer to a customer or potential customer will be 'no' or 'not yet'; but we must still maintain good customer relations with those people, keep up-to-date records of changing needs and manage expectations. Saying 'no' is not the same as delivering a poor-quality customer service; indeed Jones and Keppler (2008) look at American public services and the skill of communication in being able to say 'no' whilst still improving customer service.

Conclusion

This chapter has discussed the collection and use of information which will allow housing organisations to turn data into insight and then into improved outcomes. The rationale for using Customer Insight is two-fold: (1) improved customer service and satisfaction rates (2) better and more efficient use of public money and resources. In the financially constrained times that the public sector and social housing organisations now find themselves in – the proper use of CI becomes vitally important.

References and further reading

Chartered Institute of Housing (2008) *Customer Insight: Knowing Your Customers*, Issue 32, February 2008. Coventry: CIH.

Chartered Institute of Housing, HouseMark and Tenant Services Authority (2010) *Tenant Insight: a toolkit for landlords*. London: TSA.

Chartered Institute of Marketing (2001) *Managing the Marketing/Customer Interface*. London: CIM.

Dr Foster Research Ltd and Tetlow Associates Ltd (2007) *Guide to Segmentation, Customer Satisfaction Measures for Local Government Services*. London: LGA, IDeA and NCC.

Experian (nd) *Improve outcomes through applied customer insight*. www.experian.co.uk

Frazer-Robinson, J. (1999) *It's All About CUSTOMERS*. London: Kogan Page Ltd.

HM Government (nd) *Customer Journey Mapping: an introduction*. London: HM Government.

HouseMark (2008) *Driving up Performance; producing effective local information*. Coventry: HouseMark.

Housing Quality Network (2010) *Customer Profiling – How Would You Do Yours?* York: HQN.

Hull City Council (2010) *Improving the Collection and Use of Research and Intelligence*, Report to Cabinet, 26 April.

Hyde Group (2010) *Where are Tomorrow's Heartlanders? Unlocking the potential of social housing*. London: The Hyde Group.

Improvement and Development Agency (2010) *Customer Insight: through a Total Place lens*. London: IDeA.

Iyengar, S. (2010) *The Art of Choosing, the decisions we make every day – what they say about us and how we can improve them*. London: Little Brown.

Jones, E. and Keppler, P. (2008) 'Improving customer service and communication skills in public works: Learning to say 'no' without closing doors', *Journal of Public Works & Infrastructure*, Vol. 1, No. 2, pp.156-170.

Kotler, P. (2000) *Marketing Management – The Millennium Edition*. New Jersey: Prentice Hall.

Local Government Association (2006) *Putting the Customer First: lessons from business*. London: LGA.

Local Government Association (2009) *Is There Something I Should Know? Making the most of your information to improve services*. London: Audit Commission.

McDonald, C. and Negrin, K. (2010) *No Data – No Progress, data collection in countries participating in the decade of Roma inclusion 2005-2015*. Open Society Institute: www.soros.org

Muthiah, N. (2010) *Choice Based Lettings – what does the future hold?* Presentation by the Chief Executive of Home Connections to the Centre for Comparative Housing Research conference at De Montfort University, Leicester, 20 July.

Obama, B. (2010) *Speech following interim airline security review*, 5th January, http://news.bbc.co.uk

ODPM (2004) *The Benefits of CRM*. London: ODPM.

Perri 6, Bellamy, C, and Raab, C, (2010) 'Information-sharing dilemmas in public services: using frameworks from risk management', *Policy & Politics*, Vol. 38, No. 3, pp.465-481.

Richardson, J. (2000) *Quality and Customer Focus – Good Practice Briefing*. Coventry, Chartered Institute of Housing.

Salecl, R (2010) *Choice*. London: Profile Books Ltd.

Samson, D (2001) 'Patterns of Excellence', *Marketing Insights*, CIM July-September 2001. www.cimglobal.com

Stone, M *et al*. (2000) Customer Relationship Marketing. London: Kogan Page Ltd.

CHAPTER 8:
Brand: new products and new markets

Kerry James and Joanna Richardson

Introduction

This chapter considers why branding is important in the housing sector, and how businesses, individuals and communities are affected by it. We will explore the point of branding, how organisations, places and products are branded and the relationship between brands and customer experience.

Branding – investment or immaterial?

If someone asked you to describe a brand, how would you respond?

- a logo?
- catchy strap-line?
- product range?
- an organisation?
- an attitude?
- a story?
- something else?

And more importantly, would you think it is an area of work worth spending your time on?

A brand is all of the above things and more. It is the sum of what people perceive about an organisation. In other words, it is their experiences of your business when they have browsed your website, visited your offices, read about you in the media and interacted with your services or products (either directly or through word-of-mouth).

So if branding is about what people think of you, don't you think that it is worth your time and effort? The rewards you can reap could include more satisfied tenants, less vigilant regulation and, say, cheaper loans (just look at the competitive rates of bonds being reported in the housing press for organisations like Hyde and Notting Hill housing associations). A good brand is recognised by international money markets as well as local tenants: a good brand can result in increased value or business savings.

But what exactly do we mean by 'brand'?

Anholt (2007) suggests that:

- *A brand is a product or service or organisation, considered in combination with its name, its identity and its reputation*
- *Branding is the process of designing, planning and communicating the name and the identity, in order to build or manage the reputation* (p.4).

He also outlines four different aspects to the brand:

1. *Brand identity* – the core concept of the product, clearly and distinctively expressed
2. *Brand image* – perception of the brand in the mind of the customer
3. *Brand purpose* – the internal equivalent of brand image, the organisational culture of the brand
4. *Brand equity* – the value of a brand, which can be difficult to quantify specifically, but affects how an organisation is presented to the world (think of the difference between Aldi, Tesco and Waitrose, for example).

(adapted from pp.5-6)

Branding is an emotional response – it is a single word or concept that you can create in the mind of your target audience; it can establish or destroy reputation, it can change behaviours or attitudes, it can impact on results and it can drive sales, up or down. It is powerful and it is here to stay.

How people experience brands

People typically respond to brands in one of three ways:

- *Visual* – the things people see that they associate with your business, such as your logo, a written strapline or product design
- *Auditory* – where people associate a sound, spoken strapline or piece of music with you
- *Kinesthetic* – where people feel, or sense things that trigger familiarity with your brand. This could include physical interaction (such as picking up a lambswool jumper in a shop, or pressing buttons on a touchscreen); equally it could be that people associate a particular feeling with your brand.

The perception of a brand is experienced through a number of different expressions to a range of target audiences; some of which may be linked to the corporate strategy of the housing organisation, the neighbourhood or a place marketing initiative for a particular housing scheme – for instance the logo, the physical regeneration etc – but others will be much more personal experiences.

Figure 8.1: Perceptions of brand

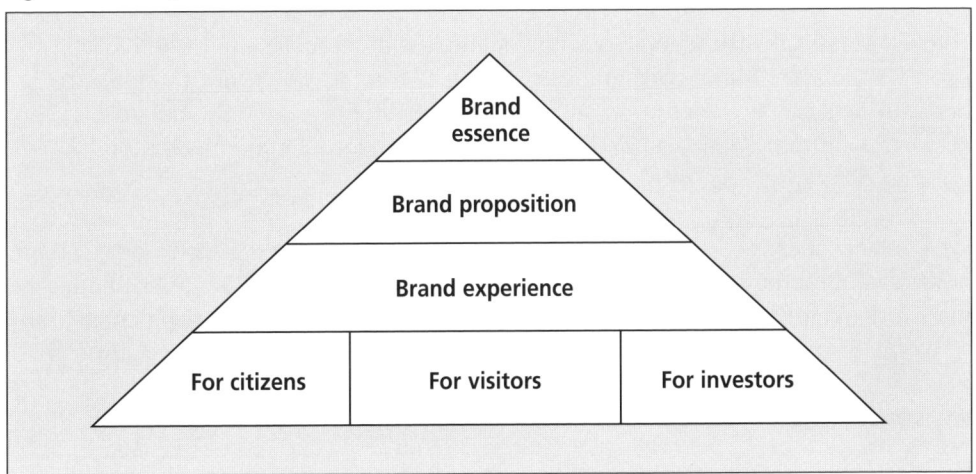

The 'personality' of a brand can be expressed to people in different ways. This might be through communicating messages about an organisation's values and personality, showing what life is like in a particular neighbourhood or marketing a product like shared ownership. There are lots of different elements involved in a brand – from visual things such as logos and picture styles, through to sounds, smells and stories. The way people interpret and respond to this collective package of elements is referred to as the brand experience.

Figure 8.2: Expression of the brand

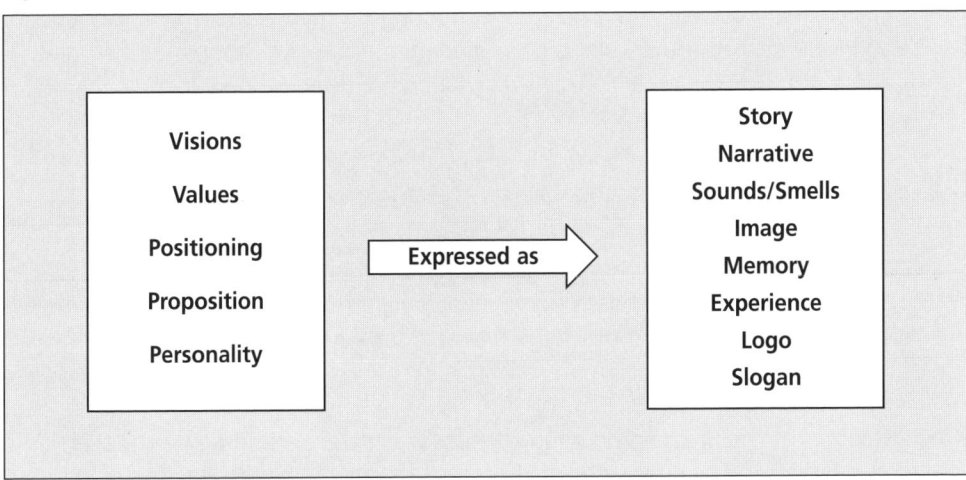

In its simplest form, a strong brand can lead to added financial value, repeat commissions or usage, positive kudos and opportunities to generate extra business. Negative brand equity, on the other hand, has the opposite effect.

Branding housing businesses

The year 2010 saw affordable housing waiting lists at a record level of 4.5 million people, regulatory frameworks under review or subject to significant change and budgets increasingly under pressure to deliver more for less. So why should branding be something that providers need to worry about when there are much more pressing priorities to deliver?

Well, mainly because strong branding is part of the day job. A well-branded, positively promoted organisation has the tools to build and maintain trust, stimulate market demand, attract partners, increase revenue and show the positive impact of its work.

Ways in which the leading sector players typically do this include:

- *Corporate accreditations* – The Sunday Times 'top 100' company status, RoSPA awards, Investors in People and the like convey good messages about an organisation's effectiveness as an employer, governing body and so on.
- *Award wins* – UK Housing Awards, Housing Heroes, Housing Design Awards and similar accreditations (such as the The Sunday Times 'top 100' and the Green Business Award etc) position providers as thought leaders or best practice organisations.
- *Alignment* – sponsoring or partnering charities, resident groups, apprentices and other philanthropic causes helps to build profile and highlight corporate social responsibility.
- *Business-to-business relationships* – attracting partners, employees, funders and regulators through relationship management, news stories, case studies and joint advertising can cement reputations and secure new income streams.
- *Business-to-tenant relationships* – maintaining relationships with customers through proactive and responsive services and a programme of regular communications can achieve better performance.
- *Developing audience-specific or product sub-brands* – for example, to generate demand for shared ownership developments, choice-based letting schemes and reward programmes, can increase income or improve performance.

When it comes to maintaining demand for services or developing new products, it is in your interests to be a 'provider of choice'. Without the desirability factor, your chances of maximising rent income, letting properties or attracting extra funds are likely to be pretty constrained.[31]

---

31 Or to put it another way: shared bedsits for the elderly, anyone?

Only as good as your last contact

McDonalds, Royal Mail, Nike, Apple, BP, Burberry – billions of pounds are spent managing these famous brands every year, but the 'personalities' of each brand are not always publicly perceived as their boards intended.

That is because unfortunately, managing reputation can be a tricky business. An unexpected accident here, whistleblowing incident there, poor customer service or inconsistent leadership can quickly damage people's views of a brand and the value of a business. And in the social media age, forget the adage of yesterday's newspapers becoming fish-and-chip wrapping in a day or two; these days, grievances can become 'trending topics' in a matter of minutes, and take on a search engine-optimised life of their own for weeks and months to come.

Housing organisations face proportionally less hazardous territory than global brands, as the majority of business is conducted on a local or regional scale. However, once damaging stories get into the public domain, they can severely affect the brands concerned. In early 2010, *Inside Housing* reported allegations of bullying in two separate housing organisations; shortly after the stories hit, concerned parties were posting commentary on internet forums and the brands subsequently went into a crisis media spiral. This damage could take months if not years to overcome.

Rational arguments

An interesting emerging trend is how changing governance structures impact on branding. In some parts of the country, housing groups are collapsing structures – that is, merging traditionally local brands (such as former stock transfer associations) into one corporate entity.

This approach presents opportunities for commercial viability, corporate growth and consistent governance; equally, it is likely to change the dynamics of the relationship between landlords and their primary resident audiences. Those historic foundations tend to be built on locality and personal connections rather than speaking the clean, corporate tones of most business-to-business branding.

The key to maintaining 'brand integrity' lies in working out what each founder brand contributes that is special or unique, and trying to make those characteristics central to the new corporate body; otherwise groups risk alienating their core consumers at the expense of financial stability.

See the case study on the next page.

Case in point: organisation branding (group merger)
Affinity Sutton Group

Organisation
A housing group managing more than 54,000 homes from Plymouth to Newcastle.

Vision
- To use our heritage, fresh thinking and commitment to help people put down roots.

Brand architecture
- The origins of the group dated back more than 100 years and involved a complex legacy of mergers, restructures and numerous brands. This stage of the process involved an amalgamation of William Sutton, Broomleigh and Downland housing associations.
- Affinity Sutton wanted to create a simpler, unified structure and achieve broader recognition of the national Affinity Sutton Homes brand – but incorporating elements of each merging brand's identity and culture.

Visual identity
- The group's executive team wanted to communicate the diversity of its work and appeal to a diverse range of audiences – including MPs, regulators, funders and resident groups.
- The desired brand 'personality' was to come across as warm, genuine, fresh and experienced. This included updating the existing Affinity Sutton logo, known as 'the marble' – but without moving too far away from what was a fairly well-known symbol.
- The agency team created a new sphere made up of soft-tone navy blue, light blue, yellow and green colours.

Roll-out
- To coincide with the launch of its new identity, Affinity Sutton pledged to plough more than £2 million each year into its neighbourhoods, as well as raising additional cash from external sources. Indeed in 2010 it announced a doubling of its annual surplus and the creation of a charitable community foundation pump-primed with £19 million.

Agency
The Team

Sources: www.creativematch.com/viewNews/?97947 and www.affinitysutton.com/about_us/finance_and_performance/annual_accounts_09-10/sustainable_communities.aspx

Branding in the social housing sector

For many years, the social housing sector has relied heavily on making best use of scarce resources. Through the passages of time, professionals have become used to making do and mending through the seasons of grant regimes, waiting lists, bidding rounds, partnership funds and so on.

But of course, measuring brand success in this industry is pretty complex; it is not all about making a profit. Things like tenancy churning, customer satisfaction, demand for housing and neighbourhood reputation are all closely linked. And external factors – such as changes in government policy and grant cuts – can also have a major impact upon the way organisations are perceived.

Your 'point of difference'

The origins of current branding in the housing sector stem from changes to housing policy in the late 1980s; the triggers were a political shift towards housing associations as preferred providers, government promotion of stock transfer and the creation of the local authority enabling role. Increased competition, combined with the removal of 100% Housing Action Grant, forced housing associations to develop more proactive brands and marketing strategies so they could:

- attract potential local authority partners and funding through joint commissioning arrangements (popularly known as 'beauty contests')
- stimulate demand for development schemes, particularly with shared ownership and low cost sale homes
- respond to political agendas around increased consumer choice.

Fast-forward to the late 1990s and turn of the twenty-first century, and housing clearly had an image problem. In a 2001 MORI poll, only 17% of people surveyed said they would want to live in social housing if they could get it. And within the industry the news wasn't much better; 81% of association chairs and chief executives thought the sector had a bad image.[32]

This state of affairs led to a new, sector-wide call to action – the birth of the 'in business for neighbourhoods' (iNbiz) brand. Launched by the National Housing Federation (NHF) in September 2003, iNbiz aimed to tackle the stigma associated with social housing, promote associations' work in supporting communities and build positive profiling and influencing opportunities. Associations across the country signed-up to supporting iNbiz – in total, covering more than three quarters of housing association stock.

---

32 http://www.southeast-ra.gov.uk/documents/committees/healthy_region_forum/2005/230605/national_housing_federation.ppt

Through iNbiz, providers commit to a set of promises, explaining what their organisation will do for its customers and communities. Information badged under the collective brand is shared regionally and nationally through the NHF; achievements are also flagged through case studies and celebrated in the 'What We Are Proud Of' awards programme. Yet alongside the collective badging, there are also benefits for individual organisations, whose achievements are recorded as a contribution towards the greater good. The brand has helped to bring together attention and focus around branding in the sector.

In addition to sector-wide branding, housing organisations are clearly branding themselves as individual organisations with unique selling propositions (USPs) in a bid to capture the essence of the customer experience and also to attract inward investment from international finance markets and (where there still are any) government funds and grants. If Mary Portas, the BBC's *Queen of Shops* were to visit a housing association or local authority[33] she would pace the streets, visit tenants in their homes, sit in the reception and talk to homeless people and applicants; then she would come back to the board or committee having established who the customer is and what they expect and say: '*That's* your point of difference'. In other words, X is what defines your brand, and it matters.

Vision and values

So what's the big idea?

John Grant (2006) argues that a brand is a 'strategic cultural idea' – for example, he cites the Blairite *New Labour, New Britain* policies as applying branding techniques to politics. Grant also points out that it is not always the brand owner that creates the idea; for example, the names individually attributed to the Spice Girls (Sporty, Scary, Posh *et al.*) came from a *Top of the Pops* magazine journalist and were incorporated into the brand later on.[34]

Developing a vision will shape the 'personality' of the brand. It is about what you stand for and what makes you stand out – like making a promise on what your brand will deliver.

Visioning should include consideration of:

- relevant history or heritage
- findings from any perception surveys or consultations (how others see you)
- a self-assessment (how you see yourself)
- target audiences and their preferences
- details of proposed business goals for the brand.

---

33 What a fantastic television programme that would make! If anyone from the BBC reads this, we are open to negotiations...
34 Presumably to give it a little 'zig-a-zig-ah'!

If you do not find the pearl hiding in the oyster at this stage, you could end up with a lot of grit. Some well-known companies paid the price because their evolving brands were not understood or accepted by key audiences – Consignia's return to the Royal Mail name being an obvious example.

And ideally, there needs to be something that is specific to you and you alone. Without your own 'unique selling proposition', how can you hope to be noticed for your special talents? You might get the job done faster than anyone else for less, have an unusual style of leadership that makes you a great employer, or your products may have extra features that residents love; whatever it is, there needs to be something that marks you out from the crowd; so find it and exploit it.

Brand identity

Logo design is often the best-known part of brand development. It is the point where the big ideas, structures, name and words are transformed into something visual, lasting and hopefully memorable – although that is not always easy, given the number of brands that compete for our attention every day.

To show how logos and brands pervade our lives each day, David Airey (2010) spent the first few minutes of a typical working day photographing each brand he came into contact with. The result? 33 logos in 33 minutes – spanning categories as broad as aftershave, toothpaste, clothing labels, electronics manufacturers, news channels and online brands.

Airey's experiment is an interesting take on the work done by American advertisers Jon Bond and Richard Kirshenbaum, which suggested people are bombarded with as many as 1,500 advertising messages each day. That is a lot of visual clutter. And if it is true, how and why does your brand stand out from anyone else in the marketplace? Is your organisation visible, memorable, likeable, desirable or just forgettable?

Most memorable brands do have something that 'hooks' the viewer or tells them a story. Just think about:

- the golden arches associated with McDonalds
- Apple's logo, with a bite taken out of it
- Amazon's 'smile from A-Z'.

Housing brands do not have to scream from the rooftops (unless you feel that is the best option for your audiences). Remember, what is important is that the final result helps to get your messages across to the right people, and achieves your business objectives.

Product branding and the diversification in service offer

The core vision and image of an organisation is what is known as the 'attack brand' – it is the 'face' of your organisation as a whole. However, there can be supplementary brands, particularly for large organisations with a diverse range of products; and these are known as 'slipstream brands'. With stock transfers declining and development schemes becoming both more competitive and difficult to achieve, some housing providers have pursued alternative business opportunities. One increasingly common option has been to expand into new products, services and markets (see chapter 3 for models of product and service growth, e.g. Ansoff and Boston Consulting Group).

Some providers have obvious opportunities to 'cross-sell' services to existing customers, such as providing handyperson services to their tenants. This model offers multiple benefits – protecting the organisation's assets, supporting older and vulnerable people in their homes at a relatively low cost and offsetting the cost of labour and materials.

Of course, the prospective customer base does not end there. In some cases, people who may not previously have thought of themselves as social housing customers are now logical targets for providers. In particular, providing maintenance services to homeowners in the vicinity is an easy 'in' for landlords with the workforce capacity and desire to grow. But this raises two key issues around branding:

- some householders may not wish to visibly purchase services from a social housing provider, so they might not want an association's van parked outside their home
- housing associations without a repairs workforce are unlikely to want someone else's brand delivering their service.

So how do you get around the stigma of the social housing 'label' and when is it appropriate to diversify into completely new products and markets? Time to get emotional…

Emotional branding

Marc Gobe (2002) describes the four pillars of emotional branding which help organisations to make successful connections with their consumers:

- *Relationship* – giving your audiences the emotional experience they want
- *Sensorial experiences* – providing memorable brand contact and creating loyalty
- *Imagination* – when designing products, packaging, retail environments and advertisements
- *Vision* – through continual reinvention and creating emotional resonance.

BRAND: NEW PRODUCTS AND NEW MARKETS

> ### Apple of the consumer's eye
>
> A classic example of a brand that connects with its customers and continually reinvents itself is Apple's iPod. The first player with a hard disk, it was seen as filling a need for high-capacity music storage. The elegant design and scroll-wheel functionality promoted the brand as a 'concept' rather than just another media player.
>
> Yet the first-generation units did not fly off the shelves initially, because at the time Microsoft cornered the mass market and the iPod depended on Mac- and iTunes- compliance. But one year and a Windows-compatible version later, sales rocketed from 150,000 units to two million a year. Since then, successive generations have emerged almost annually, alongside new products such as the iPod Shuffle, iPod Nano, iPod Touch and of course the iPad.
>
> And of course, the development of applications or 'apps' has revolutionised the marketplace. Anyone can apply to be a developer and make something to impress buyers – from games, through to social networking software, to-do list generators or route finders. It is highly lucrative for the top-selling applications (typically developers attract a 70% cut) but also tightly controlled; Apple ultimately decides which applications will make it into the App Store.

Source: Softpedia News (2005)
http://news.softpedia.com/news/iPOD-where-will-it-stop-895.shtml

All well and good, but being friendly, feely, funky and flexible are not necessarily the first things you'd look for in a housing provider's toolkit. So how is this example relevant to the sector?

Well, for many people buying an iPod or iPhone there is a clear excitement trigger; the anticipation of buying something functional, entertaining and nice to look at. The control and use lies in the hands of the consumer. Not a million miles away from the feeling you might get with the keys to a new home in your hands, in fact...

So what do many providers do at this point in the game? Often, initiate a formal sign-up procedure where people fill in lots of forms, then get the keys so they can go and get the practical stuff sorted. What about the joyous moments though? How about creating memories, visual triggers and networking opportunities to get customers co-producing information and help them to associate the 'cool stuff' with a new home? This could include:

- taking images with smartphones and incorporating them into offer letters or packs

- using tools such as Woobius Eye to show where stopcocks or meters are located
- providing colour swatches (either app-based or mini Pantone-style books) to inspire people with decorating ideas
- encouraging people to upload 'my homestyle' images to Flickr pages or YouTube channels to show how they have created a beautiful home environment.

For some people, this may well sound like a waste of money. With 25% cuts announced through the 2010 emergency budget – and regulatory changes almost a constant issue – it is likely that economic restraint will force many providers back to focusing on core activities such as housing management, maintenance and rent collection.

But if you have got a logical reason to expand or improve customer satisfaction, board support and a robust business plan, the feeling you create with a new customer at the 'point of sale' (or rent) will significantly influence how they will perceive you in the months and years to come.

So, if you have the wherewithal to invest in new services such as domiciliary care, marketing or helpdesk support, why not make it memorable? And if you need to target a particular audience segment (say young people), will a corporate video, letter and set of keys create the same effect as a blog, Facebook page or text competition? As a former housing minister might say, 'What matters is what works'.

Reputation across the channels

Branding and reputation are intrinsically linked. Reputation with customers matters, at least as much as it does with your investors and regulators. There are other key measures of reputation too; for example the UK Councils monthly social media reputation index which compares across a range of metrics including overall council satisfaction and CouncilMonitor[35] sentiment scores. CouncilMonitor also include a total monthly buzz chart,[36] where spikes in mentions can be seen to coincide with periods where there was high news value – such as the budget, or in local areas where findings in a particular case or review are published. This level of media monitoring is an interesting proxy for reputation – remembering that not all news is good news, and a high buzz spike can represent opportunities for poor reputation as well as good.

The Local Government Association (LGA, 2010) Reputation Guide suggests that for good reputation there are three crucial issues to get right:

---

35 www.councilmonitor.com
36 Total amount of mentions and references to UK councils online.

1. Leadership
2. Brand
3. Communications.

They suggest five rules of reputation:

- prove you provide value for money
- always inform and engage residents and staff
- build trust and confidence in what you do
- improve key services and show you are doing so
- focus on changing lives for the better.

LGA has a wider campaign on reputation management[37] for councils; a range of guides are available including one (2008) called *A Councillor's Guide to Getting the Credit in Residents' Eyes*. The guide advises on promoting the positive aspects of council services, engaging with the public and being more efficient. The content of the guide is sensible and public minded, even if the title of it could be seen to be a little defensive.

Qube (2010) also offers guidance for online reputation management in the public sector; it suggests that organisations should:

1. listen to relevant conversations (monitor what people are saying about your services online)
2. build on your online reputation (by listening to the audience, monitor which themes are of most importance and then feed this into your own online presence so that the services and information are of value to customers)
3. defend your online reputation (do not stifle or censor debate, but if harmful messages are damaging your reputation then you need to defend the organisation).
(adapted from Qube, 2010, pp.9-12)

The politics of branding

Branding is not always an easy journey. In fact, some types of brand development present implementation challenges – particularly where there is a lack of shared vision or purpose, or active opposition to a process.

Stock transfer campaigns in the 1990s and 2000s are a case in point. Successive government policies encouraged the transfer of homes from local councils to housing associations. Enabling associations to borrow funds for investment in home and environmental improvements served as an incentive to change ownership – subject to the majority of voting council tenants saying 'yes' to transfer.

---

37 www.reputation.lga.gov.uk

Case in point: organisation branding (post-transfer)
Wellingborough Homes

Organisation
A stock transfer association created in December 2007, to meet the housing needs of people in Wellingborough and the surrounding areas.

Vision and values
- *Vision* – creating a better place to live through quality, well-maintained homes and improved services.
- *Values* – to be professional, confident, enthusiastic, caring, communicative and ready to embrace change.

Brand architecture
- As a new stand-alone association, there was a logo identity (created through consultation) but no other brand elements.

Name
- Like many stock transfers, locality was the key driver in establishing this new stand-alone association; Wellingborough Homes 'did what it said on the tin' and was an easy-to-remember option.

Visual identity
- The executive team wanted to create a vibrant, accessible brand that spoke to the primary resident audience, but would also interest secondary business stakeholders. The creative brief was to produce a look that was very different from the local council, to create differentiation from the transferring authority to the new provider.
- Resident consultation showed a preference for bright colours, a friendly tone of voice and 'not too slick' feel. The agency hand-drew a series of easy-to-understand, colour-coded icons to represent core elements of the new association's services – such as repairs, rents and customer involvement.

Roll-out
- The new brand was expanded across all resident-facing communications, including a new website, customer magazine, tenant handbook, suite of literature, signage and vehicle livery.
- For business partners, a slightly more muted approach was taken – the distinctive icons were still used to reflect service provision, but used in conjunction with the navy and maroon colourways from the logo rather than colour-coding communications.

Agency
The Bridge Group

BRAND: NEW PRODUCTS AND NEW MARKETS

Of course, the relative value of home improvements as an incentive to transfer was perceived very differently among different groups of tenants. For some people, the apparent medium-term benefit of new doors and windows (for example) was countered by uncertainties about a change in landlord and fears of tenants' rights being reduced. And some opposition groups, ideologically opposed to the process, communicated anti-transfer messages to dissuade people from voting in support.

Whilst getting the transfer offer right was a driving force, branding and communications also became an integral part of many transfer campaigns – used as a tool to establish dialogue with proposed new landlords and, in some cases, to create 'home-grown' brands for fledgling transfer associations and community gateways. This two-way dialogue was often a critical part of the debate in the run-up to a ballot; strong Customer Insight and familiarity with highly localised issues could sometimes be the difference between a 'yes' and 'no' vote.

Transfers were susceptible to highly local influences and new stand-alone associations often reflected this; names, identities and strategies were frequently linked to geographical features or historical connections to reinforce trust and security in a changing world.

As a result, many stock transfer associations are firmly rooted in local engagement; and without that early resident support, it is unlikely that more than one million homes would have transferred out of local authority ownership between 1988 and 2008. The question is whether those roots will stand the test of time post-recession, as some groups choose to test the value and power of monolithic brands whilst others need to restructure their businesses in line with sector spending cuts and revised business plan projections. And on the other side of the coin, housing policy appears to have come full circle, as the 'single conversation' places greater influence in the hands of the local authority strategic role.

Place branding

Place branding started to gather momentum in the UK during the 1990s, with the adoption of choice-based lettings (or 'the Delft model' as it was then known) and a greater focus on factors which affected desirability of accommodation. Wide-scale approaches to regeneration and increased political focus on competition and collaboration also encouraged housing organisations to take a more active role as community facilitators and champions.

In recent years, the topic of 'place branding' has become more widespread as local authorities, regeneration partnerships and housing providers aim to attract investment, tourists, shoppers, businesses and residents to their areas. Place branding is not just about a logo, but a visual element may well be a part of it (think of the 'I ♥ NY' logo as an example of a place logo).

So, what do we mean by 'place'?

Figure 8.3: Kinds of place

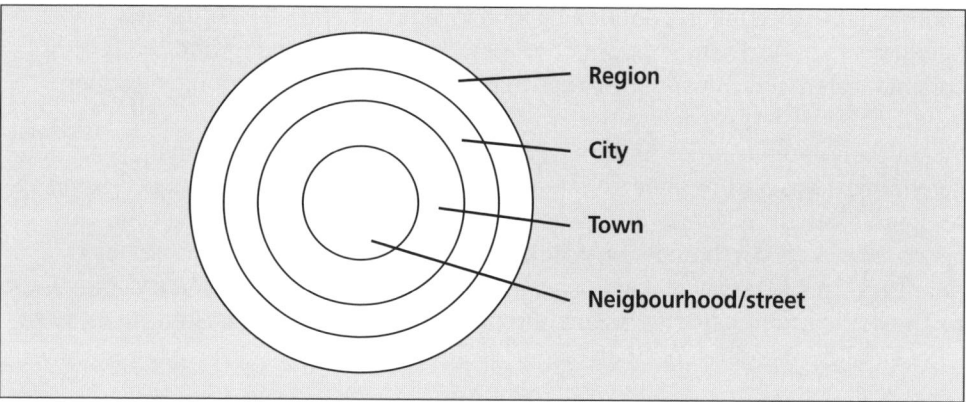

There are a range of places that residents and visitors connect with. For international investment opportunities, this might involve countries or even continents; but looking at housing and 'liveability', we will probably consider regions, sub-regions, cities, towns, villages, neighbourhoods, estates or streets. Residents' perceptions of place often do not match legal and administrative official boundaries – they may be much more fluid and informal. There may be places that naturally fit with each other on a number of issues, and where that applies, marketing locations together will attract better investment, visitor numbers and resident retention.

It is also important to remember that place branding is not all about inward investment and attracting new residents into new properties, it is about retaining a good relationship with existing citizens in a place. So any image that is being used in a particular campaign must resonate with a truthful yet attractive image, or it will alienate those residents already there.

Branding places to reduce stigma

But why brand places? Branding on its own cannot 'stop the rot' in places that are deteriorating. However, as part of an overall regeneration package, place marketing and place branding are key to attracting investment (whether from government or private business). It may also be the case that the physical place, and indeed other indicators such as levels of anti-social behaviour, unemployment and educational attainment, suggest that a place is actually attractive in all but name; and that some degree of branding might help to reduce undeserved stigma. The (2006) ODPM report *State of the English Cities*, also noted this importance of 'place' and the international recognition, and economic importance of English cities. This suggests that place marketing should then be an ongoing process, that adapts to demographic and other changes that occur in places.

Kotler *et al.* (1993) outline an example of the cyclical dynamics of city decay to show why place branding matters and can save money in the longer term:

Figure 8.4: City decay dynamics

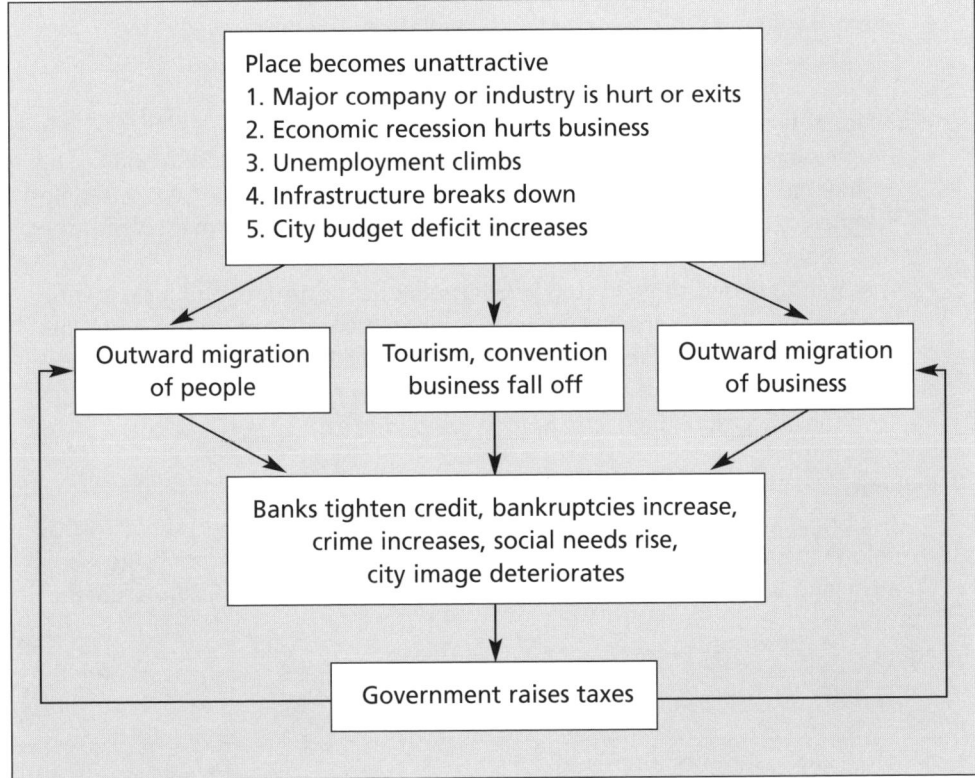

Kotler, P et al. (1993), p.7.

Perception of place

Measuring stakeholder perception and influencing attitudes and behaviours are at the core of place branding. This is big business; in the Liverpool One example, the rebuilding project exceeded £1 billion.

> **Case in point: place branding**
> **Liverpool One**
>
> **Place**
> Liverpool One covers a 42-acre site between the city centre and docks – a £1 billion development that incorporates more than 30 individually designed buildings in distinct districts, each with a different character and design.

> **Vision**
> - To achieve a retail-led development city centre in time for the city to maximise the benefit of 2008 European Capital of Culture Status, and get people returning to Liverpool to spend leisure time and money.
> - There was also a financial target to lease 95% of the development by completion.
>
> **Visual identity**
> - The new brand needed to work in both business-to-business (B2B) and business-to-consumer (B2C) markets. The brand values were to be big, simple in concept, unique and true to the development and transformation of Liverpool.
> - The brand needed to be rooted in Liverpool's own attitudes and local identity. Naming the place Liverpool One both marked the postcode and an ambition to make the city the number one shopping choice in the north-west.
> - The core rules behind the brand were 'make new rules', 'involve everyone', 'love the city', 'think big', 'create more' and 'be best'.
>
> **Roll-out**
> - The brand was launched in 2005, whilst construction was progressing. This helped the developers to sign-up retailers. By June 2009, Liverpool One was attracting 500,000 visitors a week, and the shop units were 98.5% occupied.
>
> **Agency**
> Wolff Olins

http://www.admotusmarketing.com/PB_pb200919.pdf
http://www.wolffolins.com/media/case_studies/Liverpool1_case_study.pdf

But assessing and responding to people's perceptions is arguably old hat for housing providers. For example, the National Housing Federation's STATUS survey model is more than 10 years old and is still used as a key indicator in regulatory judgments; local authorities also use this model, but with a different methodology and frequency. So the tools used to gauge residents' views are already well known; it is how you respond to the findings that is significant for your brand.

More recently the 2008 Place Survey required local authorities to ask residents for their perceptions about the areas in which they live. This approach was intended to capture residents' views on local services and interventions – including issues such as anti-social behaviour, mutual respect and fair treatment by local services – and see how far people felt listened to by their council. However, the number of indicators was cut from 18 to 13 in April 2010 and then councils were advised not to proceed with the autumn 2010 survey.

The introduction of the 'Total Place' initiative was to explore how efficient local government is at delivering local services – and identify potential for improving efficiency whilst also reducing costs. Thirteen pilot areas were chosen, representing different geographical, economic and demographic profiles across England – and each focusing on a particular theme, such as housing, crime and mental health services – to see how money flowed and whether services could be delivered more effectively.

> The **Croydon** pilot won the Total Place Achievement of the Year award in June 2010. Focusing on the needs of young children, partners identified that they could shave more than 5% off the £206 million joint budget by changing the way they do things together. Greater co-operation and clear agreements between the local council, NHS, Jobcentre Plus and other public agencies and joined-up government policies were the triggers to making this happen.

This section highlights that place branding is about much more than the identity of individual housing organisations or local authorities. It involves interaction between people, engagement between residents and their localities and a complex mix of environmental, social and communication factors. There are opportunities for housing providers to help shape the agenda, but rarely to control it.

Conclusion and next steps

We hope that this chapter has convinced you that branding matters for social housing. It is vital to understand how your customers perceive you, so you can attract and retain customers and forms of investment, and maintain a high degree of quality in your housing product, services and overall reputation – and in so doing also influence the overall brand of social housing.

This chapter has aimed to demonstrate the depth and reach of the housing 'brand' and, as with many other elements of customer focus and marketing that have been discussed in the book, show that it is part of your core business. Forget any notions of slapping on a logo; branding matters.

References and further reading

Admotus Marketing (2009) *Moving Millions: the marketing programme behind Liverpool One*. London: Admotus Marketing.

Airey, D. (2010) *Logo Design Love*. Harlow: New Riders.

Anholt, S. (2007) *Competitive Identity, The New Brand Management for Nations, Cities and Regions*. Basingstoke: Palgrave Macmillan.

CouncilMonitor: www.councilmonitor.com

Eshius, J. and Edelenbos, J. (2009) 'Branding in urban regeneration', *Journal of Urban Regeneration and Renewal*, Vol. 2, No. 3, pp.272-282.

Gobe, M. (2002) *Emotional Branding*. New York: Allworth Press.

Grant, J. (2006) *The Brand Innovation Manifesto*. Chichester: John Wiley & Sons Ltd.

Harrison, S. (2009) *How to Do Better Creative Work*. New Jersey: Pearson Education Limited.

Kotler, P., Haider, D.H. and Rein, I. (1993) *Marketing Places: Attracting Investment, Industry and Tourism to Cities, States and Nations*. New York: The Free Press.

Local Government Association (2010) *New Reputation Guide*. London: LGA. www.lga.gov.uk/reputation

Local Government Association (2008) *A Councillor's Guide to Getting the Credit in Residents' Eyes*. www.lga.gov.uk/reputation

Mono (2004) *Branding – From Brief to Finished Solution*. Hove: Rotovision SA.

ODPM (2006) *State of the English Cities*. London: ODPM.

Qube (2010) *Online Reputation Management in the Public Sector*, July. www.qubemedia.net

Taylor, D. (2007) *Never Mind The Sizzle ... Where's the Sausage?* Chichester: John Wiley & Sons Ltd.

Wheeler, A. (2003) *Designing Brand Identity: A Complete Guide to Creating, Building and Maintaining Strong Brands*. Chichester: John Wiley & Sons Ltd.

CHAPTER 9:
Putting the 'social' into marketing

Joanna Richardson

Introduction

Social marketing is not a new phenomenon in the public sector. Government has been using campaigns to promote behaviour change for years (COI, 2008 and Halpern et al., 2004) on issues such as drink-driving, wearing seatbelts, healthy eating, conserving energy, switching to renewable sources of energy, recycling and even how to stay composed during the World War II effort.

Governments across the world are increasingly turning to social marketing to change behaviours (Australian Public Service Commission, 2007) and there are increasing numbers of toolkits offering support.[38] Social marketing is difficult and is not always a success, but the results can be powerful for customers with improved life experiences in the places they live.

Earls (2009) refers to 'herd' behaviour suggesting that individual marketing is difficult and that herd marketing is even harder. However, later in the chapter we will look at

---

38 e.g. the Canadian www.toolsofchange.com

experiments on 'think' techniques from researchers which show that the power of the collective can help to change behaviours for social benefit. Earls uses seven principles to define herd marketing, of which one relates to 'co-production'. This theme is dealt with in a number of other chapters in this book (for example chapter 10 on the power of communication) and this also applies to a range of ideas which are relevant not just to social marketing, but to other customer-focus ideals of service delivery that are analysed throughout the book.

This chapter will aim to define social marketing, to look at some theoretical explanations, such as 'nudge' and 'think', to examine the social marketing mix and some key steps; as well as some housing and other examples of social marketing in action.

What is social marketing?

The National Social Marketing Centre define social marketing as:

> ...the systematic application of marketing alongside other concepts and techniques to achieve specific behavioural goals, for a social good (www.nsmc.org.uk).

Social marketing is part of an overall marketing approach, but rather than trying to influence decisions on buying/consuming a product or service, the focus is instead on influencing behaviour on a wider level which will achieve a social or public benefit.

Social marketing works alongside other policies and techniques; it is not a panacea. So, marketing, social research, public health/housing/sustainability policies will work together. Moreover, it is important to note that objectives should still be 'SMART', just because an objective is to change a social behaviour does not mean that it should not be specific and measurable.

As with core marketing functions, there is still a requirement to:

- **Know your customers** – socio-economic data along with attitudes and beliefs will help a housing organisation to know their customers' orientation on a range of issues.
- **Know what you want to achieve** – what behaviour are you trying to affect? Is it anti-social behaviour, encouraging tenants to support new housing development, pay the rent on time – Be SMART in setting objectives for social marketing campaigns.
- **Understand existing behaviours** – what behaviours do you want to change, what influences these behaviours? It is important to look at the bigger picture.

- **Segmentation** – if a housing organisation is already involved in a process of Customer Insight, then segmentation of housing customers for social marketing purposes will be second nature. This allows targeted solutions from a mix of approaches.
- **Engage with the marketing mix** – there will be no single solution, but instead a range of measures and interventions which when used in conjunction with one another can achieve a desired goal.
- **Cost and competition** – some behaviour changes may be small 'nudges' which require a housing customer to invest only a short amount of time, for a reasonable incentive (e.g. vouchers, better service, money off, lower tax etc) but other changes will require a more in-depth 'think' and this can cost time and energy for a benefit that may only be seen in the longer term and to the wider community rather than the individual. Housing organisations need to understand the cost and competition in drawing up any strategy on social marketing, or there is a danger of low take-up in the community.

Successful social marketing campaigns use techniques that understand and connect with their audience so well, that the commercial marketing sector is trying to learn the lessons (CIM, 2009). However it goes beyond just understanding and reason to an emotional connection. Later on in the chapter we will briefly examine the cognitive dissonance between what we know and how we act (for example 'I know that smoking is bad for me, but I want a cigarette at this party; it gives me confidence and is part of who I am.'). It takes an emotional connection to start to break down this juxtaposition of knowledge and action – just think of the television adverts where children plead with their parents to stop smoking.

So, social marketing starts with an understanding, then goes through an emotional connection – it makes a plea for action rather than just thought (give up smoking NOW). The key clue of social marketing is in its label – social. So, still with the smoking example, it is more than your own individual health, there are issues of passive smoking, and also the hopes of your children that are being used in the message to urge you to change your behaviour. As Simpson (2009) says *'We is stronger than me'*. The social housing sector has many examples of collective action for the wider social good and so many elements of social marketing will be seen in the way that residents' groups lobby for play equipment, or monitor anti-social behaviour on an estate.

Kotler and Lee (2007) suggest that there are 12 core principles to a successful social marketing campaign; and these can apply to situations in social housing:

1. Take advantage of prior and existing successful campaigns – publicise outcomes from other campaigns, perhaps a community has purchased some

new play equipment after saving 'rewards' from an incentive scheme, e.g. Irwell Valley's Gold scheme.[39]
2. Start with target markets most ready for action – Customer Insight and segmentation may highlight neighbourhoods or particular groups of tenants that are more likely to participate straightaway.
3. Promote single, simple, doable behaviours – one at a time. SMART objectives will help achieve this, as smaller measurable behaviour changes are easier to sign up to.
4. Identify and remove barriers to behaviour change – these might be within the housing organisation or local authority itself, or there may be local political or ideological resistance to social marketing. It is important to ensure the culture, as well as the policies and the procedures of the organisation, are ready to help implement the change.
5. Bring real benefits into the present – again if outcomes are measured, it will be easier for members of the community to see when goals are reached. If the behaviour change results in lower-level incidence of littering or anti-social behaviour on an estate then the benefits will be seen by residents first.
6. Highlight costs of competing behaviours – tenancy agreements can demonstrate the individual punitive costs of behaviours, e.g. eviction if rent is not paid or anti-social behaviour is committed. However, wider community-level costs of certain behaviours can also be highlighted that go beyond the cost to the individual.
7. Promote a tangible object of service to help target audiences perform the behaviour – for example some mediation schemes in neighbourhoods have produced a small laminated card with key bullet points to remind someone how to stop a conflict spiralling out of control.
8. Consider non-monetary incentives in the form of recognition and appreciation – a reward scheme may not just be about financial incentives and vouchers, but can also be a way of saying 'thank you' – we can see that you have done this and it is appreciated.
9. Have a little fun with messages – an example later in this chapter shows a council in Derbyshire doing just this with their 'Are you a banana?' campaign.
10. Use media channels at the point of decision-making – in their book, Kotler and Lee cite an example of a sign by a lake showing the number of people who have drowned in the lake not wearing a lifejacket (113) and the number of people wearing a lifejacket (0) – this is at the point that someone might be about to launch their boat and they may think twice about wearing a lifejacket.
11. Get Commitments and Pledges – later on in the chapter we look at the approach of 'think' as well as 'nudge' and it may be that group thinking and deliberation is more likely to result in commitment to the behaviour.

---

39 In September 2009 Irwell Valley introduced the Golden Foundation, a new £1 million grant fund scheme, where small grants can be made to small groups and larger grants up to £5,000 can be made to recognised community groups. Irwell Valley also asks for ideas on projects to be considered by the Foundation Panel: www.irwellvalleyha.co.uk

12. Use prompts for sustainability – continue to encourage neighbourhoods to work together on social projects such as reducing ASB or increasing take-up of recycling and other sustainability projects through encouraging feedback.

The social marketing mix

The use of the marketing mix is important to ensure a range of approaches depending on the target audience. One can apply the social marketing mix to housing, for example asking a local community to stop their objection to proposals for a new affordable housing development.

Figure 9.1: 'Selling' new affordable housing development to a local community

Segment	Product	Place	Price	Promotion
Older residents	1. Sustainability of the village, younger people able to stay and support local Post Office, shops and other services. 2. Potential incentives through some type of planning gain.	Local newspaper articles, newsletters etc, highlighting the problems for the area if new housing is not built.	Free if using advertorials, providing copy to local publications.	Involve younger people in raising awareness of the problem, through an event or exhibition locally.
Local politicians	1. Growing and thriving community/constituency. 2. Support for this type of approach from the coalition government with the added benefit of potential incentives to improve infrastructure and perhaps lower taxes (which will please voters).	Committee and board meetings at local authorities and housing associations	Free	It is important to get the chair of the board, the portfolio-holder or chair of the council to support the idea and 'sell' it to others.
Younger residents	1. New and affordable homes in your area. 2. A neighbourhood with a future that young people will want to stay in and be part of.	Again, articles in local newspapers, but also updates on the organisation's Twitter, Facebook or local politicians' blogs.	Free	Potentially less of a need to promote as this group will have the most tangible benefit – affordable new homes.

Behavioural insight

In chapter 7 we examined Customer Insight which was the process of turning data into information by connecting the dots. Here we look at 'behaviour insight' to see what factors might influence behaviour.

A number of factors can impact upon individual and group behaviour.

Figure 9.2: Factors influencing behaviour

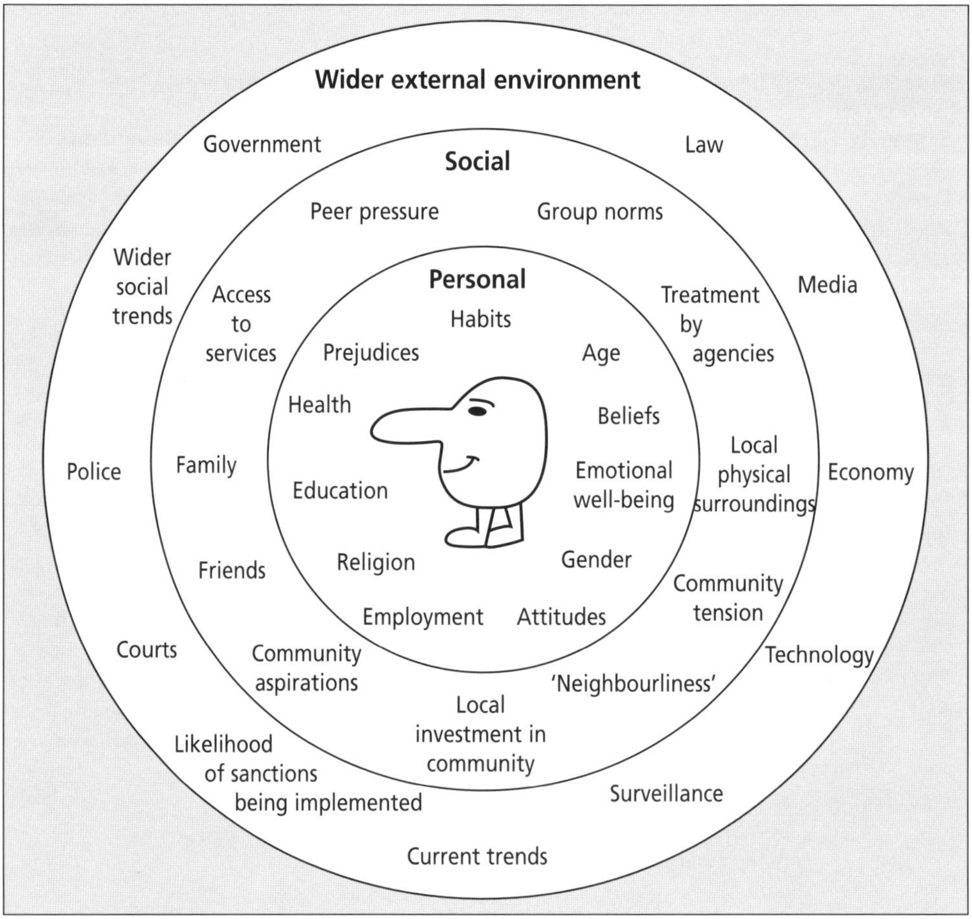

In social marketing campaigns it is important to segment customers and profile values and behaviours to better understand how you might influence them – for example understanding young men with driving offences might provide ideas on how to influence their behaviour and to reduce the chances of recidivist behaviour on drink-driving or speeding. On estates, as well as looking at the physical surroundings and opportunities for young people committing noise-nuisance, organisations may find behaviour insight sheds new light on how to influence more social behaviour.

Nudge

Thaler and Sunstein (2008) refer to social marketing, in some aspects, as 'gentle nudging'. They suggest also that the approach is not entirely paternalistic, but instead offer the term 'libertarian paternalism'. Whilst libertarian and paternalism may appear to be mutually opposing views, Thaler and Sunstein say that social marketing is aiming to change people's behaviour (paternalism), but that this is through making choices (libertarian). They make two key claims:

> *The first is that seemingly small features of social situations can have massive effects on people's behavior; nudges are everywhere, even if we do not see them. Choice architecture, both good and bad, is pervasive and unavoidable, and it greatly affects our decisions. The second claim is that libertarian paternalism is not an oxymoron. Choice architects can preserve freedom of choice while also nudging people in directions that will improve their lives* (Thaler and Sunstein, 2008, p.252).

Cialdini (2007) uses six principles of persuasion (or 'weapons of influence') in his work, and he claims that these principles can be used to influence, or be used to defend against being influenced by 'compliance professionals':

- Consistency (seen as an important value – consistency between what we say and what we do; however, the downside is automatic consistency even where this is not the best outcome in a particular situation)
- Reciprocation (this rule is overpowering, and even overpowers likeability)
- Social Proof (tendency to assume an action is more correct if others are doing it – e.g. 'best selling' as an advertising hook)
- Authority (obedience to authority)
- Liking (more likely to buy from someone you like – particularly friends, e.g. Tupperware parties)
- Scarcity (potential availability of a good or service only 'while stocks last').

He refers to 'material self-interest' as a further factor, but states that this is 'a given' in most acts of persuasion and that it should be acknowledged, but does not need to be extensively examined.

Cialdini also discusses the 'perceptual contrast principle' (p.12) where the context and order in which alternatives are given, has a bearing on the choices made. For example if one lifts a light object and then a heavy object, the latter seems to be heavier than if it had been lifted first, or on its own. Individuals shown pictures of an 'average'-looking man or woman were harsher about their appearance if they had first been shown pictures of a model, than if they looked solely at the 'average' picture. So, if a choice is available in any negotiation, then the framing of those choices and the order in which they are given are crucial to the outcome.

This notion of framing choices is important also in reasserting an individual's own values. People may know very well that eating too much fatty food, or smoking cigarettes can cause heart disease, but this knowledge may not always turn into positive action – there can be a gap between what we know and what we do, which is known as cognitive dissonance, and can manifest in any of the numerous decisions we take every day.

Figure 9.3 Cognitive dissonance (or the value/action gap)

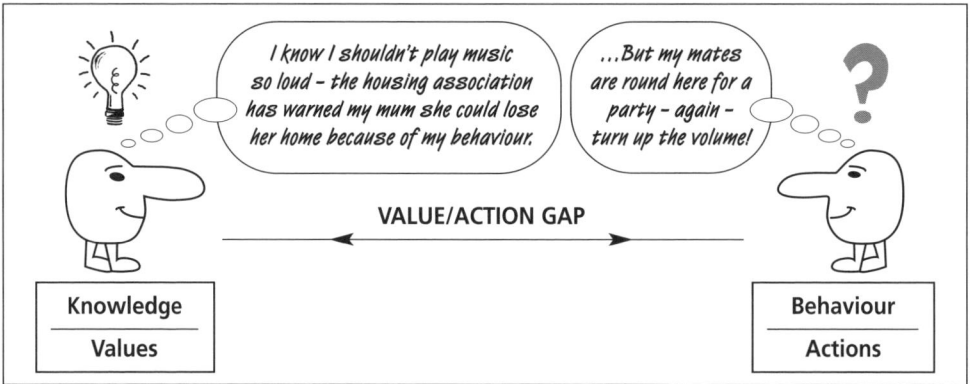

Cognitive dissonance demonstrates quite well King's (2003) caution that promoting certain responsible types of behaviour goes beyond a simple provocation and response. There are so many hidden facets to individuals' and communities' values that any government or public agency social marketing campaign needs to deeply understand the complexities and rationales for certain types of behaviour. Flint (2004) discusses the shaping of 'responsible and responsive' tenants as part of a wider politics of the governance of behaviour; and we can see that in the use of social marketing on a community level.

> **Change 4 Life** is a key public health campaign initiated by the previous Labour government devised on social marketing principles of changing behaviours and attitudes towards food and exercise. The campaign had a £75 million budget over three years and was part of the wider Healthy Weight, Healthy Lives strategy for England (HM Government, 2008). It was launched in January 2009 and a one-year review was published in February 2010 showing that targets on campaign recognition and sustained interest had been exceeded and that there were some emerging positive indicators of behaviour change as a result of the campaign. Businesses had come on board too and pledged £200 million 'in-kind' support (e.g. through placing the logo and through using their marketing and advertising skills). These Business4Life partners ranged from healthcare providers, to media and television companies to big organisations such as Tesco, Kellogg's, Mars, Pepsi and Kraft.

The coalition government in July 2010 announced that the £75 million budget would be cut so that Change4Life became *'less a government campaign and more a social movement'*. However the Health Secretary Andrew Lansley suggested that businesses should step in to pay the bill for the social marketing campaign and that in return for 'actual funding' rather than in-kind contributions there would be no additional regulation or legislation on the food industry (Lansley, 2010).

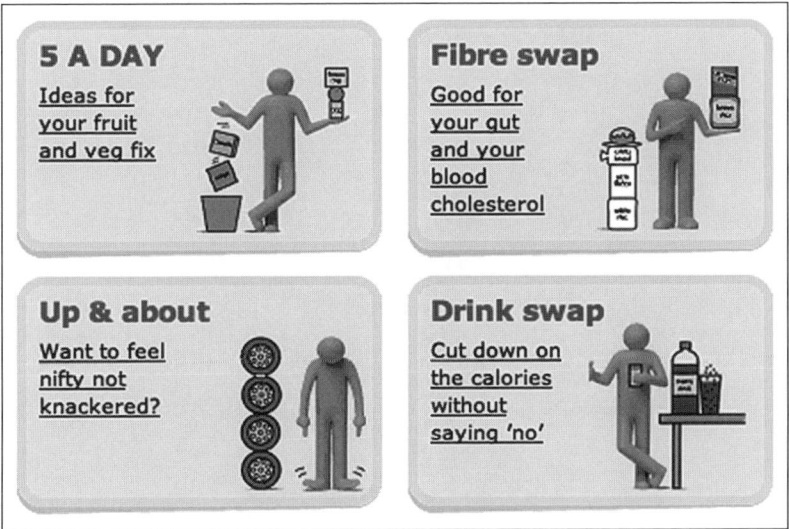

Inclusion of marginalised groups

Social Marketing could be used across the public sector, and particularly in housing, not just to change the behaviour of individuals for their own benefit (e.g. by having a healthier and longer life) but to benefit wider communities and to include previously excluded groups.

In Spain, the Fundación Secretariado Gitano (FSG) found that despite the progress that had been made in recent decades, the Roma minority were still the group facing the greatest social rejection. As part of the Acceder employment programme, the FSG produced a campaign aimed at changing people's views of Roma and particularly encouraging them to include Roma through employment as a way to achieve integration. They produced two television and two radio advertising spots, along with posters, tee-shirts, bags and other merchandising. The key message of the campaign is that Roma are 'boxed in' by perceptions and that it is very difficult for them to break out of that box. Many of the posters (see example on the next page) and the television spot show a person moving around with a white box drawn around them that moves with them and that they cannot step outside of. It is quite a powerful presentation of a core message aimed at the wider community to think differently and allow the Roma to step out of the box.

HOUSING AND THE CUSTOMER

A micro-website of the FSG was used to host all of the campaign material, along with reports and video explaining the Gitanos y Empleo (Roma and Employment) programme that had started in 2000, www.gitanos.org/iguales

FSG Employment makes us equal campaign
www.gitanos.org

Involving residents to encourage support for new housing development

Along similar lines to FSG's attempt (above) to encourage a change of perception of and behaviour towards the Roma people in Spain, there is a need to change behaviours regarding development of new accommodation. It is not just the more contentious developments (Gypsy sites (see further Richardson, 2007), wind farms, energy and recycling plants) that face a blanket 'no' from residents in some areas – but ordinary 'affordable' housing too. There is a buffet of acronyms relating to the proposal of new schemes and the people who say 'no' – the most famous of these is *NIMBY* (Not in My Back Yard), but also consider:

- *NIMTO*: Not in My Term of Office (relating to councillors and MPs who fight against new developments that may make them less electable in the future).

- *BANANA*: Build Absolutely Nothing Anywhere Near Anyone
- *LULU*: Local Unwanted Land Use

But now consider: **WIMBY** – Welcome into My Back Yard! This project in the Netherlands focused on redevelopment of Hoogvliet. The members of the WIMBY organisations, in telling their story, told of fighting mediocrity of ideas and opposition from the establishment. They struck upon the analogy of 'acupuncture' to explain the variety and boldness of the different initiatives and developments:

> *Pricking with a pin at precisely the right moment automatically liberates new energy and creates a new balance, allowing space and tolerance for initiatives that are unexpected and different* (Provoost (Ed.) 2007, pp.411-412).

In **Derbyshire** the Derbyshire Dales District Council has also tried to tackle the BANANA issue head on by allowing open debate with residents and highlighting the need for affordable housing. They asked 'are you a banana?' of residents as a way of getting people to think about their attitude to new affordable housing in a particular area – this was not a hostile challenge, but a 'nudge' to make people think more about their attitudes and behaviour and to prompt a genuine conversation about future housing in the area.

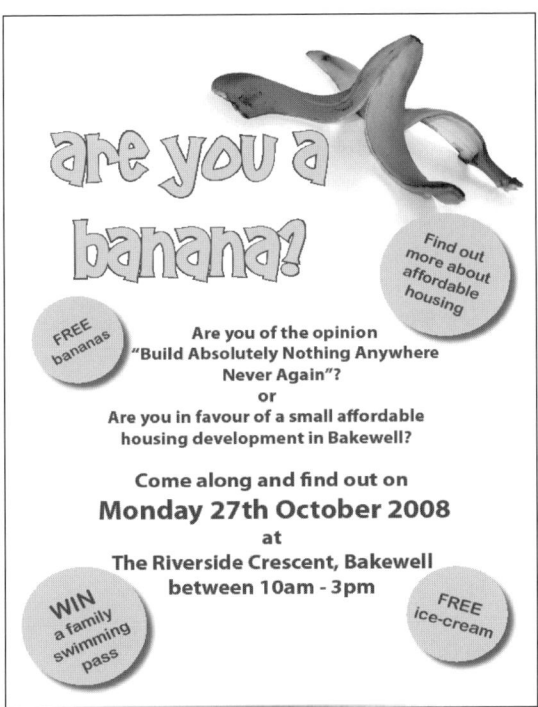

Derbyshire Dales District Council poster

Leunig (2007) suggests ways that land value can be captured by the local authority to pass on in the form of financial incentives (e.g. nil council tax for a number of years) in order to 'nudge' residents to accept new development in an area. Based on the premise of offering below market price, but significantly more than 'fair' price for agricultural land, local authorities will be able to capture a proportion of land value for the benefit of the wider community, rather than just the individual landowner.

The coalition government seems to like the idea of incentives to nudge communities to allow development with Pickles (2010a) saying *'These incentives[40] will encourage local authorities and communities to increase their aspirations for housing and economic growth...'* and Shapps (2009) suggesting that NIMBYs can be *'turned into YIMBYs'*[41] through the use of incentives. He said prior to the election that a future Conservative government would *'...guarantee 125 pence for every pound received in council tax from new social homes...'* and referred to benefits coming out of new development to include: regenerated town centres, lower council tax bills, support for post offices and local schools.

Encouraging recycling – nudging and thinking

One more example of behaviour and attitudes has been analysed by John *et al.* (2009). The researchers make clear that nudging is not telling people what to do or how to behave, but instead asking people to think about making choices in different ways so that outcomes can benefit not just the individual making the choice but also benefit their fellow citizens. However, they offer an alternative approach of 'think' which they suggest *'Through deliberation and dialogue, citizens can make informed and better choices about collective actions and the direction of public policy'* (p.361). John *et al.* (2009) suggest that nudge and think are two quite differently rooted aspects of behavioural economics (nudge) and deliberative democracy (think), but that they are not mutually exclusive – a nudge might lead to a think and a think might lead to a nudge. See Figure 9.4.

One of the experiments feeding into John *et al.*'s (2009) understanding of nudge and think was an experiment[42] using feedback to enhance uptake of recycling in an area. Some 318 streets in Oldham were assigned to either a 'treatment' or 'control' group. The treatment group received feedback to tell them how their street was doing in terms of recycling food waste. The feedback consisted of postcards with a smiley face ☺ if participation in the scheme was above average, and a frown face if below average. The control group received no feedback. The experiment showed that the treatment group's performance improved by 3% because those receiving smiley faces

---

40 Although the government did not map out what exactly the incentives would be, saying that practical details would emerge later.
41 Yes In My Back Yard.
42 For more information see *Rediscovering the civic and achieving better outcomes in public policy*, policy briefing number 5 www.civicbehaviour.org.uk

Figure 9.4: Nudge/Think

Nudge	Think
Individuals make their own decisions in a limited knowledge of the context and of the options available. They do not think about every available option – mainstream economic assumptions of 'perfect' information cannot be made.	The public nature of deliberation is crucial.[43]
Selective searches may be based on partial ignorance of the context and incomplete information – irrational preferences and false beliefs may rule the choice made.	Government needs to provide the context, the information and the institutions to allow citizens to deliberate and then follow up on outcomes to keep 'thinkers' engaged in the process for the future.
Preferences may become fixed and choices may be made on premises from past decision-making.	Preferences and assumptions can change through thinking and deliberating with others.
Investment from individuals is presumed to be low, only brief periods of time will be needed to engage with a nudge; however investment from the state may need to include 'incentives' to change behaviour.	Investment from thinkers is higher; they will need to spend more time over a longer period to deliberate choices and the civic impact of outcomes. Government will also need to invest time and resource to follow up outcomes to keep thinkers engaged.

Adapted from John *et al.*, 2009, pp.362-367.

were encouraged to carry on and those receiving frowns persuaded those not already participating in the scheme to join in. Incentives and feedback are an important part of 'nudge' and 'think' mechanisms.

> To 'nudge' residents' behaviour on recycling in **Windsor and Maidenhead**, the council has implemented a reward scheme to incentivise take-up. Partners involved in the scheme include Marks & Spencer, the primary school and the leisure centre – residents can be rewarded with vouchers redeemable against their shopping as an incentive to recycle more, or they may be donated to local schools.

---

43 John *et al.* refer to individuals keeping themselves in check in public debates, but the reverse can also be true if a situation is poorly managed, for example consultations on Gypsy and Traveller sites can see individuals fire one another up rather than keep one another in check.

The new coalition government likes the 'nudge' approach to encouraging recycling. The Conservative Secretary of State for Communities and Local Government suggested that 'bin taxes' were too heavy-handed and may result in fly-tipping and backyard burning. He instead referred to the Windsor and Maidenhead scheme as providing an incentive to get involved – the 'big society' in action (Pickles, 2010).

Social marketing on social media

Increasingly public sector organisations are turning to social media outlets for their social marketing campaigns.

> **Brighton & Hove City Council**[44] ran a campaign to engage people in the area on their travel behaviour in an attempt to encourage people to drive less and either walk or use public transport instead. A Twitter initiative was developed @Twago to track daily habits and to monitor any changes that residents were reporting in their travel behaviour.

Some campaigns can have a dual outcome of finding out more about the population and engaging with them on their preferred media. Where a service is delivered online then efforts to raise the profile of, and traffic to, that site will be the main focus of a marketing campaign on social media.

> **Connexions**[45] ran a social media campaign. First, they profiled the online community of 13-19 year olds and then after finding out what they preferred to engage with, they developed a strategy that bridged young people's interests with Connexions' needs which resulted in the IMPACT challenge. This was a competition for young people to design the next Connexions advertising campaign and the winner saw their advert on buses all over Sussex. The competition created increased web traffic on the Connexions website as part of the 'public vote' for the winner.

Conclusion

Social Marketing is an important factor in housing organisations' and public agencies' toolkits in creating sustainable communities. It can help to change specific behaviours in order to improve how estates look, how tenants behave towards one another and how open communities are to new affordable housing development. It should not be seen as a costly adjunct to an already busy and diverse workload, but instead should be a further opportunity to find out who our customers are and how we can create and manage spaces that they want to live in.

---

44 www.qubemedia.net
45 *ibid.*

References and further reading

Australian Public Service Commission (2007) *Changing Behaviour, a public policy perspective.* Available at: www.apsc.gov.au

Central Office of Information (2008) *How public service advertising works.* London: COI.

Chartered Institute of Marketing (2009) *Less smoke, more fire: The benefits and impacts of social marketing.* Available at: www.cim.co.uk

Cialdini, R. (2007) *Influence: The Psychology of Persuasion.* New York: Harper Collins.

Earls, M. (2009) *Herd, how to change mass behaviour by harnessing our true nature.* Chichester: John Wiley and Sons.

Flint, J. (2004) 'The Responsible Tenant: Housing Governance and the Politics of Behaviour', *Housing Studies,* Vol. 19, No. 6, pp.893-909.

Fundación Secretariado Gitano (2007) *Annual Report 07.* Madrid: FSG.

Halpern, D., Bates, C., Mulgan, G. and Aldridge, S. with Beales, G. and Heathfield, A. (2004) *Personal Responsibility and Changing Behviour: the state of knowledge and its implications for public policy.* London: The Prime Minister's Strategy Unit.

HM Government (2008) *Health Weight, Healthy Lives: A Cross-Government Strategy for England,* London: HM Government.

HM Government (2010) *Change4Life One Year On, in support of healthy weight, healthy lives.* London: HM Government.

John, P., Smith, G. and Stoker, G. (2009) 'Nudge Nudge, Think Think: Two Strategies for Changing Civic Behaviour', *The Political Quarterly,* Vol. 80, No. 3, pp.361-370.

King, P. (2003) *A Social Philosophy of Housing.* London: Ashgate.

Kotler, P. and Lee, N. (2007) *Marketing in the public sector, a roadmap for improved performance.* New Jersey: Pearson Education.

Kotler, P. and Lee, N. (2008) *Social Marketing* (3rd ed.). London: Sage.

Kotler, P. and Lee, N. (2008) *Social Marketing, influencing behaviours for good* (3rd ed.). London: Sage.

Lansley, A. (2010) *Speech to the UK Faculty of Public Health Annual Conference,* 7th July. Available at www.dh.gov.uk

Leunig, T. (2007) *In my back yard: unlocking the planning system.* Policy Paper. London: CentreForum.

National Social Marketing Centre (nd) *Social Marketing Works.* Available at www.nsms.org.uk

Pickles, E. (2010) *We'll boost recycling with a gentle nudge,* 8th June 2010. Available at www.guardian.co.uk

Pickles, E. (2010a) *Revoking Regional Strategies.* Written Statement 6th July. Available at www.communities.gov.uk

Provoost, M. (ed.) (2007) *WIMBY! Hoogvliet future, past and present of a new town, or: The Big Wimby Book.* Rotterdam: Nai Publishers.

Richardson, J. (2007) *Providing Gypsy and Traveller Sites: Contentious Spaces.* Coventry: CIH for the Joseph Rowntree Foundation.

Shapps, G. (2009) *Labour have created a generation of NIMBYs.* Blog 27th October 2008. Available at www.conservatives.com

Simpson, J. (2009) 'Lessons from social marketing', *The Guardian Public*, 1st October. Available at www.guardianpublic.co.uk

Thaler, R. and Sunstein, C. (2008) *Nudge: Improving decisions about health, wealth and happiness.* New Haven: Yale University Press.

CHAPTER 10:
The power of communication – talking and listening to the customer

Kerry James, Joanna Richardson and Nicola Winn

Introduction

Good communications are vital – that is listening as well as talking. However, we do not just advocate the importance of communications strategies for particular schemes or campaigns. Instead good communications should be occurring 24/7 as part of everyday transactions with the customer. Remember the example from Solihull Community Housing in chapter 7, where someone in the call centre did not just deal with a repair but, through listening to clues, found out that the customer needed help and adaptations in their home, all from one telephone conversation. This is the essence of good everyday communication – a good outcome for the customer and efficient for the housing organisation.

One of the reasons that proper two-way communication is so vital, is that it is a way of giving customers a voice in a system. The word 'empowerment' can be overused, but in the case of good communications which listen to the customer rather than talk at them, tenants can be empowered and can be given a voice (see further chapter 2 of this book, where Brown, Richardson and Yates examined choice and voice in the social housing sector). The limitations of choice to exit the sector, and the threat to strength of voice with cuts in funding to organisations like the National Tenant Voice (NTV) mean that, on an organisational level, listening to and talking with customers is essential in making sure public services are accountable.

Good communications can help you understand staff and customers better, can help to target services to where they are most needed and can pick up clues in the short term that save resources in the longer term. This chapter examines a number of elements of good communication planning and refers to some examples from the housing sector and beyond to illustrate key points.

Confused, confounded and communicated

Of course, the first question to consider is what we really mean by the term 'communications'. These days, the word can mean many things to different people –

HOUSING AND THE CUSTOMER

the action of communicating, the technology we use or even a department responsible for making things happen!

In this chapter, we will think of communications as something you need, or want, to say to someone to get your message across. You might want to shout your achievements from the rooftops, persuade people to behave in a different way or defend your doorstep when a crisis descends; whatever the situation, there are tools available that can help you be represented as accurately and effectively as possible.

Examples of situations where communications can help housing organisations to succeed include:

- Recruiting, keeping, developing and motivating team members
- Building and maintaining strong relationships with lenders and investors
- Positioning the unique strengths or aspirations of the business to help attract income or new business
- Managing relationships with customers and stakeholders to safeguard the future of the business and enhance levels of customer satisfaction
- Connecting people across defined places or organisations, helping them to share resources and/or develop networks
- Submitting a 'right to reply' to public criticisms or media enquiries.

As we saw in chapter 7, profiling and segmenting your customer audience is important in providing the right service to meet need – the position is the same for communications. If an organisation knows its customer base (or audience) and can provide communications in a preferred way for a particular segment, then the message is more likely to be received and understood.

Communications models

Figure 10.1: Communications model

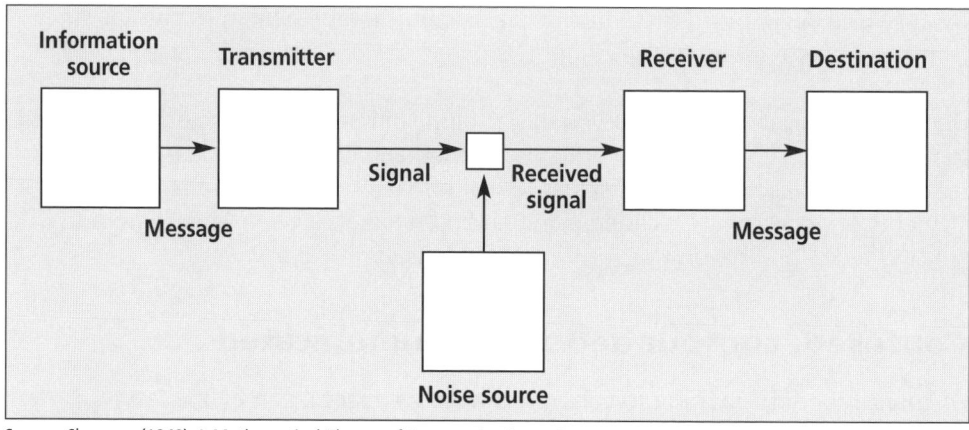

Source: Shannon (1948) *A Mathematical Theory of Communication*, p.2.

The illustration in Shannon's paper *A Mathematical Theory of Communication* shows a communication system as a linear process with a start and an end point. It is based on just transmission of communication. However, in 1949 the Shannon-Weaver Model was improved with the addition of a further element of feedback, added by Weiner, which makes the process circular and ongoing. The Shannon-Weaver model proposes that all communication must include six elements:

- a source
- an encoder
- a message
- a channel
- a decoder
- a receiver.

The role of communications

In a conference presentation[46] The Cabinet Office (2009) outlined the government's priorities and the role of public sector communications (see box).

Figure 10.2: Government priorities and role of communications

Priority	Role of communications
Supporting people through the recession and building a strong recovery.	• Access to support services • Connecting to opportunities • Sustainable behaviour
Reforming and modernising our public services and national infrastructure.	• Public in control • Staff involvement/engagement
Restoring trust and accountability in the political system.	• Transparency • Public engagement

Whilst there was a change of government in 2010, and the budget for public services, inevitably including communications, was severely reduced – the fundamental lessons in the role of communications and the priorities at a local government and housing-provider level clearly remain relevant.

Why is this so? Well, primarily for the same reasons we explored in chapter 8; a well-branded, positively promoted organisation can build and maintain trust, enhance customer satisfaction, stimulate market demand, bring in more money, attract the right partners and show how it makes a difference. Without strong and effective communications in the toolkit, your chances of making this happen are slim.

---

46 23 June 2009 Haymarket conference in London, *Engage the Public*, presentation by Michael Warren 'Next Steps on Insight: the innovation challenge for government communications'.

A case for communicating

Let us pretend a new bidding round is being launched, the 'Tailored for Tenants Fund' – which will grant cash to housing providers who hand over management of services directly to tenants.[47] No surprises that this imaginary fund has a limited pot of money available. So how will something like this be decided? Well, typically one or more of the following scenarios will determine the success of bids:

1. You have brilliant ideas and can prove why they will work
2. You are part of an alliance that will save money training tenants together and delegating services over a broader area
3. Your track record in resident consultation and involvement will make a difference
4. Your organisation can make the changes happen and achieve quick wins publicly faster than anybody else.

All of those scenarios are dependent on great communications in one form or another:

1. persuading and influencing people
2. managing complex dialogue in groups
3. proactively listening and responding to feedback and
4. spreading the word quickly and efficiently.

So the better equipped you are as an organisation on each of these points, the better your chances are of 'bagging the budget'.

Communications in the social housing sector

In this chapter we are exploring the role and function of communications across a range of functions in the social housing sector. On many occasions the communication will be outward-facing, with the customer, or wider society, through

Figure 10.3: Communications triangle

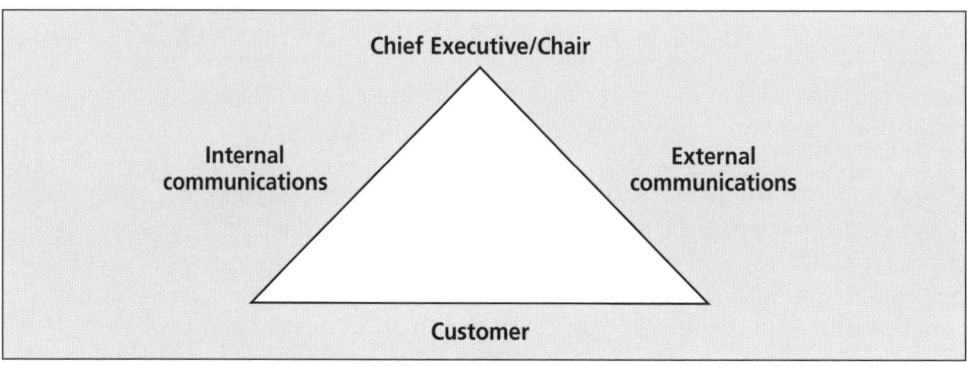

---

47 Yes, this does sound similar to Section 16 funding doesn't it – the three of us have worked in the social housing sector longer than you think!

THE POWER OF COMMUNICATION

a variety of media. It is vital, however, not to underestimate the basics of everyday communication with customers and with staff on the most routine transactions, but also with internal staff. Failure to communicate with staff will result in a failure of ensuring a consistent and embedded end message to external audiences. See Figure 10.3.

Partners in delivery of services are also important to include in communications strategies, so that they are aware of day-to-day issues as well as broader challenges and responses.

> Keepmoat has written a book (2010) *One Company, many solutions*, with the aim of telling some of the challenges faced by partner organisations and highlighting ways that Keepmoat has worked with them.

Organisations should have a general communications plan which covers the basics of who you need to communicate with and how this can best be achieved. Different media may be required depending on the relative segments of the audience. So let us take tenants, for example: a 'one size fits all' approach would not successfully reach the following:

- Young teenagers
- Tenant board members
- Families
- Older residents
- People with learning difficulties.

As well as needing to have alternative languages, or Braille/moon/audio available, it is important to think about how much notice an individual will take of the message according to the medium in which it is delivered. Common media used in the housing sector for different groups include:

- Newsletters
- Website
- Texts (e.g. for rent arrears)
- Residents' meetings
- Board meetings
- Email.

The diagram on the next page is just one example of the many and varied ways that social housing organisations talk to their customers.

Others, like Spire Homes, are developing schemes that reward residents each time they give feedback – without enforcing a regular commitment to formal participation.

Figure 10.4: Harvest Housing Group customer involvement mechanisms

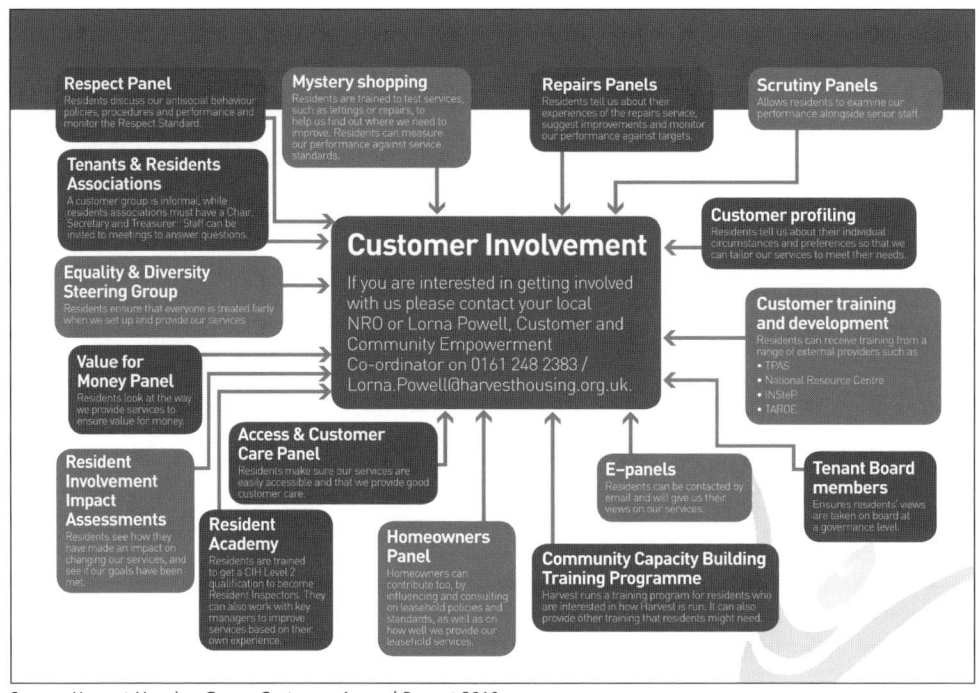

Source: Harvest Housing Group *Customer Annual Report 2010*.

The provider/customer relationship

Historically, the role of communications in social housing organisations has often focused on the relationship between provider and customer, for example:

- Asking for customer feedback on the quality of services, such as repairs
- Involving tenants (leaseholders, residents or customers) in service planning and/or decision-making
- Helping tenants to take on the responsibility for day-to-day management of their homes, through the Right to Manage
- Reporting performance information to tenants, through the annual report framework and recommendations in the CIH's Practice Online.[48]

Some of these responsibilities may seem very current (for example, involving residents in developing services) but have actually existed for decades in various forms. As early as July 1969 – the same month that Neil Armstrong took his first steps on the moon – there was also a giant leap for resident involvement, with the publication of Sherry R Arnstein's article *'A ladder of citizen participation'*. This document set out ways of involving citizens in planning in the United States.

---

48 Formerly known as the Housing Management Standards Manual.

Arnstein described levels of involvement through which people could voice their opinions and attain a degree of 'power' – or conversely, be educated, manipulated or subjected to tokenistic consultation without really having much influence over the process or result. The highest rungs on the ladder were where the most meaningful consultation was said to occur – with partnerships, delegated powers and, ultimately, control by people themselves seen as the most effective means.

So is Arnstein's model still relevant more than 40 years on? To a degree, yes; clearly by engaging customers in service planning, delivery and monitoring, housing organisations can better understand what people think about their work, look for ways of doing things more quickly, cheaply or efficiently and build endorsements for their individual brands. And giving people meaningful opportunities to shape and influence their communities where they want to do so is much more likely to engender neighbourhood sustainability than managing a survey process ever could. Whether that is enough to create the government's 'big society' vision, only time will tell.

The power of communications

Our sector is peppered with events that have shaken the world. 24 Dash (2009) published the top 10 events that shaped social housing, selected by a panel of expert judges. One of the key defining moments was the BBC broadcast of the Jeremy Sandford play, *'Cathy Come Home'*, in November 1966. Together with the coincidental launch of charity Shelter a few days later, homelessness was acknowledged as a key challenge facing society rather than a niche problem; collectively, these campaigns were instrumental in building political momentum for the Housing (Homeless Persons) Act 1977.

Despite these prominent examples, communications strategies were a twinkle in the eye for most housing organisations even by the late 1980s, and marketing plans generally existed only where housing associations had big development programmes (as a tool to sell low cost home ownership). The advent of estate regeneration changed all that; it made organisations think more about how they developed partnerships and relationships. In some cases, providers had to convince people about the prospect of change; otherwise key business objectives – such as decanting hundreds of people to alternative homes – could not be met.

Seddon (2008) has highlighted the concept of 'failure demand' – previously mentioned in chapters 2 and 6 – where a lack of planning can cause problems for an organisation's customers, and ultimately its business. Cautionary communications tales that fit this concept include:

- Organisations posting customer mail-outs for new services but forgetting to tell staff in the customer service centre, who were listed as the main contacts and consequently had no idea how to advise callers

- Contentious rent statement letters going out the day before the technical spokesperson went on holiday
- Chief executives and board representatives speaking separately to the media (and not each other)
- Disgruntled employees posting 'nobody told us' messages on internet forums
- Press releases being posted on social media several days before emailing the final version to journalists (by which time, the story was old news).

The secret to not getting tangled in these webs is simple – get strategic.

Getting strategic with communications

If your business needs to set up or review its approach to communications, you will need the following items in place as a minimum:

- *Communications strategy* – that explains your business objectives, shows how communications will help you achieve them, lists your target audiences, identifies your key messages, shows people's responsibilities and considers how best you can connect with your target audiences

- *Customer involvement strategy* – that shows how you will engage your customers in shaping services and business priorities

- *Timetabled communications plan* – that provides the 'nuts and bolts' of what you will communicate (how, to whom and when, plus individual tasks and progress notes)

- *Media protocol* – which explains how to deal with proactive press releases and crisis media enquiries and who has authority to speak on behalf of the organisation and about what

- *Media release template* – to make sure you stay faithful to the brand and do not accidentally overwrite any critical work with vigorous cutting and pasting

- *List of emergency contacts* – so if you need key people in a hurry, you do not have to hope they are in the office or pray someone knows their mobile number

- *Social media policy* – because even if you do not Tweet or use Facebook, chances are members of your team do – and being clear about the rules will help preserve your collective and individual reputations

- *Customer Insight* – turn your knowledge into insight – through better understanding of customer needs by properly analysing data and then communicating how you will meet that need with your audiences (see further chapter 7 in this book).

Get tactical

Tactical communications fall into two camps – proactive (when you want to positively promote your organisation) and reactive (when your actions or inactions are put into the spotlight by others).

Proactive communications

If you have got something positive to say, there are plenty of ways in which you can spread the word. The key to success is:

- *Understanding who your most influential audiences are* – and the things that will interest, impress or annoy them
- *Knowing what type of recognition will help achieve your business objectives* – do you want to be seen as a 'green' developer, the best care provider or something else? If you are not clear about this, why should anyone else be?
- *Getting positive results with as little effort as possible* – so you can get on with the rest of the day job.

Once you know whom you want to target, what you want to achieve and how much time you can spare, you can spend time working up your tactics. Let us look at a real-life example…

Case in point: the house that Jennifer built
Matrix Housing Partnership/Accord Group

Objectives
- To raise awareness of a school competition to build the eco-home of the future, and align with Accord's 'goal to be greenest' PR campaign.

Messaging
- Matrix Housing Partnership has developed some exemplar low-carbon homes and is committed to building the eco-homes of the future.
- The partnership is encouraging young people to design a sustainable property that can, and will, be built in real life.

Channels
- *Press releases* – issued to 12 different regional newspapers (to reflect short-listed students in different areas), plus offers of radio and television broadcast opportunities.
- *Award entries* – submitted for a CIH Midlands Best Practice Award and *Inside Housing* Sustainable Housing Award.
- *DVD* – to showcase the winning student (Jennifer Brook), her school and design, this was launched at the CIH conference in 2008.

→

> **Impact**
> - More than 60 media articles, including an *Inside Housing* feature.
> - The campaign was covered in a national feature on *BBC Newsround*.
> - Accord Group won the 2009 CIH Midlands Best Practice Award for its 'unique approach to sustainability'.
> - The campaign was a commended finalist at the 2008 *Inside Housing* Sustainable Housing Awards, in the 'community engagement' category.
> - The winning student's school received £4,000 towards an eco-project and consultancy from SUSTAIN to help with project management.
> - The winning design is now being taken forward as a development project in Redditch, and is currently at planning application stage.
>
> **Agency**
> None (in-house campaign developed by Accord Group)

Your business needs may be very different. You may want more customers, subscribers, or demand for specific property types; or maybe less of something, like abandonments, empty properties or evictions. But the same principles apply:

- Be clear about what you want to achieve
- Think about who you need to woo and win, influence, involve or keep informed
- Crystalise your messages
- Think creatively about how to reach the segments of your audience
- Tell them more than once, and in a variety of ways, in a carefully timed and executed way.

Reactive communications

The way you handle reactive communications – especially in a crisis, such as death, major emergencies or service failure – can make a big impact on the success of your organisation. Barry (2004) says:

> *How a company acts in the face of a single disaster or major problem often carries more weight than years of exemplary behaviour. No matter what size a business is, negative or crisis issues can arise out of nowhere and pose a real threat to reputation and survival.*

Social housing is not immune to such scenarios, for example, explosions and carbon monoxide poisoning incidents have caused fatalities for residents and catapulted providers into the headlines. Fire, flood or financial disaster, enforced supervisions and building failure can all have a catastrophic effect on both individual lives and your reputation. So you need to assess the risks facing your business and have a ready-made plan that will help you to spring into action if the worst happens.

If a situation happens, do not panic; try the following communications tips for responding to a crisis as a starting point:

- *Consider how the general public may respond to the topic emotionally* – think like an independent observer rather than someone invested in your business as loyalty can cloud your judgment (and make you vulnerable later)
- *Find your weaknesses and plug the gaps* – this could be anything from a service failure to a refusal to share information between agencies; whatever the flaws, find the extent of the problem and take steps so it will not happen again
- *Explore how special interest groups and the media may engage* – so you can anticipate their views on the issue and likely public-awareness campaigns
- *Anticipate early warnings and put monitoring arrangements in place* – this will help you to communicate developments quickly and efficiently across the business (clearly defined policies and a robust communications strategy will help)
- *Accept that you cannot always change public opinion* – focus on using language that will reduce public anxiety and build trust that you will contain or reduce the risk
- *Speak as one voice* – make sure your business presents a united front to the world and agree designated spokespeople and messages in advance
- *State your position simply* – you need to tell a story that people can understand. There may be tricky technical issues to deal with, but baffling people will work against you (especially if you are heading into broadcast or social media and competing against emotive pictures). Find the soundbites and the things that prove you are on the case
- *Work with the media* – explain the context and things you think people need to know, using extra information to prove your point. And if you can offer up sympathetic spokespeople to state your case and reassure audiences, this may well help you; conversely withholding information or providing information on or over deadline will not help your cause.
- *Do not forget your own people* – it is so easy to concentrate on the challenges given to you by the media that you may lose sight of the internal gossip-mongers and those genuinely feeling worried or in the dark. Plan simple and regular briefings to keep staff and board members posted so they do not see something in the paper, or hear it on the airwaves first
- *Remember social networks* – the world has changed and your external reputation can spin out of control without you even knowing anything about it. Make sure you know who is saying what about you and think tactically about how to handle the results.

(Adapted from Regester and Larkin, 2010, pp.100-104).

Data dangers

Now and again communication between agencies comes under the spotlight. This can be due to information gaps, unwillingness to share information or fears of non-compliance with data protection laws.

Housing organisations already hold, and continue to collect, a range of data on their customers. The law requires a privacy statement to be provided to the customer; often incorporated into tenancy agreements or forms, this statement tells the customer what information you will hold about them, whom you will share it with and what it will be used for.

Data protection legislation does not prevent agencies from sharing important information with partners, but it does need managing carefully. When passing qualifying information to partners, the original information-holder must still make sure their partner adheres to eight legal principles. Detailed legal advice is beyond the remit of this chapter, but guides exist (e.g. Hall 2010) that explain the subject further. The key issue is that data protection should not be used as a way of avoiding passing on 'need-to-know' information; managed properly, partners can provide life-saving public services together.

Case in point: disseminating data protection training
Orbit Group

Objectives
- To increase employee awareness of data protection legislation, ensuring all personal and sensitive personal information was processed in line with customer and employee rights.
- To support Orbit Group to develop an educational board game and supporting tools to embed the principles of data protection.

Messaging
- To empower and enable staff to embed the eight data protection principles and understand how they affect their day-to-day job.

Channels
- A bespoke educational board game, 'You're Secure', was developed as a training tool for employees. This featured a set of eight illustrated characters, each representing one of the core data protection principles. A bespoke set of 'Golden Rule' key-ring cards – depicting the eight characters together with a 'plain English' summary of the law applying to each – was produced. Banner stands featuring the same characters used in the board game were also produced to increase visibility of the initiative in the offices.
- Posters – a set of posters featuring the characters were used to highlight different elements of the law across the office environment.

→

> **Impact**
> - All levels of staff at Orbit Group have been able to increase their knowledge of data protection and have been empowered to make protecting individuals' information an integral part of their work. Analysis of the training has resulted in a 99.9% satisfaction rating with the content and tools used as part of the training. Every person doing the training was set a series of questions to answer on data protection. They then answered these questions again after finishing the training. The pre- and post-awareness analysis in the data protection mini tests has resulted in a 99% increase in knowledge and awareness. Orbit is now looking at using this model in future to support training on information, governance and security. The group will be working with The Bridge Group again to extend their toolkit.
>
> **Agency**
> The Bridge Group

Choose your channels

Now you know the who (audience), why (tactics) and what (messages) you want to get out, it is time for 'how' – that is, which channels or media are right for you to use to get your points across.

Winn's wheel

These days, customers are faced with more choices, more messages and more hectic lifestyles than their predecessors. So what if they do not want to get involved today, tomorrow, or at all; and how about if they want to vary their interactions with you from passive to highly participative at different times?

Another factor to consider is the blurring of boundaries between traditional engagement and communications models. It is now much easier for all your stakeholder audiences to both influence and be influenced by news articles, blogs, online and offline forums and pressure groups; so why not have a model that brings together historically separate disciplines and audiences? Enter our suggested new model, 'Winn's wheel', on the next page, as a starting point for discussion.

As you can see, the wheel splits into three separate groups – information, interaction and influence:

- *Information* – the options in this group (such as press releases, award entries and case studies) involve housing organisations 'pushing' news and data out to audiences to inform, influence and educate people

HOUSING AND THE CUSTOMER

- *Interaction* – which may involve both pushing out content and encouraging feedback from key audiences about business issues
- *Influence* – where customers and stakeholders take a lead in shaping and directing business.

Figure 10.5: Winn's Wheel: different approaches to communication and engagement

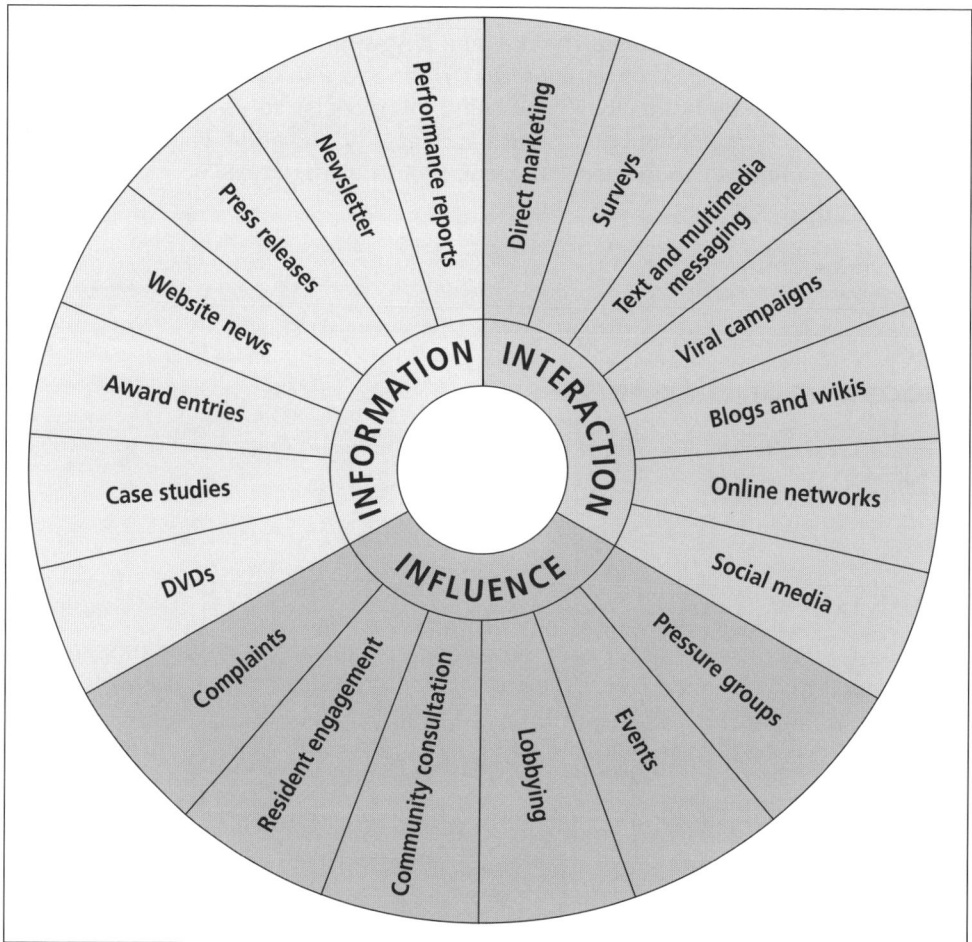

Using a wheel analogy achieves three things. First, it shows how providers can integrate communications and engagement methods to achieve two-way dialogue with a range of audiences, including (but not restricted to) residents. Second, it reinforces that the whole point of communicating is to drive change through stakeholder influence. And third, it offers flexible, interchangeable options, rather than depending upon people progressing 'up' or 'down' a scale; so people can choose to opt-in or opt-out (and the level at which they want to engage) from one day to the next.

All aboard the 'Cluetrain'

Levine *et al.* (2009) remind us that customers want to talk to their service provider; that an ongoing conversation is the basis for a well-functioning market, and that providers should be receptive to new ideas and views. In a commentary at the end of the book, McKee (2009) gave an example of how Lego 'caught the cluetrain' when it finally understood that its customers (particularly adult fans of Lego) wanted to suggest ideas for new products. After years of defensive behaviour around communications from and to the organisation, a new executive director of Lego Direct posted a communication onto a hobby forum which included the message:[49]

Whether you are an AFOL,[50] or a parent purchasing a first DUPLO set, or a KABOB (Kid with a Bunch of Bricks – we just made that up), here are some words that should gladden your hearts: We are listening.

Hundreds of responses were received from customers straightaway. Now on www.lugnet.com there is an ambassador programme advertised to allow AFOLs direct representation at the company. The company also devised a product (Design by ME) that would allow customers to 'dream, build and design' their own Lego masterpieces.[51]

The big question is how flexible providers can afford to be. If I want to text my views on repairs today, submit a business idea online tomorrow and pop over to your board meeting next Friday, can your organisation cope with that without forcing me to fill in loads of paperwork, inputting to multiple databases or bugging me with updates that I have not asked for? If the answer is yes – and you can show me proof that I have made a difference – you are definitely onto a winner. And you will hopefully save time, money and scarce resources by cutting back on needless processes.

Proactive channels

Having suggested an overall approach, let us look at a few of the more popular methods you can use as part of your overall communications strategy:

- *News releases* – the 'bread and butter' of any communications function. When using them, make sure that every release a) has significance for one or more of your key audiences, b) considers the publication(s) you are targeting, c) has a clear, explanatory introduction d) is to the point and e) does not hit newsdesks three minutes before the title goes to print!

---

49 Message from Lego Direct Executive Leader on www.lugnet.com in December 1999, as cited in McKee, 2009: p.272.
50 Adult Fan of Lego.
51 Thanks to my own KABOB, Edward and AFOL, David Richardson for my growing knowledge of the world of Lego!

- *Features* – more detailed and less time-critical than news releases, typically these cover a particular area of business or people profiles. Use to showcase unique achievements (a business win does not count)
- *Advertorials* – a combination of 'advert' and 'editorial', these are essentially paid-for sales pitches written to look like editorial content. Often used in trade journals where your partners will be asked to purchase space to show their commitment to working with you (and maybe other partners they work with…)
- *Comment pieces* – opportunities for individuals to vent their opinion on a given subject. These tend to have more impact for known celebrities or people with strong views (although you may need to consider risks depending on the subject and strength of opinion)
- *Case studies* – explain how products or services work in real life, typically supplied with partner or customer endorsements and photography; these can work well as business-to-business communications or in regional, national and trade publications
- *Awards* – wins show that you are a sector leader in a particular field, short-lists are still pretty good to be on. Make sure any award entries you write focus on the end results achieved, not the processes you followed (that happens more than you might think)
- *Blogs* – short for 'weblog', this is where you produce and upload your own web articles, and wait for people to comment. A useful medium alongside social media, or to offer people content that can show you off as a 'thought leader' in a particular area over time
- *Websites* – another way of producing and uploading things that you want to say, but keep them newsworthy as people can spot 'spin' a mile off and provide as many transactions as you can (that is what keeps people coming back for more); if you are due to be inspected make sure you have checked how accessible your site is (does it offer colour contrast, translation options, text enlargement facilities, screen readers, etc?)
- *Video* – fairly popular in the industry, for general communications it is better to produce subject-specific content above corporate offerings; if you are uploading to YouTube make your video content fast, funny or fervent
- *Newsletters and magazines* – another staple in the housing provider's toolkit, these tend to be aimed at particular audiences (tenant newsletters with local or community content and partner magazines for business achievements and endorsements). Global trends are highlighting 'social magazines' which work online – say for the iPad – and it will be interesting to see if housing moves down this route
- *Media events* – these can include anything from launches and open days to media briefings and editorial lunches. Use them as networking opportunities with people who count
- *Publications* – not heavily used but can be a useful way of showcasing successes and sponsorships; for example, the Keepmoat (2010) book mentioned earlier

- *Wikis* – where you create information that others can add to (think Wikipedia). Pretty scarce in social housing but may be one to watch in future, if there is significant good practice potential?

Reactive channels

If a problem comes up or someone is unhappy with your organisation, you may have to respond to media or public attention. The most common ways of responding are:

- *Press statements* – outline the situation, details of any areas or personnel affected and provide contact details for further enquiries; in some cases you will need legal or professional advice to make sure that you are disclosing the right messages at the right time and not putting the business at risk
- *Interviews* – sometimes it will be helpful to have a senior or technical spokesperson to act as the face of your organisation; where this happens make sure s/he is properly briefed – knowing whether it is a live or recorded chat, TV or radio broadcast, the first question that will be asked and so on will help preparations
- *Social media* – speed of response is very important with this medium as messages travel so quickly; if you have had social and traditional media enquiries, try to respond to them simultaneously.

If you have ever thought that not commenting is a good option, think again! In some cases this will be the only opportunity to put the situation into context, express sympathy or concern on behalf of your organisation and reassure people of the actions you are taking.

There are very few times when responding will make things worse; apart from getting into 'tit-for-tat' games with people or groups who want an argument, and know public opinion is likely to be against you.

One word of caution – when you have dark clouds on the horizon, do remember to keep other people informed. The last thing you want is employees or board members hearing about a problem on the regional evening news, so use whatever internal channels are available to you; this will also help if key contacts are approached separately.

Communications and technology

The use of information and communications technology is not something that housing providers can ignore as part of their overall communications strategies. The *2020 Public Services Trust* recognised this:

> ...public services need to embed information and communications technology (ICT) more boldly and systematically in planning, delivery and evaluation in order to radically improve efficiency, quality and citizen control (p.6).

Over the last couple of years, the use of electronic media has become much more widespread in the UK. Many people now routinely use online technologies (such as services, applications and websites) as part of everyday life. A basic computer, laptop or mobile phone allows speedy access to all sorts of activities, including:

- Reading, sharing and filtering news
- Researching information
- Collaborating on files and wikis
- Commenting on blog posts
- Listening to music
- Reviewing customer service
- Watching video content
- Playing online games
- Taking part in competitions
- Networking with contacts.

A report produced by Comscore (2009) showed that from the 36.8 million unique UK internet visitors in May 2009, almost 30 million people participated in social network activity, such as Twitter and Facebook. What is more, this activity is particularly high for the 15-24 and 25-39 age groups, so if you are targeting these segments it makes sense to include an element of social media in your communications strategy.

There is an increasing phenomenon of the use of electronic media, and viral messaging, used in the commercial sector, so think about:

- Word of mouth
- Wikis
- Blogs
- Social networking sites such as Facebook and Twitter.[52]

Some of these options may not be appropriate for those who like more traditional media, but if you are seeking the views of people who are computer literate and united by a common interest – whether that is crime, gardening or spending priorities – then using blogs or wikis can work in the right circumstances. It is the diversity of communication streams that is important. Think back to chapter 7 in this book where we explored customer profiling as part of gaining Customer Insight. Tools like Mosaic divide the customer base into groups based on preferences and characteristics, and within those preferences are issues related to communications and how particular customers like, or are able, to talk to their housing provider.

---

[52] Many housing organisations have a Twitter presence, not just providers, but also trade magazines, professional bodies, government agencies and so on (even DMU housing lecturers!) – it is not just Stephen Fry, e.g. @CIH, @Insidehousing and @Socialhousing

THE POWER OF COMMUNICATION

Mathematical and network theories might offer some ideas for understanding the power of the internet – we need to remember the reach of internet communications just in sheer numbers of people who may read and write about your organisation online. Reed (1999) referred to a huge underestimation of the growth in number of users of the internet, based on previous mathematical models suggesting that a network grows in proportion to the square of the number of users (n^2), when in fact Reed stated that group formation was the key – so not one user talking to one user, but groups of 2, 3 and so on. The exponential growth in connections due to the advance of technology must be taken into account in assessing the potential of online communications with customers, but also the risk of adverse views being quickly and widely publicised. Organisations also need to take the message to well-used forums rather than expect customers to visit their website, and many housing providers now have Facebook and Twitter sites to enable them to join in the wider online conversation and the community.

Even though customer-reach is variable for other household types, it is still worth considering online networks as part of your communications mix. With such a big chunk of the population online – plus increased availability of electronic channels through digital television, free library access and various bidding initiatives – then obviously housing providers need to be open to using these media to engage audiences.

Social and anti-social media

David Armano (2006) created this diagram to show how social networks operate. As you can see, there are series of tightly knit 'community clusters' that interact both individually, and with other clusters – creating powerful networks that reach across the globe.

Figure 10.6: Me and my network community

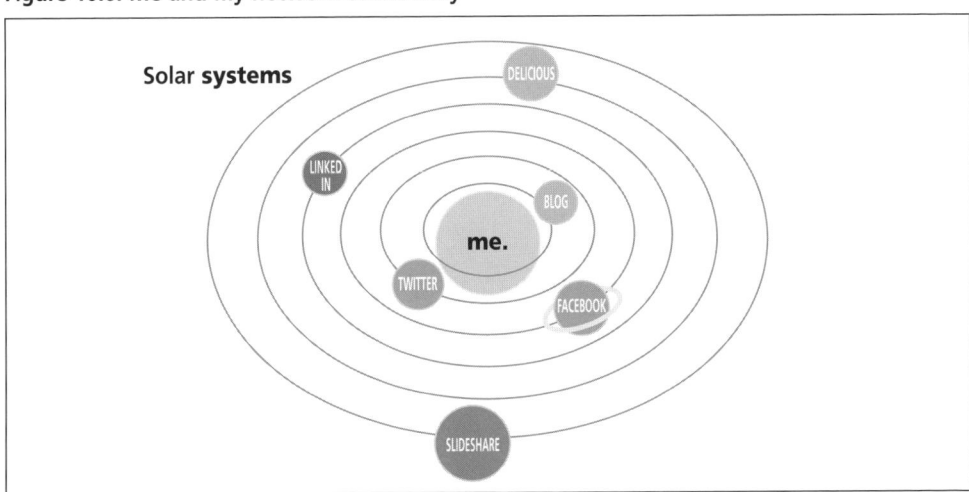

Illustration by David Armano, www.darmano.typepad.com

As people build connections and trust through these new hubs, it has become very easy to share information online in a matter of minutes – whether that means filming a plane crash in the Hudson and posting the pictures on Twitter, or announcing a government policy change (such as the anticipated abolition of the Tenant Services Authority) on the web.

An important thing to remember about social networking is that you cannot control it. This medium has a life of its own, so do not ever imagine you can completely influence what happens on your page or profile; there are plenty of examples where organisations have tried to exert influence and ended up the worse for it, including:

- *Birmingham City Council 'Twittergate'* (Qube, 2010) – following critical feedback on the council's new website, the authority said the website was created for constituents not the 'Twitterati' – only to produce an even more critical story and news item
- *Cardiff City Council Facebook 'Scouse slur'* (Inside Housing, 2009) – where a housing officer rowed with his neighbour about anti-social behaviour on their street, leading to national newspaper coverage
- *Brighton and Hove Council YouTube postings* (Qube, 2010) – where a local councillor posted meetings on YouTube and faced suspension following complaints from peers, after which the story made news headlines and the council was accused of having something to hide.

As we can see, a sense of 'crowd influence' and community pressure starts to emerge. Howe (2008) refers to crowdsourcing and suggests that there are four primary categories to consider (which can overlap or be used together). See Figure 10.7.

The best that you can do on social media is present an orderly, united front for your organisation. Having a clear policy to say what people can and cannot post online – and the implications for anyone who breaches these rules – is essential. Offering training to representatives may also help you to protect their profiles and your business, which is handy if people are members of controversial groups or networks (it does happen!).

You can also monitor online buzz through free services like SocialMention or Google Alerts, which keep track of what people are saying about you. As the immediacy of the medium means that reputations can change by the minute, that is a definite benefit. As Mark Twain famously said: *'A lie can travel halfway around the world while the truth is putting on its shoes.'* In social media, it could probably lap the runner!

Of course there are lots of grey areas, such as what employees and board representatives can post in their own time; but at least by opening the debate, you can anticipate and plan for risks. That is a lot easier than having to deal with a journalist enquiry via Twitter with a fast approaching deadline...

Figure 10.7: Types of crowdsourcing

Description	Premise	Examples
Collective intelligence or 'crowd wisdom'	Groups contain more knowledge than individuals; the sum is greater than its parts	• Barack Obama using online and social networking tools (such as his online Town Hall meeting in March 2009) as part of the presidential campaign • Grant Shapps responding to Twitter questions during his ministerial address to the 2010 CIH conference • http:ideajam.net collects technical problem-solving wisdom from IBM Lotus Software customers, and the ideas submitted affect customer online popularity
Crowd creation	Crowds possess creative energy to design and redesign products and services, and campaign for change	• Lego forum-based dialogue (mentioned earlier) • Iran's Green Revolution
Crowd voting	Crowds are asked to organise major amounts of information by carefully judging what it reads online, buys or uses (notwithstanding that some providers are accountable to small, but highly marginalised groups)	• Google determines website rankings based on search results, prioritising those with the greatest number of hits
Crowd funding	The crowd offers to pay a given amount of money in return for a product or service	• Sellaband website, where artists post their music and fans offer to pay what they feel is an appropriate amount; when the target is hit, Sellaband produces the album • Irwell Valley Gold Scheme, which allows customers to accrue money for schemes such as community play equipment in particular neighbourhoods • The new government's Spending Challenge in the wake of the June 2010 emergency budget (or is that 'crowd cutting'?)

Based on four categories from Howe, 2008: pp.280-281.

The Local Government Association has produced guidance on managing social media, and beginner's guides are also available from The Bridge Group's hub website, www.tbghub.co.uk

Measure up

So how do you know if your communications activity is hitting the mark? Time to measure the value of that hard work.

Here are a few suggested ways of showing you have made an impact:

- Evidence of extra take-up (if you have been promoting new developments or services)
- Reduction in a service problem (such as empty homes, abandonments and so on)
- Replies to a bespoke contact number or address
- Award wins
- Securing funding or sponsorship
- Increases in customer satisfaction on a given topic
- Hits to a designated page on your website
- More enquiries about the subject you have been promoting (ideally with your team members asking people where they heard about it…).

Does this surprise you? Often people expect that the ultimate goal should be a 'hit' in publication X or Y, or appearing on television. Those things can be achieved if you really want them, but remember the whole point is to base communications around your business objectives. If one of your top priorities is to let empty homes, some local coverage that gets those voids filled will be a lot more useful than a photo in *Society Guardian*, no matter how much that may appeal!

There are other ways that you can measure your achievements. For example, if you work with a communications agency, chances are at some point you will come across the term Advertising Value Equivalent, or AVE for short. That is a way of calculating the area of a publication taken up by your media coverage, and comparing it with the advertising space cost for an equivalent area. Or with major campaigns, you can buy in consultancy support to measure things like public awareness of your brand or services.

Periodically, it is useful to review the type and level of communications coverage that you are achieving, to see how far your activity is supporting your stated business goals. If you are getting the results you want, keep doing what you are doing; if not, try reviewing either the tools that you are using, publications that you are targeting or subjects that you are focusing on.

Conclusions

This chapter has shown us that communication is not just a process; it is something you have to plan, monitor and manage so that you can achieve the right results for both housing provider and customer.

In an industry where our relationships with customers can last a lifetime and involve personal, vital experiences such as providing a home, or care services, it is critical that we connect with people appropriately and sensitively.

Tapscott and Williams (2008: 3) discuss *Wikinomics* in the context of

> ...deep changes in the structure and modus operandi of the corporation and our economy, based on new competitive principles such as openness, peering, sharing and acting globally.

By creating opportunities for people to communicate with us and influence our work – maybe even thinking of them as co-producers of services, campaigns and messages – we can bring about services that best fit their needs and often, provide more efficient methods of delivery; that is critical against a backdrop of the public sector financial crisis and 25% budget cuts.

References and further reading

2020 Public Services Trust (2010) *Online or In-line: the future of information and communication technology in public services*. London: 2020 Public Services Trust.

24housing (2009) *Reform & Revolution – the top 10 events that shaped social housing*. Available at www.24dash.com/news/housing/2010-01-04-Reform-and-Revolution-The-top-10-events-that-shaped-social-housing

Arnstein, S. (1969) 'A ladder of participation in the USA', *Journal of the American Institute of Planners,* July, quoted in M. Stewart and M. Taylor (1995) *Empowerment and Estate Regeneration*. Bristol: The Policy Press.

Barry, A. (2004) *PR Power: Inside secrets from the world of spin*. Warwick Business School.

Cabinet Office (2009) 'Next Steps on Insight: the innovation challenge for government communications' presentation by Michael Warren to the *Engage the Public* conference, 23rd June, London.

Comscore (2009), *Nine Out of Ten 25-34 Year Old U.K. Internet Users Visited a Social Networking Site in May 2009*. Available at www.comscore.com

Hall, D. (2010) *Data protection for frontline staff – quick legal guidance on eight topics*. York: Housing Quality Network.

Howe, J. (2008) *Crowdsourcing: how the power of the crowd is driving the future of business*. London: Random House Business Books.

Inside Housing (2009), *Housing officer in Facebook 'Scouse' slur*. Available at www.insidehousing.co.uk/ihstory.aspx?storycode=6506064

James, K. (2010) *From uh-oh to 2.0: a beginner's guide to social media – parts one and two*. Coventry: The Bridge Group.

Keepmoat (2010) *One Company, many solutions*. Doncaster: Keepmoat.

Keller, J. (2010) *Evaluating Iran's Twitter Revolution* Blog on www.theatlantic.com/science/archive/2010/06, June 18th.

Levine, R., Locke, C., Searls, D. and Weinberger, D. (2009) *The Cluetrain Manifesto* (2nd ed.). New York: Basic Books.

McKee, J. (2009) 'How Lego Caught the Cluetrain' in R. Levine, C. Locke, D. Searls and D. Weinberger (2009) *The Cluetrain Manifesto* (2nd ed.). New York: Basic Books.

Neighbourhood Renewal Unit (2003) *Media and PR Toolkit, How to create effective, engaging communications*. London: ODPM.

Qube (2010) *Online Reputation Management in the Public Sector*, July. Available at www.qubemedia.net

Ramesh, R. (2010) 'NHS spends millions on websites that fail patients', *The Guardian*, 5th August: p.1.

Reed, D. (1999) 'Weapon of Math Destruction, a simple formula explains why the internet is wreaking havoc on business models', *Context*, Spring Issue. Available at www.contextmag.com

Regester, M. and Larkin, J. (2010) *Risk Issues and Crisis Management in Public Relations*. London: CIPR.

Seddon, J. (2008) *Systems Thinking in the Public Sector*. Axminster: Triarchy Press.

Shannon, C.E. (1948) 'A Mathematical Theory of Communication', *The Bell System Technical Journal,* 27, pp.379-423.

Shannon, C. E. and Weaver, W. (1949) *A Mathematical Model of Communication*. Urbana, Illinois: University of Illinois Press.

Tapscott, D. and Williams, A. (2008) *Wikinomics: how mass collaboration changes everything*. London: Atlantic Books.

Wilson, D. (2010) *Targets Choice and Voice: Accountability in Public Services*. London: 2020 Public Services Trust.

CHAPTER 11:
'Selling' social housing: marketing campaigns and advertising

Kerry James and Nicola Winn

Introduction

Marketing in social housing is often misunderstood, and occasionally maligned. We have heard people describe it as advertising; 'selling' services; and producing a leaflet or poster for an open day. At the other end of the scale, some organisations use highly sophisticated profiling techniques, strategies and creative tools to raise cash, change public opinion and change people's behaviours.

Chapter 10 discussed the importance of measuring communications activity, and ways that housing providers can prove they are making an impact (such as reducing empty homes or increasing customer satisfaction). Marketing works in the same way. By understanding what people want and need, you can provide services to suit them, adapt your work to changing demand and maintain positive relationships with your customers.

This chapter shows how you can use marketing and advertising techniques to find out what makes your customers 'tick', and then develop plans and messages to achieve your business objectives. There are also some examples of marketing campaigns from the sector to show how other organisations have approached particular challenges.

The point of marketing housing

The Chartered Institute of Marketing (CIM, 2009a) describes marketing as '...*the management process responsible for identifying, anticipating and satisfying customer requirements profitably*'. It's a bit of a mouthful, but it highlights that the customer is at the heart of marketing, and businesses ignore this at their peril.

By understanding people's needs and preferences, housing providers can:

- Negotiate service provision and standards with residents – which offers opportunities to adapt or even cut out activity if residents think the money would be better spent elsewhere

- Spot ways of increasing and/or maintaining demand for services that generate valuable income and can be re-invested into the business (such as selling maintenance services)
- Focus communications on the things that matter most, and at times to suit residents (for example, changing newsletter length or frequency, or moving to more flexible formats)
- Build long-term relationships with customers, and business stakeholders such as funders, regulators and local agencies
- Position their businesses to reflect what they do differently and better than anyone else.

Yet it is not that long ago that housing providers rarely needed to market their goods or services to customers. In the early 1990s, the combination of high housing need, rising homelessness and recession meant that landlords were the keepers of the keys and controllers of opportunity; allocations systems operated on a 'points make prizes' system with needs assessed based on factors such as shared facilities, household composition and medical conditions.

As a result, housing organisations did not need to worry about acquiring and keeping customers unless they had pockets of low-demand property, a mismatch of service provision or new development schemes to promote. This meant marketing was often seen as an add-on activity rather than a professional skill.

How things have changed. The development of the Citizen's Charter, Compulsory Competitive Tendering and choice-based lettings systems were key milestones in the shift towards customer empowerment. Since then, resident engagement has gradually become a fundamental part of sector regulation; and the introduction of local standards and reporting arrangements means landlords need to know what makes them genuinely 'different' and position themselves accordingly.

Property vs profitability

We agree with the CIM that the customer is central to marketing, but, in social housing, many people find the concept of profitability tricky and that is perhaps a tension that needs resolution. Some people might argue that even today, customers do not have unlimited property choices in the way you might choose an iTunes track or chocolate bar; there is a perception that housing is different.

Certainly lots of individuals come into the sector to make a difference and generally people do just that – through preventing homelessness, providing safe, warm properties, helping people to access benefits and much more besides. But does that mean that we should look at customers as charitable objects, or as people who can make their own informed choices?

'SELLING' SOCIAL HOUSING

In a world where budgets are sharply declining, regulators being streamlined and efficiency savings now part of an everyday cycle, increasingly managing with very scarce resources overrides the natural desire to provide a 'social good'. For example, the coalition government's proposals to end lifetime tenancies in August sparked an immediate outrage from some quarters. The story made front-page lead for *Inside Housing* and sparked anger from various sector sources about potential impacts on the poorest members of society. Similarly the prospect of housing benefit calculations being based on the Consumer Price Index rather than Retail Price Index has caused concern among some sector commentators, with warnings of significant income drops for many housing providers in the next few years; assuming that income and materials costs will continue to rise, it is likely the sector will feel the squeeze sooner rather than later.

With limited resources, the need for good marketing is even more important; you need to maintain demand for services and find ways of keeping your brand in people's minds on a limited budget. That means knowing your audience inside out, and talking to them in the right ways and at the right times.

Marketing from A to B

Whilst budgets may be declining, the challenges and demands placed upon housing organisations certainly are not. So how can marketing help? Well, we often describe it as a way of helping you get from one place to another – from point A to point B.

Your point A and point B may be unique to you, or a situation common to many housing providers. For example, your organisation may be a transfer association with 3,000 homes (point A) but your business plan aims to grow to 5,000 homes in the next five years (point B). You may be launching a new service that currently has no customers (A), but needs at least 50 for the service to keep running (B). Or your latest STATUS survey may show 60% customer satisfaction (A), when your board expects at least 70% (B).

Figure 11.1: From point A to point B

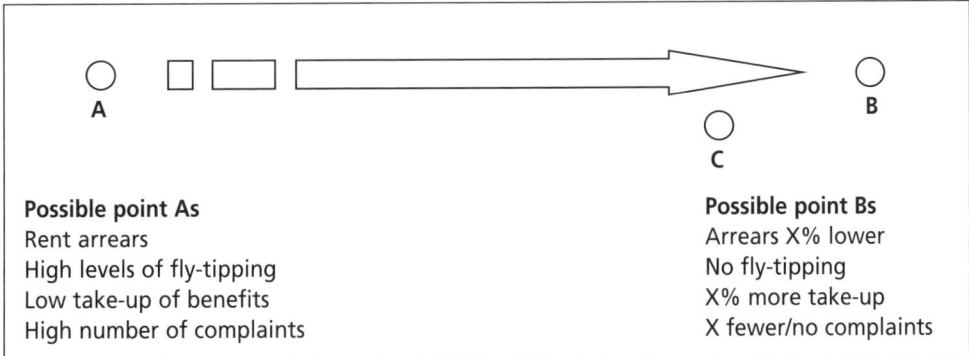

As you can see from the above diagram, the point As in life are generally problems, challenges or 'before' situations in your life that you need to sort out; the rent arrears, neighbourhood problems, low service take-ups and complaints in your world. So they should be easy to spot.

Point Bs, on the other hand, are targets, solutions or 'after' scenarios that you want to achieve. You must be as specific as you can with these – ideally, they will be a clear benefit or result that you can measure. So 'raised awareness' is a bit vague, but '10% more awareness of campaign' might be clear if you planned to do a survey to test people's views. In other words, you need 'SMART' objectives:

- *Specific* – so you know exactly what needs to be done, such as build 100 new homes
- *Measurable* – in a way that you can show whether or not you have met your targets
- *Achievable* – because if you are miles away from the goal and cannot realistically hit it, you are in danger of hurting colleagues' morale (or your own) for nothing
- *Realistic* – in that you have suitable staff time, money and resources to make it happen
- *Timebound* – so you know when you will have achieved the objective(s) and can review your progress on the way.

And why is there a point C? Because sometimes things will not end up as you expect. You can have a clear direction, plan carefully, work hard, review like mad and still end up somewhere different. But with the right marketing planning and tools, your chances of ending up at point B are much higher than having no plan at all!

In the mix

So let us assume you know what needs to change, and what a good result looks like for your organisation, how do you go about pursuing your objectives? The marketing mix, also described as the '7Ps of marketing'; this was examined by Garry and Richardson in chapter 3, but here is a brief reminder:

- *Product* – what do your customers want or need? You need to understand this to develop the right products or services, and understand what level of quality will meet customer requirements now and in the future
- *Price* – how much can and will they pay? This step involves making sure services or products are priced competitively; and working out if you want to add extra services or details that will offer customers better value for money. There is an obvious link between the type and condition of property and its perceived desirability, which also links to customer experience and physical evidence of your performance through regulation
- *Place* – where will people access your services? The place of product or service delivery must be appropriate and convenient for the customer; that is, it is

available in the right place, at the right time and in the right quantity. Increasingly these days it is easier to put transactions online, but that obviously depends on how many of your customers can access and use the web
- *Promotion* – how will you tell people? You need to communicate what the organisation does and what it offers customers, through activities such as advertising, branding, PR, corporate identity and exhibitions
- *People* – how good is your team? The brand's reputation is in their hands, so organisations should make sure that representatives of the organisation are appropriately trained, well motivated and have the right attitude
- *Process* – how strong are your systems? Credible information, strong technology and clear procedures will help to create strong customer service
- *Physical evidence* – how can you prove your quality? Providing information and examples will show customers that the organisation keeps its promises, for example through a clean and tidy reception, case studies and customer feedback (regulatory judgments are another obvious example for housing organisations).

(Adapted from CIM (2009), pp.4-7.)

The CIM points out that each of these seven 'ingredients' in the mix is vital to success. For example, you cannot develop a new service without thinking about how much it will cost or where the customer will access it; this needs to be carefully planned. Time to put together a marketing strategy…

Simply strategic

To make sure you are taking a strategic approach to marketing, it is important to link any related plans and activity to your business objectives.

Hatton (2000) identifies a strategic planning hierarchy, which runs from the business (or corporate) plan through the entire organisation:

- *Business plan* – at the top of the tree, this plan sets the long-term direction for the organisation. It typically includes an environmental analysis, details of the markets to be competed in, proposed scope of activities and resources available
- *Functional or operational plans* – these both influence business plan development (in assessing existing service strengths and weaknesses) and follow the lead of the business plan. Typically a marketing plan will fall into this category and include an audit of resources, situational analysis, service objectives and overview strategies for different elements of the proposed marketing mix
- *Tactical plans* – these transform the operational plans into lower-level actions that meet the above objectives; for example, some marketing plans may include proposed actions and channels for public relations, marketing,

research and advertising. Kotler and Armstrong highlight that this part of the process includes answering key questions: *What* will be done? *When* will it be done? *Who* is responsible for doing it? *How* much will it cost?

Competitor analysis

The CIM says that:

> *The best way of 'beating your competitors' and providing your company with an added advantage is to learn more about them and understand where they are strong and where they are weak. You can then compare this information with your own view of your company and look for opportunities where your product or service can provide an additional benefit* (CIM, 2009a, pp.4-6).

There are numerous techniques for analysing your organisation's performance against your competitors. Probably the best-known of these is the 'strengths, weaknesses, opportunities and threats' (SWOT) model – given its widespread use, we have not covered SWOT here.

Management writer Michael Porter describes five forces that affect organisational performance and the relative competitiveness within an industry. He recommends analysing changes in these forces when preparing marketing strategies and plans, as follows:

- *Ease of entry* – how quickly and easily can new competitors enter and compete against you? (For example, setting up a new registered provider takes substantial time and clearance; launching a small home maintenance service is much quicker and may need less investment)
- *Competition* – is the existing marketplace very competitive, based on investment requirements, sector knowledge and customer acquisition time/costs? What are the advantages and disadvantages for your organisation?
- *Substitute products/services* – can your services be substituted for any competitors' offerings? And do your prices put you at an advantage or disadvantage?
- *Supplier power* – are the suppliers to the market buoyant? Do they have a specialist remit? How many other businesses exist in their line of work?
- *Buyer power* – are customers loyal or receptive to approaches from competitors? What are the costs of moving supplier in terms of time, money and effort? Are there procurement consortia or benchmarking clubs in place to force pricing down?

From prospects to pals

In chapter 10, we spoke about the different audiences that housing organisations typically communicate with every day – from internal contacts through to business partners, politicians and wider publics.

Using marketing techniques can help you to understand people better and anticipate what they need from you – and then communicate in ways that make them feel listened to, valued and positive towards your organisation. Drayton Bird (2007) says the object of business is to '...*locate a* prospect, *make that prospect a* customer *and then turn that* customer *into a friend. The secret of success is to treat people in a way which matches the nature of the relationship'.*

Bird also argues that you should decide how to communicate with your prospects and customers depending on how *friendly* you are with them. From this perspective, 'good friends' might get weekly contact, whilst strangers would be much less frequent; and the things that you say would vary substantially between friends and acquaintances.

In an ideal world, you will have access to customer profile data that tells you which customers like texting, who prefers meetings, how many use the internet and so on. That means you have automatic clues on how people might be open to helping you shape products and influence service delivery. The key lies in integrating your marketing and community engagement data, particularly if you have separate teams performing these functions. If you currently hold information completely separately, it may be worth checking your data protection registration details to see if you can combine information to consult and communicate with people in a more streamlined way.

Most housing providers will also have access to substantial data resources – from waiting lists to complaints, housing needs and stock condition surveys, CORE data, survey results and service register – which may give you pointers about how you are perceived, service demand and option for expanding, improving or cutting provision.

If your data is patchy to start with, you will need to make some intelligent assumptions about how to 'hook' people in. And do not forget that some people may need help to connect with you, say through language translations, audio tapes, Braille documents or picture cards...by keeping your databases updated you can show that you have listened and made an effort to support someone's individual needs.

Bird (2007, pp.22-23) summarises the beauty of customer profiling, and the long-term business benefits of this approach:

> ...*when you isolate someone as an individual this automatically implies that you discover what differentiates them from other individuals. What are their special characteristics? And by speaking to them as individuals, using the knowledge you acquire about them and their relationship with you, you will be able to make appeals which are far more relevant to them...your success revolves around how well you respond to their needs and their desires.*

Suss out your segments

Segmentation is not, surprisingly, a way of unwrapping a certain brand of tasty chocolate orange. It involves thinking about groups or sub-groups of people who share certain characteristics. Bush and Webber (2006) describe it as *'...all about grouping: using the information gained through profiling to divide up the customer and prospect universe into smaller groups depending on the activity'*.

For many housing providers, your key customers are visible by the products they use; they will be your tenants, or service users. But that is just top-level information. Some people will form a sub-grouping because of where they live. Others might use particular services, such as sheltered housing, and form another sub-grouping. Depending on the resources at your disposal, you can build much more sophisticated pictures of your residents and start to make more informed assumptions about their lifestyles, communications preferences and so on.

Let us look at a specific example. Imagine you are about to launch a new home insurance scheme to your tenants. Thinking about customers as a whole, what sort of messages do you think might interest people in joining? Write down as many things as you can think of.

Now consider three specific customer segments that you might come into contact with:

1. People aged 18-25 years in their first tenancy
2. Pensioners living in sheltered housing
3. Tenant board members.

What do you think makes each of these groups different? (Think about people's incomes, priorities, lifestyles and interests as a starting point.) Jot down the differences for each group.

Now go back to your overall messages (the things you thought would generally be interesting to tenants). If you were talking to a younger tenant, are there any things you might add in or leave out? Would an older person see things any differently? And what might a tenant board member need to know that other customers would not?

Finally, once you know what needs to be said, you should spend time thinking about the tools or 'channels' you will use to get your message across to your different audience segments. Or to put it another way – who will notice you if you use texts, or newsletters, or your website, to make a point?

Once you understand your audience segments, you can start exploring ways of making them feel welcome or valued. Examples might include:

- Sending welcome cards to new residents just after they have moved in, with contact details and personal introductions from patch staff
- Sending thank-you letters with loyalty rewards to residents on the anniversary of their tenancy
- Creating personalised options for competitions based on customer profile data, so people can win different prizes depending on their circumstances
- Extending opening hours or call centre times to meet the needs of particular groups
- Providing access to different web content for regular resident participants, based on them choosing from a range of interests
- Delivering differently sized newsletters to customers where they have asked you for more, or less, information
- Creating different types of information (for example, blogs or ezines) for people who do not like printed material.

Express yourself

Now that we have touched on marketing strategy and you have thought about audience needs, let us take a look at how you can transform business objectives into captivating creative work.

Great, creative marketing is like going on a hot date. It involves big ideas, positioning, propositions, briefs, technique and results. Let us look at each of those points in turn.

Big ideas

Steve Harrison (2009) introduces the concept of the 'big marketing idea' and explains how to go about it:

> ...people notice things that are useful to them. So if you're going to get their attention and impress them you need to work out how the thing you are selling can help them. To be more specific, you should look for ways in which you can solve their problems.
> Find this simple problem/solution dynamic and you'll have found your big marketing idea. Once you have that, you'll be on your way to producing something truly effective. You may even make history.

Of course, with social marketing the 'problem' may concern your target audience themselves; Harrison relates the topics of obesity and smoking during pregnancy, for example. With this type of challenge, your role is to be a facilitator rather than offering a direct solution – you need to come up with something compelling enough to make people want to change their behaviour. And to make that happen – whether you want to shift perceptions, behaviours or loyalty – then you'll need to motivate the audience in some way. Considering the potential 'carrots' and 'sticks' of what you are proposing may be useful:

- *Carrots* are incentives or positives; your audience will respond favourably to these because they offer a perceived benefit. Examples might include policy changes which benefit cutomers (such as extra rent-free weeks), gifts or vouchers, free or discounted services and family fun days
- *Sticks* are disincentives or negatives; things that your audience will want to avoid or move away from – such as penalty charges, court action or service cuts.

The classic 'carrot' approach dates back to 1998, with the launch of Irwell Valley Housing Association's Gold Service. The first housing association to launch a rewards and incentive scheme for its customers, Irwell Valley wanted to reward the loyalty of customers who paid their rent on time and kept to the terms of their tenancy agreements. The association did this by introducing ongoing membership criteria (such as paying rent on time), and offering a range of benefits to members who continually kept to the scheme rules. The benefits package includes cashback, debit card loyalty points, quicker repairs, access to training grants and access to a back-to-work fund. Long-term members automatically upgrade to higher-level benefits, including anniversary payments and an unconditional service guarantee.

Positioning

The next challenge is to work out how you can best position your organisation or product in the minds of the customers you want to reach. What makes you different? How are you special? What do you do better than your competitors?

Your SWOT assessment and competitor analysis will help kick-start this process. Ries and Trout (2000) also make some key points to help businesses position themselves and their products effectively:

- *Understanding your fit in the marketplace* – are you the leader or a follower? If key players were ranked on a ladder, would you be nearer the top or bottom rung and why? Being first into the market is a definite advantage here
- *Reality check* – if you are on the bottom rung, it is unlikely you will challenge the leader from there so where are the gaps to differentiate yourself – quality, price, location or something else?
- *Mind over matter* – how can you get into the mind of your customer and stay there? What are your natural advantages and where can you beat your competitors?

- *Name game* – is your organisation or product name relevant and memorable to your audience?
- *Simplicity* – how can you whittle down the volume of material you communicate to create clear, unambiguous messages that will leave customers with no doubt about your offer and advantages?

Steel (1998) relates the story of a meeting with a specialist accounting firm, where different partners gave different perspectives based on their own jobs rather than what would be useful to say to customers. In the end, Steel took a more direct approach to get the result he needed:

> *Finally, I asked one of the partners if he had any children. Yes, he told me, a little puzzled by my question, he had two kids. I asked him how old they were.*
> *'A boy of six and a girl of four.'*
> *'So when they ask you what you do at work, what do you tell them?'*
> *His eyes lit up. He had, he said, tried to explain it to them only the other day. Something like, 'Daddy helps make other people's businesses more efficient... er...run better. Like the coach on your Little League team tells you how to hit better, or catch better, or throw better, that's what Daddy does for people who want to make more money.'*

This breakthrough ended up transforming the brief, because it changed the language and perceptions being used and helped to focus on what was important for the customer in plain and simple terms.

Dave Trott (2009) relates the story of snake-oil salesmen in the Wild West, and how they learned to charm gullible customers into buying a product that did not really do anything for the buyer. He explains that over time, customer admiration and trust turned to disillusionment and advertising got a bad reputation; so the Unique Selling Proposition (USP) was born. But, he argues, '*...advertising became really boring*' as a result of USPs, because some people resorted to lazy thinking – they would look for a difference, however, small, and then stop there.

Knight (2004) is an advocate of the elevator pitch. He says, *'if you can't describe, compellingly, your business to an audience of one, how on earth can you expect a group of people, possibly thousands, to understand or be interested in your advertisement or other communication?'*

So if we apply this technique to social housing providers, would your customers associate you with 'creating communities where people want to live and take pride in?' And would you want them to remember you for that before (say) the quality of your services, the security that your financial strength offers, your brand personality or your knowledge of a particular area better than anyone else? Just a thought...

Propositions: USP

Unique Selling Point (USP) is vital to the marketing of a product or service.

> *With many products and services that we buy in our everyday lives, there is very little distinguishable difference between one provider and another. However for a good promotion, you need to tell your customers why they should buy from you and not another similar provider – you need a USP. In some cases you may want to consult with your existing customers or clients and find out why they bought from you – they may tell you your USP. There are many ways of eliciting this feedback, such as focus groups, surveys and so on* (Richardson, 2009).

Barry (2009) develops this idea, saying, *'The key is to say one thing that's different about your product (of genuine interest to the consumer), or be the first to say something that the competition could say, but has yet to realize it'*.

Dave Trott (2009) points out:

> *The two magic words here are "unique" and "selling".*
> *What you talk about has to be unique, not just a marginal improvement on what everyone else offers.*
> *Plus, for it to be "selling", it has to be something that people truly want.*
> *Not just any old point of difference.*
> *Unique on its own isn't enough.*

If you are finding it hard to distinguish the difference between your services and a competitor's, it may be worth considering whether you offer any 'added value' (such as higher service standards, longer opening hours, freephone helplines and so on) that will help you to develop your USP.

Briefs

The creative brief is the point where you throw all the key ingredients into a bowl and get ready to mix them creatively.

Harrison (2009) says: *'you should dedicate a lot of time to writing the brief. In fact, as a general rule, you should spend twice as long on the brief as you do on the creative'*.

Housing professionals may find themselves contributing to a brief now and again, and maybe preparing some in-house materials; marketers will probably have to produce briefs more regularly. So when you're producing creative work, it is useful to have a process to follow and questions that you routinely ask yourself. Figure 11.2 offers an example of this.

Figure 11.2: Flow chart for creative brief

Know your needs
What is your point A and your point B?
How will you measure the journey?

Face the facts
Hunt for information, talk to colleagues, download data, consult customers, get as much inspiration as you can…

Assess your audience
Who are you targeting? (Customer segments, needs, wants, interests, preferred communication methods and so on)

Consider your competitors
What are they doing? What is their brand like?
How will you differentiate?

Be on brand
Are there clear brand guidelines?
Do you look visually consistent?

Mull over your message
What do you need to say? Is it clear?
What tone are you speaking in?

Balance your budget
How much can you spend? Does that include materials and print?
Is in-house or agency better for this?

Choose your channels
Is it some words? Is it a campaign? Is it a super advert?
Method must work for audience (see Winn's wheel, chapter 10)

Test the timing
Can you 'piggyback' any big events or news stories?
Is it appropriate to send with other stuff? Can you miss holidays?

Confirm the call
How do you need people to respond?
Do you want them to sign up, sound off or take part in something?

Once you have drawn up your brief, it is important to test it with someone before letting your creative brains loose on it; do not just assume you have got it right because sometimes little details can make a big difference. So maybe test it out and even ask a colleague for their view; you can then decide if anything is missing or needs adjusting.

Before we move on, it is useful to highlight another useful term which is often used in advertising – AIDA. This stands for 'attention, interest, desire, action'. Or as Dave Trott (2009) puts it:

> How does advertising work?
> It works the same way as every other purchase decision.
> Every purchase decision is a combination of 'desire' and 'permission'.
> Without those two elements nothing happens.
> If you want to buy something, but you can't justify it in any way, you don't buy it.
> If you can justify buying something, but you don't want it, you don't buy it.
> It's that simple.
> You've got to want something, and it's got to be okay for you to have it.

Technique

This is where the creatives come out to play (this may either be design professionals or you or your colleagues unleashing your own inner artist!). The task is to produce work that meets your brief and will convey the desired message to your priority audience(s), so you can keep building and maintaining strong relationships.

If you have commissioned an agency, you are paying for creative input and will often be better off letting them go and play – after all, if your brief is strong, then you should end up with good results. But if you need to produce something in-house, Young (2003) originally developed a classic technique for developing ideas in the 1960s, which we have adapted below:

- Absorb as much raw material as you can – not just about your product/service and customer, but also films, internet, art galleries and anything else that inspires you; keep a scrapbook, folder or 'funky box' if it helps
- Read, digest and combine ideas; look for patterns, ideas and meaning
- Stop, move away from the cookie jar, and go and do something else for a bit so your brain can ferment for a while – sing, dance, have an exciting evening out!
- Be ready to capture the flash of inspiration that strikes when you least expect it
- Note the emerging ideas down, filter them and rework until you get a gem.

It is also important not to discard ideas too early. Barry (2009) describes the greatest barriers to creativity:

- Fear of the unknown
- Fear of looking stupid
- Premature judgment of ideas
- Attachment
    - Attachment to old ideas
    - Attachment to past successes
    - Resistance to change
    - Reluctance to explore better methods
    - Stopping at the first good idea.

So if you have a little spark niggling away in your brain, do not ditch it until you have taken a second opinion.

Results

The final step in the process involves agreeing how you will measure the journey from your point A to point B – in short, how you will keep track of the results.

Great creative work will always have a call-to-action – that is, you are inviting the customer to do something. This might include:

- Visiting a specific page on your website
- Signing up for an event
- Buying a product
- Catching up with their payments
- Applying for a service
- Becoming a member of a group or panel
- Passing on information
- Giving you feedback about a service
- Forwarding a link, video or piece of news to someone they know
- Recommending a friend as a potential customer.

Friendship Care and Housing has run a successful 'Money Matters' campaign around financial exclusion. This approach – which includes a tenant guide, money advice surgeries, Christmas doorstep lender warnings, website updates, newsletters and conferences – included calls-to-action in the form of ranked feedback for an advice guide and invitations to a conference. 100% of respondents ranked the guide at least 8 out of 10, and 250 delegates attended the 2009 conference (a big increase on the preceding year).

Including tangible calls-to-action means that you then have something to measure – such as how many people went straight to the right page on your website, who made a payment after your work went out, or how many recommended-friend forms you have received. You can also include less tangible examples, such as the total number of people who visited your website after a particular mailing, or clicks from a specific button; it is just that you might not necessarily know whether your marketing or speculative visits were the driver.

Where possible, we would also recommend you show the benefits of the call-to-action to encourage people to take part. You can do this by offering people free content if they subscribe to something, proposing loyalty points or gifts for people who recommend others to you, and so on.

Putting it all together

The brief in action

Let us apply a specific case to this brief, to test if it works. Imagine that your point A is that one of your neighbourhoods has 30 garages with low demand, and your point B is to advertise and fill all of those vacancies within two months. That is your need identified.

Looking at the *facts*, you will want to pull out as much information as you can about the area, such as layout, garage occupancy rates, reasons for people quitting, demographic data, turnover trends, and so on. It might also help to talk to customers and patch teams to see if anything else needs to happen before your advertising campaign is launched.

From an *audience* perspective, you want to identify those people who are most likely to be interested. That might include people living in the neighbourhood or surrounding area, broken down into people who own or rent cars, those with motorcycles and people with other qualifying vehicles (maybe trailers). So you will need to compile a list of audience segments and check your customer profile data – maybe tenants, waiting-list applicants in and around the neighbourhood – to gauge just how sophisticated you can be in targeting prospects. You will also want to generate a list of other people who might be interested (say if you were targeting family members, local community groups, private tenants in the area and so on).

Next up is the *competitor* analysis. If there are other providers in your vicinity, you would need to check whether they have similar problems. If they do, are they advertising too? What are they saying and how can you differentiate? Obviously you would want to think things through before going head-to-head for potentially the same customer groups.

On *branding*, you will need to set some parameters for whoever will be doing the creative work later – an agency, or design colleague, or yourself depending on the circumstances. That way, you will look consistent and co-ordinated with any other material produced by your team – using the right typeface, appropriate images and so on.

Message-wise, it is time to start thinking about the audience(s) that you need to attract. Will one message fit everyone or do you need to produce different materials for people with different vehicles, living in different areas and so on? For example, if the neighbourhood had has a lot of on-street car theft, you might want to mention the opportunities for security. Or if your garages are cheaper than anyone else's, you might present price as your 'hook'; it depends how many audience segments you have identified.

Budget next. How much have you got to play with? This will determine which channels you use and who does the creative work.

Which brings us to *channels*. There are a range of things you might choose from, such as website advertising, area noticeboards, office displays, newspaper editorial, posters in shop windows, leaflets and word-of-mouth. Having absorbed your customer profiles, you need to work out which of these channels are most likely to work with your various audiences (that might mean using different tools for different targets, of course).

To test the *timing*, you will want to check whether any local events are timed to coincide with your launch; you might also want to avoid holiday periods, when people are less likely to connect with you (unless they are getting a car for the festive season!).

Then, your *call*-to-action needs to give people a quick and easy way to respond. If you are sending emails, it might be a click to an application form. If you are putting up posters, it might be a number or drop-in facility. Whatever you decide, make sure you are helping people to connect with you efficiently.

Real-life examples

Finally, let us look at two case studies to show how key marketing objectives and messages were translated into strong creative output. Both examples involve homelessness charities, but the approach and channels were very different.

Case in point: driving donations for the homeless
Pathways to Housing

Campaign objectives
- To raise awareness of homelessness in New York, by creating a virtual homeless person that is impossible to ignore.

Messaging
- There are over 40,000 people homeless in NYC we walk by everyday.

Channels
- Installation/mobile – featuring a life-size video of a homeless man digitally projected onto Manhattan buildings. The man shivers as he sleeps on the street; a message then pops up inviting people to move the virtual person by texting. The text triggers another video, showing a door to a new home, which the man walks through; finally, the passer-by then gets a text message code that allows them to donate to Pathways to Housing.

Impact
- Within a one-week period 200 people sent text messages, and more than 30 made a mobile donation
- Pathways to Housing also had an increase in traffic to its website and rising numbers of fans on its Facebook page
- The campaign was featured on numerous websites and blogs, including the globally renowned Huffington Post.

Agency
Sarkissian Mason

Case in point: communicating rises in repossessions
Shelter

Campaign objectives
- To highlight a dramatic rise in projected repossessions (from 45,000 to 75,000 a year) as a consequence of the credit crunch, higher interest rates and rising unemployment.

Messaging
- People's homes are at risk as a consequence of the fragile housing market
- Every eight minutes, someone loses their home
- If this affects your household, come to Shelter for support *(bearing in mind that a lot of the target audience may not have considered this previously)*.

Channels
- *TV advertising* – showing a real landscape, then a house built from playing cards that would tumble down in the wind
- *Posters* – based on the TV advertising, and highlighting that someone was losing their home every eight minutes (based on the projected repossession figures)
- *Direct mailing* – based on the TV advertising
- *News stories* – based on the TV advertising
- *House of cards exhibition* – to complement the visually striking imagery, Shelter persuaded over 50 famous global artists and designers (including Damien Hirst and Vivienne Westwood) to create a unique piece of artwork. Each artist donated a unique design for one playing card, knowing that their contribution would feature in an exhibition organised by Shelter
- *Create your own card competition* – A standalone website was launched where Shelter invited the public to design a bespoke card, which would feature in the forthcoming exhibition; this campaign, run in partnership with the *Metro* title, captured substantial blogging and social media attention, creating a buzz where would-be designers were canvassing their contacts for votes
- *Bespoke pack of cards* – a special 'limited edition' pack of the designed playing cards was printed and sold at £70 per unit.

Impact
- More than £100,000 was raised, from auctioning the 52 designer cards and sales of the limited edition packs
- Independent research by consultancy nfpSynergy showed increased brand awareness over the period – especially in London, which received the most media coverage.

Agency
Leo Burnett

For many housing providers, television advertisements and virtual people are very expensive – and this might not work for your specific target audiences. But if there is a particular topic that you and several business partners are lobbying on, sharing campaigns and costs can make more expensive channels viable…

Indeed, with increased focus on scarce public resources, it is a good time to look for ways of sharing – from cross-partner newsletters through to joint procurement. These types of projects usually need a longer lead-in time and you may find political tensions arise from time to time; but with careful thought, energy and imagination you can reach a much broader audience and boost your reputation in the bargain.

Conclusions

This chapter has examined practical marketing campaigns in the social housing sector and further afield. We looked back to some of the theories and frameworks outlined in chapter 3 to provide context for the practical ideas and real-life examples that work.

References and further reading

Barry, P. (2009) *The advertising concept book: a complete guide to creative ideas, strategies and campaigns*. London: Thames & Hudson.

Bird, D. (2007) *Commonsense direct & digital marketing* (5th ed.). London: Kogan Page Limited.

Bush, R. and Webber, R. (2006) *The IDM Marketing Guide* (chapter 2.6). London: The Institute of Direct Marketing.

Chartered Institute of Marketing (2009) *Marketing and the 7Ps*. London: CIM.

Chartered Institute of Marketing (2009a) *Marketing planning toolkit for small business*. London: CIM.

Harrison, S. (2009) *How to do better creative work*. New Jersey: Pearson Education Limited.

Inside Housing (2010) 'Cameron's U-turn on security of tenure', *Inside Housing*. Available at www.InsideHousing.co.uk/news/housing-management/cameron's-u-turn-on-security-of-tenure/6511043.article

Macdonald, S. (2010) 'Find the right formula', *Inside Housing* (27 August) Available at www.InsideHousing.co.uk//6511365.article

Richardson, J. (2009) *Branding and Advertising* (from Housing and the Customer Module). Leicester: De Montfort University.

Ries, A. (2001) *Positioning: the battle for your mind* (20th anniversary ed.). Columbus, Ohio: McGraw-Hill.

Steel, J. (1998) *Truth, lies and advertising: the art of account planning*. London: John Wiley & Sons Inc.

Trott, D. (2009) *Creative Mischief*. London: Loaf Marketing Ltd.

Wallace, N. (2010) *Using light display to raise awareness and money, The Chronicle of Philanthropy.* Available at http://philanthropy.com/blogPost/Using-Light-Display-to-Raise/21696/

Young, J. W. (2003) *A technique for producing ideas*. Columbus, Ohio: McGraw-Hill.

CHAPTER 12:
Change management

Joanna Richardson

Introduction

Change is something that we have to deal with all the time at work and at home. Change itself cannot be stopped, but it can be managed to help people come to terms with the impact and to work to make the change a success. If people feel threatened by change, then it is the role of good housing leadership to help open eyes to the positive attributes of change, or indeed to manage responses and provide support where the change inevitably has a disappointing impact for some individuals.

Good management skills, leadership and communication, are vital to the success of a business in periods of stability and of change.

Changes in context

In recent times there have been so many changes that it is difficult to distinguish distinct programmes of change that have been underway in the public sector, and particularly for social housing. One way that an organisation can start to examine what is going on, and what responses might be needed in the future, is through a PEST type of analysis. By outlining a very brief analysis for the social housing sector, we can see just how many changes we have to deal with, and what might be changing in the future.

Political/ regulatory	A new Conservative-Liberal Democrat coalition government. Whilst on some issues there is a rapport (surprisingly on the speed and level of public sector cuts), other issues such as voting reform in the Commons, and suggestions on reviewing 'lifetime' council tenancies show ideological clear water between the political parties.
	There has been a bonfire of 'Quangos'. Not only was the TSA under review but regional planning bodies, leadership boards and government offices in the regions have gone. The regional spatial strategies (RSSs)[53] have gone leaving a vacuum in understanding of 'where next'[54] for housing provision.

→

53 Which provided a strategic framework for planning.
54 This is particularly manifest in the provision of sites for Gypsies and Travellers with councils slowing or halting their development plan documents because pitch requirement numbers in the RSS are not seen as applicable.

Economic	The recession of 2008 and the financial and economic crisis that followed (see further Richardson, 2010) is clearly the biggest change the public sector has faced for a long time. What started as a private sector crisis has ended in public sector chaos with huge budget cuts affecting all areas, including the housing sector, and fears of the impact of public sector cuts on private contracts can spark fears of 'double dip' recession. It is difficult to plan for services for customers in this economic climate as budgets are down between 25% and 40% in many areas. Back office functions, and even chief executive roles are merging across organisations in a drive to create efficiency savings, and there are redundancies and service closures. All of this affects management and morale of staff significantly.
Social	The so-called demographic 'time bomb' of an ageing population in the UK has a huge impact on the provision of housing and ancillary support services for older people. There are also issues around immigration and the changes and diversity of population in particular areas of the country and their needs for housing.
Technological/ legal	There were 23 Bills in the Queen's Speech in 2010 including the Local Government Bill. There has been much debate and suggestion which will shape the bills as they go through Parliament, and there will be a need for more law to enact, for example, the abolition of the TSA which was created under the Housing and Regeneration Act 2008. There is also case law which affects changes not just on the level of managing tenancies, but also how housing organisations see themselves – e.g. the issue of whether a housing association is a public body. European law also impacts here.

The PEST analysis is just a flavour of the issues that housing organisations should be discussing and planning for. There are many more points to add to the illustration above, but that is a whole other book!

What is change?

The Audit Commission (2001) suggest that there are four types of change:

Operational gains	This is an incremental, directive approach. Change is programmed in detail with a controlled and monitored approach. This approach does not count on changes which might come from the external environment – it is to do with the function of the organisation and is tightly programmed.
Surgery	Is also a directive approach, but this is a 'step-change'. A step-change is a big, whole-sale change to the organisation and it is radical for the organisation; however because it is directive – it is controlled more by the organisation – the organisation has chosen to undertake this change for internal reasons, rather than in a direct response to the external environment.
Evolutionary learning	This is an incremental change (like operational gains) but it is organic rather than directive. It occurs where an organisation knows where it is going and is clear on its strategy, but it operates in an uncertain environment – one could think of the police and hospitals as people who work in an uncertain environment; they cannot be sure of how many people will commit crimes or fall ill.
Transformation	The final type of change is 'transformation' and the Audit Commission suggests that this is the most relevant type of change for many public service sectors today. Transformation rather does what it says on the tin – it is organic, responding to changes in the external environment, but it is a step-change. It can be risky, so it needs clear leadership, but also involvement of all key stakeholders.

Good management techniques are important for a successful business and this is especially important during times of change. One has to be prepared for resistance to the proposed change and employ the management techniques and leadership skills to help dissipate that resistance. The key techniques to dealing with resistance to change are:

- Communication with and involvement of stakeholders
- Motivate staff
- Explain why the change is necessary and what benefits can be derived
- As with any 'sale' of a product or idea think on behalf of your staff or customers 'What's in it for me?' (WIIFM).

Another framework for examining change is through a Restorative Practices (RP)[55] approach. Costello and Wachtel (2009) offer an organisational change window:

	SUPPORT (encouragement, nurture)	
	TO	**WITH**
PRESSURE (mandate, requirement) HIGH	Managed strategic change Top-down imposed change	Connecting personal and professional growth Self-managed project
	NOT	**FOR**
	Cosmetic change (faddism) Avoiding/resisting change	Management consultants Best practice emulation
	LOW	HIGH

In an emerging context of 'big society' and localism, this RP change management framework and its emphasis on connecting with, rather than doing for or to people, has some resonance. Changes in the way that public services will be delivered, including social housing, especially along the lines of co-production and 'big society' as mooted by the coalition government, will mean that the change management process should itself be co-produced with staff and service users.

Individuals dealing with change

When looking at taking an organisation through a transformational change, it can be difficult to remember that every individual working for, and a customer of, that organisation will have issues around the change and they will have questions on how they will be affected. It is important to anticipate these issues as much as possible in the planning stage.

When first facing change, people's first instinct may tend to deny that it will ever happen and put their head in the sand – this is where a PEST analysis, clearly communicated, can help individuals to understand the rationale for change. The next step someone might take is to resist a change – this can manifest in sabotage of meetings, gossip on the office grapevine and passive aggression in just not implementing ideas; which is all in a bid to undermine the change and the leadership; however where handled well and allowed within limits, resistance can be healthy, empowering and positively inform the change. There are also more direct

---

55 With its roots in Restorative Justice which is largely a reactive approach to a wrongdoing, Restorative Practices take a proactive approach to building community capacity to deal with conflict and issues. See further www.iirp.org

acts of resistance, for example strikes in the workplace, or 'NIMBY' campaigns in communities where new developments are proposed. With the right information, reassurance and support though, it is possible to move people on from resistance to a period of reflection and contemplation of the alternatives being proposed. Individuals will do their own research to see how the changes will affect them; it is in the organisation's interest to assist with this research and to supply information that will help individuals get on board with the change process. The final step for an individual is either to commit to the changing organisation or to exit. Following denial, resistance and then exploration of options an individual will know whether they want to commit to the change or not.

Figure: 12.1: Individual responses to change

Broadly then, there are some key stages that housing organisations must plan for by understanding individuals' emotional responses to change:

Individual reaction to change	Organisational leadership response
Deny	*Wake up call – create a sense of urgency* Tell people that the change is really happening and provide a rationale (PEST)
Resist	*Allow resistance within limits* But manage it so that the process does not destroy morale across the whole organisation. →

Explore	*Maintain focus on the core objective* Project manage the change and keep people focused on the end goal with SMART targets.[56] Focus also needs to remain on the customer, houses still need to be repaired and tenancies managed during the process of change.
Commit	*Review, learn, act – monitor the change* Learn from the change process to see what might be done more effectively next time.

There are a number of writers on this subject of individual reaction to change, e.g. Fisher (2005) and Kübler-Ross (1969); these particularly examine the psychological responses to change and why we react in the way that we do.

Organisational change

Whilst it is important to look at change from a bottom-up perspective, e.g. individuals' reactions to change, there is also a need to examine the organisational perspective – to look at the organisation as a whole. The Burke-Litwin (1992) model does this by looking at what they refer to as 'culture' and 'climate' variables. Climate is easier for people in an organisation to see, it is the foreground – for example how they are managed, and how they work with colleagues. Culture is in the background and perhaps a little more ingrained, and therefore less visible – culture refers to the set of norms and beliefs – the invisible social hierarchy.

Burke-Litwin also debate the type of change organisations undergo, and they refer to transformational and transactional change. Remember the four types of change that the Audit Commission report (2001) discussed (incremental/step-change/directive/organic). Here, transactional change could relate to incremental change, and transformational change could relate to a step-change. Burke-Litwin claim that transformational change needs good leadership, and transactional change needs good management.

The change process

There are many models and frameworks that one can use to describe, analyse and manage the change process. It is probably best to keep things as simple as possible, and for this reason the model by John Kotter (1996) can be particularly helpful. Kotter refers to an eight-stage process of creating major change (p.21):

1. Establish a sense of urgency
2. Create a guiding coalition (not just an individual leader)
3. Develop a vision and strategy

---

56 Specific, Measurable, Attainable, Relevant, Time-bound.

4. Communicate the change vision
5. Empower broad-based action
6. Generate short-term wins
7. Consolidate gains and produce more change
8. Anchor the new approaches in the business culture.

There are a number of 'business' books and fables which fly off the shelves and deal with a range of management issues. One example is Spencer Johnson (1998) who wrote the bestselling change management book *Who Moved My Cheese?*[57] The story behind this change management fable is centred on two mice called Sniff and Scurry and two small men called Hem and Haw. They live in a maze and wake up one day to find that their usual supply of cheese is not in the usual place. The mice quickly move on, while the two men take different lengths of time to move on and adapt in order to find 'new' cheese; with one of the men learning more quickly to look out for change and adapt. The basic entertaining premise is:

Change Happens	They Keep Moving The Cheese
Anticipate Change	Get Ready For The Cheese To Move
Monitor Change	Smell The Cheese Often So You Know When It Is Getting Old
Adapt To Change Quickly	The Quicker You Let Go Of Old Cheese, The Sooner You Can Enjoy New Cheese
Change	Move With The Cheese
Enjoy Change!	Savor The Adventure And Enjoy The Taste Of New Cheese!
Be Ready To Change Quickly And Enjoy It Again & Again	They Keep Moving The Cheese

Kotter also produced a fable, *Our Iceberg is Melting*, with Rathberger (2005) grounded in his earlier eight-step model but using the story of penguins having to find a new home because their iceberg is melting. Another entertaining read for the train, but Kotter and Rathberger illustrate very well in this fable the difficulty with establishing a sense of urgency if everyone has their heads metaphorically buried in the sand. If most of the penguins do not believe their iceberg is melting, because they have not seen the crack below the surface of the water then the hero penguin of the day (Fred)[58] must convince them with evidence of the problem and must urge them to take urgent action. It is the role of housing leaders to make their staff and customers see the changing context around them and, like Fred the penguin, take the necessary steps to ensure a secure and sustainable future through managing the change.

---
57 If you like business fables then this is an enjoyable half hour read on the train, if not then the fundamental principles of change management can still be drawn from models like Kotter's.
58 Yes, really – Fred the penguin, it is worth a read!

Jeanie Daniel Duck (2001) in her book *The Change Monster* also refers to the need to help people to see the truth – or recognise and diagnose the condition – and this reflects Kotter's first step above. Daniel Duck's work is referenced quite widely in management studies and it is worth a read. She sets out changes in a business environment, but illustrates this with personal stories too.

Resistance to change

Resistance is not something one should aspire to avoid, it is a natural process of change and should be allowed to occur – however it should be managed and not ignored. It is interesting to examine in each case what the barriers to change are. A poll for government suggested the following barriers to change:

The most frequently encountered barriers	% of respondents citing the barrier
Inadequate leadership	51%
Competing resources	48%
Functional boundaries blocking action	44%
Lack of change management skills	42%
Middle management opposition	38%
Long IT lead times	35%
Inadequate communication	34%
Failure to address people issues	33%
Initiative fatigue	32%
Unrealistic timescales	31%

PWC/Mori survey, 1997, cited in DTLR, 2002, *Good Practice Briefing 2, Managing Change Results*, p.3.

More recently, Cumming (2010) for the 2020 Commission suggested (adapted from p.40) that there were some cultural characteristics of the public sector that impose barriers to transformation:

- *Culture, incentives and accountability*. The culture in the public sector tends to focus on risk avoidance as opposed to value creation
- *Credibility*. One way for politicians to make policy commitments credible is to enact legislation or purposely embed institutions to make reform difficult
- *Cost of exit*. The costs of changing institutional arrangements increase over time, so that when there is pressure to change, individuals and organisations seek first to adapt within the existing institutional framework rather than pay the price of exit[59]
- *Powerful actors favouring the status quo*. These powerful actors are usually rational agents seeking to set agendas to retain power in their own favour
- *Focus on the short term*. Transformation takes time and often energy goes into quick wins rather than transformation for the long term.

---

[59] Although this does not seem to be a barrier for the coalition government who are 'exiting' all manner of public bodies.

Whilst it is important to allow some resistance in order that staff can properly understand the situation and be empowered as part of the process; it is necessary to manage resistance and to eventually overcome persistent barriers to the change.

John Kotter and Leo Schlesinger (1979) (in Buchanan and Huczynski) identify six methods for overcoming resistance:

1. **Education and commitment**
   Managers should share their perceptions, knowledge and objectives with those affected by change.

2. **Participation and involvement**
   Those who might resist change should be involved in planning and implementing it. Collaboration can have the effect of reducing opposition and encouraging commitment.

3. **Facilitation and support**
   Employees may need help to overcome fears and anxieties about change and support in managing their response to change.

4. **Negotiation and agreement**
   It may be necessary to reach a mutually agreeable compromise. The nature of a particular change may have to be adjusted to meet the needs and interest of potential and powerful resistors. Kotter and Schlesinger view this as bargaining which may set unwelcome precedents for the future. However compromise and agreement is more likely to result in long-term implementation of the change, and the process of communication and negotiation may add good ideas from staff consultation which will enhance the change process.

5. **Manipulation and co-optation**
   This involves covert attempts to sidestep potential resistance. This step by Kotter and Schlesinger seems quite Machiavellian, playing to particular individual interests and key players. They also refer to co-optation, which involves giving key resistors direct access to the decision-making process, perhaps giving them well-paid, high-status management positions.[60]

6. **Implicit and explicit coercion**
   Management here abandons any attempt to achieve consensus. Fundamentally in this step, if a small number of staff in a housing organisation are still resisting and are actually causing trouble for their colleagues and customers, and if it is felt that resistance cannot be overcome soon then it may be the time for individual and organisation to part company.

---

60 It is possible that some Liberal Democrat supporters feel that their party was co-opted by the Conservatives in the 2010 election result decision-making process. It can be quite effective having a potential member of the 'opposition' as Deputy PM or Chief Secretary to the Treasury – it is more difficult to object to issues once you've been 'co-opted'.

As with any of the models discussed in this chapter, steps can be used in isolation, or in conjunction, depending on the situation. Organisations should always consider their own situation and adapt a framework rather than adopt it wholesale and without critical reflection on whether it suits their needs.

Another expert in the field (Fons Trompenaars, 2004) has suggested a series of lessons learnt in examining corporate change that can help get support for the change and can decrease resistance (pp.218-219):

- Know where you start from: study the existing culture and its strengths/weaknesses
- Use the reconciling corporate culture concept to explain that change is a process of 'continuity through renewal'
- Involve people in the process: discuss real dilemmas, challenges and hindrances
- Delegate responsibility and empower people to implement concrete change
- Over-communication is better than under-communication in a corporate change process
- Define project roles: sponsors, 'culture change' agents, facilitators
- Make the corporate culture change process part of the existing organisational programs
- Work on profound change (at the level of basic assumptions and core values) and on making organisational and behavioural changes to bring the desired culture to life
- Make sure that high-level executives walk the talk as well
- A meaningful set of corporate values is a mix of existing core values and new, aspirational values
- Culture change is about managing tension:
  - between old and new, change and continuity
  - between global and local
  - between results focus and people focus.

During analysis of the WIMBY! Project in Hoogvliet in the Netherlands, a question on breaking down opposition to change was asked of the Alderman of Urban Development at the time, and the answer suggested:

Take the space you are given. Take on more responsibilities. Assume authority and get things done. Commit to a goal. Make use of the possibilities you have. Many people simply don't feel like taking action. You can choose for the easy way out: if anything goes wrong blame someone else. That's what most administrators do and they reach their retirement doing it. But if you really want something, you have to keep dragging them along (Provoost (Ed.) 2007, p.98).

Stakeholders and change

As part of managing a programme of change, it is important to identify the key stakeholders in any situation:

- Draw up a list of stakeholders affected by the changes proposed
- Establish what each will gain or lose if the change goes ahead
- Use the potential benefits to strengthen support for the proposals
- Find ways to address the concerns of those who feel they will lose out, by altering the nature of the changes proposed, perhaps, or offering to reduce losses in other ways.

Gerard Egan (1994) (in Buchanan and Huczynski) identifies nine types of stakeholder:

1. Your *partners* are those who support your agenda
2. Your *allies* are those who will support you, given encouragement
3. Your *fellow travellers* are passive supporters, who may be committed to the agenda but not to you personally
4. The *fencesitters* are those whose allegiances are not clear
5. *Loose cannons* are dangerous because they can vote against agendas in which they have no direct interest
6. Your *opponents* are players who oppose your agenda but not you personally
7. Your *adversaries* are players who oppose both you and your agenda
8. *Bedfellows* are those who support the agenda but may not know or trust you
9. The *voiceless* are stakeholders who will be affected by the agenda but have little power to promote or oppose and who lack advocates.

Egan argues that different stakeholders must be managed differently. Partners and allies need to be encouraged, to be 'kept on side'. Opponents need to be converted. Adversaries have to be discredited and marginalised. Egan suggests that the needs of 'the voiceless' should be addressed in case they are 'recruited' by adversaries and used against the change agenda.

Force field analysis

This is an approach which has already been considered in the context of managing change in housing organisations by Holder *et al.* (1998). This type of analysis basically requires you to consider carefully what the drivers for change are and where the resistors to change might be. There are varying degrees of complexity that can be added to Force Field and it is probably worth including a grade for each factor, as below. We discussed earlier that drivers for change might be change agents, and indeed leaders who motivate people to change. We also considered a few ideas around resistance and barriers to change. These methods may be worth reconsidering when completing a force field analysis. In fact, undertaking a Force Field analysis is very similar in approach (particularly when ranking factors) to a health and safety assessment, where you consider all the likely events that may possibly occur and then rank them according to how probable it is that each scenario might take place, and also rank the impact on the individual and the organisation should such a situation occur. See Figure 12.2.

Figure 12.2: Force field analysis

Force field analysis For a potential scenario where a housing organisation wants to revise neighbourhood management service, requiring changes to team structure, staffing arrangements and workload			
Forces assisting	**Rank/strength**		**Forces resisting**
Urgent need for efficiencies to be made whilst retaining good quality service	5	3	Existing staff across a number of teams in the service are nervous about their individual jobs
Customer complaints and Audit Commission inspection report show that having one neighbourhood manager for an area is preference of customer	3	4	Rent arrears team and ASB team take pride in their specialist role and do not want generic patch roles
New Chief Executive has outlined his vision to all staff in the organisation, and has booked a meeting with teams involved in neighbourhood management service next week	4	4	Gossip in the office that the meeting is to announce redundancies – defensive staff and low morale in some areas
A small amount of money available to train staff or send them on courses to refresh their skills	2	3	The computer system is old and will not cope with reporting on new neighbourhood management patches; there is no money for new software

This scenario is fictitious, but represents some of the changes that organisations are thinking about. In individual organisations and particular scenarios there will be good information to rank the strength of each factor. In the example above, rank is scored out of 5 – and the idea of this is to see where urgent priorities lie and where key assets to the change process are. If a strong resisting factor can be managed quickly from the start, and if weak forces assisting can be bolstered then, in theory, a change process should be a little smoother.

Conflict management and change

As suggested earlier, resistance should be allowed (albeit managed) in the change process. From resistance comes empowerment, and from empowerment come good ideas and commitment. However, there may be situations where resistance turns into open conflict; and this must be dealt with firmly and effectively. Conflict mapping (in addition to Force Field analysis) can help identify priorities and key allies. Some work was undertaken, in research for the Joseph Rowntree Foundation, on conflict mapping a situation arising out of proposals for a new Gypsy and Traveller site. Diagrammatically showing where tensions and strengths in relationships lay can be advantageous in managing conflict and change (see further Richardson, 2007).

Leadership – change should be positive!

The Audit Commission (2001) suggest that there are four key dimensions needed to lead change:

- *Navigate* (set direction and prioritise, co-ordinate, and set targets)
- *Inspire* (develop vision, provide role models, coach, counsel, sponsor)
- *Mobilise* (sell the vision to target communities, listen and respond, proactively manage stakeholders)
- *Enable* (allocate adequate resources and skills, decide and delegate).

Moss-Kanter (1988) talked about change being a necessary and positive context for encouraging companies to be innovative. She outlined three sets of skills needed to manage effectively in such 'high innovation' and changing organisations:

1. Power skills – persuading others to invest information, support and resources in new initiatives
2. Ability to manage the problems associated with the greater use of teams and employee participation
3. Understanding how change is designed and constructed in an organisation – how the micro-changes introduced by the individual relate to the macro-changes or strategic reorientations.

(Moss-Kanter, 1988, adapted pp.35-36)

Leading transformative change through valuing staff in Solihull Community Housing

- Vision and values are promoted at staff conferences
- CEO 'lunch-bag briefings' with staff to talk over what is happening with the business and make staff feel valued and informed
- Incentive schemes like the 'Shining Star' for going the extra mile for customers, makes staff feel valued and more likely to adapt to changes which will benefit the customer and the organisation
- Celebrating diversity, e.g. the Diwali event in November 2007 and the Caribbean event in January 2009
- Staff are encouraged to share good practice and enter their projects and initiatives into awards.

Moss-Kanter also discusses the 'architecture of change' and she discusses the link between the external context for change, meaning ascribed to that context, and the actual change itself. The culture of the organisation will affect the meanings put on the change process – for example a segmentalist (controlled/structured) organisation will be restricting in the way it allows change to happen. She states that:

> *Organizations may not respond to environments so much as 'enact' them – create them by the choice to selectively define certain things as important...a company with a diverse group in the 'dominant coalition' at the top – more fields and functions represented, more diversity in sex, race and culture – is more likely to pick up on more external cues...* (p.281).

And she outlines 'distortions' in the process of change:

- Individuals disappear into collectives
- Conflicts disappear into consensus
- Equally plausible alternatives disappear into obvious choices
- Accidents, uncertainties and muddle-headed confusions disappear into clear-sighted strategies
- Multiple events disappear into single thematic events
- The fragility of changes (that exist alongside the residues of the old system) disappear into images of solidity and full actuality.

(Adapted pp.284-287)

In line with other models (such as Kotter) Moss-Kanter suggests that 'announcing change' is a power move used by some leaders in order to construct positive change and to get others to ascribe to it. Overall she suggests that the essence of the change process is as follows:

> *Organizational change consists in part of a series of emerging constructions of reality, including revision of the past, to correspond with the requisites of new players and new demands* (Moss-Kanter, 1988, p.287).

Finally, from Moss-Kanter's *Change Masters* text there is an example of the importance of recognising how successful initiatives came about. She tells the 'Roast Pig' story (p.302):

> *I call this the 'Roast Pig' problem after Charles Lamb's classic 1822 essay 'A Dissertation on Roast Pig', a satirical account of how the art of roasting was discovered in a Chinese village that did not cook its food. A mischievous child accidentally set fire to a house with a pig inside, and the villagers poking around in the embers discovered a new delicacy. This eventually led to a rash of house fires. The moral of the story is: when you do not understand how the pig gets cooked, you have to burn a whole house down every time you want a roast-pork dinner.*

Roll the Dice

For a tongue-in-cheek look at change management in the social housing sector, have a go at the 'snakes and ladders' game on the next page.

Conclusion

Change is always on the horizon, and sometimes organisations can still be reeling from the last transformation of the business, when the next big idea is suggested, or when events overtake and immediate change is thrust on the business. This chapter has aimed to give a flavour of the myriad approaches that can help leaders manage change in housing organisations; but the messages are consistent with other areas of this book – communication is key and good information is vital to success.

References and further reading

Audit Commission (2001) *Change Here! – Managing Change to Improve Local Services*. London: Audit Commission.

Audit Commission (2007): *Seeing the Light – Innovation in the Public Sector*. London: Audit Commission.

Beer, M., Eisenstat, R. A., and Spector, B. (1990): 'Why Change Programs Don't Produce Change', *Harvard Business Review*, 68(6), pp.158-166.

Boddy, D. and Paton, R. (1998) *Management, an introduction*. London: Prentice Hall.

Buchanan, D. and Huczynski, A. (2003) *Organisational Behaviour: An Introductory Text*. London: Prentice Hall.

Burke, W. and Litwin, G. (1992) 'A Causal Model of Organizational Performance and Change' in W. Burke, D. Lake and J. Paine (1992) *Organization Change: A Comprehensive Reader*. London: Jossey Bass Wiley.

Cameron, E. and Green, M. (2009) *Making Sense of Change Management* (2nd ed.). London: Kogan Page.

Catterick, P. (1995) *Business Planning for Housing*. Coventry: CIH and HSA.

CIH (2007) 'Spotlight on Customer Insight', *Housing Spotlight* 22, pp.2-3.

Cole, G.A. (1996) *Management Theory and Practice*. London: Continuum.

Costello, B., Wachtel, J. and Wachtel, T. (2009) *The Restorative Practices Handbook*. Pennsylvania: International Institute of Restorative Practices.

Cumming, L. (2010) *2020 Vision: A far-sighted approach to transforming public services*. London: 2020 Public Services Trust.

Daniel Duck, J. (2001) *The Change Monster: the human forces that fuel or foil corporate transformation and change*. New York: Three Rivers Press.

CHANGE MANAGEMENT

Figure 12.3: Snakes and ladders of change management

FINISH HERE 11. You've done it – the service is more efficient, the majority of staff and customers are happy and this is reflected in your PIs and in the budget. *Give your organisation a gold star!*	10. Embed the change into the climate and culture of the whole organisation and keep the process under review.	Brilliant – the Chair of the Board updates on progress and consolidates the gains for the organisation and for customers. Prizes and commendations awarded to staff who helped 'make it happen'.	9. Ensure you have empowered staff to take action and decisions where necessary to keep momentum for the change.	'Computer says no' – the IT system won't allow a change in reporting that you want. The customer advisors say 'we'd have told you this if you asked us at the beginning'!
7. Through a number of communication channels (web/meetings) publicise quick wins. Tell staff and customers that some targets have already been met and some improvements to service have been achieved.	What a muddle – different people are working to different aims and people have lost focus!	8. Manage resistance – don't deny it but help individuals to see the WIIFM of the change. Listen to views and take comments on board as appropriate.	Oops – word on the grapevine is there will be mass redundancies as a result of the change. Low morale and commitment to change programme.	5. Commit resources (if not money then at least time and expertise) to seminars/training/counselling for staff to communicate the change.
Great – one of the tenant representatives on the Board has given a speech to tenants and staff at the annual family fun day and said how much the change is needed and how it will benefit tenants and the organisation alike.	6. Keep communicating the vision and strategy – remind people why change is necessary.	Front page news – the local paper has run a story that services to tenants will be reduced and that the housing organisation is short of money.	Oh good – the change champions in each department and the online social networks have responded quickly and are spreading the real message of the change, rather than the rumours.	4. Make sure customers and board members/councillors are kept aware of progress. Run through the communications strategy with them – try to avoid 'rogue' messages in the media from individuals.
1. Communicate the change to the organisation, all stakeholders and customers – say clearly what the rationale is and why it needs to happen now. A meeting for all staff with the Chief Executive and directors taking the lead.	Oh dear – some members of staff say they saw the organisation try this 20 years ago – it didn't work then and it'll never work now.	2. Create a team of leaders and champions for the change – not just at director level, but involve enthusiastic staff throughout the organisation.	Wow – others think the service has needed a revamp for a while and they are twittering the Chief Executive with proposals and solutions.	3. Use a force field analysis to plot key facilitators and barriers to the change; or even try applying a seven Ps marketing mix and think of the change as a product you need to 'sell'.
START HERE Change is imminent; efficiencies are needed in the housing management service.				

Snakes and ladders graphics: VladStameny/istockphoto

Deming, W.E. (1986) *Out of the Crisis*. Massachusetts: MIT.

DTLR (2002) *Good Practice Briefing 2, Managing Change Results*. London: DTLR.

Falletta, S. (2005) *Organizational Diagnostic Models: Review & Synthesis*. Available at http://www.leadersphere.com/img/OrgmodelsR2009.pdf (accessed 15.2.08).

Fisher, J. (2005) 'A Time for Change?', *Human Resource Development International*, 8(2), pp.257-263.

Greenfield, A. (2008) *The 5 Forces of Change*. Cirencester: Management Books 2000.

Herzberg, F. (1959) *The Motivation to Work*. New York: Transaction Publishers.

Holder, A., McQuillan, W., Fitzgeorge-Butler, A. and Williams, P. (1998) *Surviving or Thriving? Managing change in housing organisations*. Coventry: CIH.

Hudson, M. (1999) *Managing Without Profit*. London: Penguin.

Johnson, S. (1998) *Who Moved My Cheese?* London: Random House.

Kotter, J. (1996) *Leading Change*. Boston: Harvard Business School Press.

Kotter, J. and Rathberger, H. (2006) *Our Iceberg is Melting, changing and succeeding under any conditions*. London: Macmillan.

Kübler-Ross, E. (1969) *On Death and Dying*. London: Routledge.

Moss-Kanter, R. (1988) *Change Masters*. London: Jossey Bass Wiley.

ODPM/DTLR (2002) *Good Practice Briefing Note Number 2, Managing Change Results*. London: ODPM.

Pettigrew, A., Ferlie, E. and McKee, L. (1992) *Shaping Strategic Change*. London: Sage.

Provoost, M. (Ed.) (2007) *WIMBY! Hoogvliet future, past and present of a new town, or: The Big Wimby Book*. Rotterdam: Nai Publishers.

Richardson, J. (2000) *Quality and Customer Focus – Good Practice Briefing*. Coventry: Chartered Institute of Housing.

Richardson, J. (2007) *Providing Gypsy and Traveller Sites: Contentious Spaces*. Coventry: CIH for the Joseph Rowntree Foundation.

Richardson, J. (Ed.) (2010) *From Recession to Renewal: the impact of the financial crisis on local government and public services*. Bristol: Policy Press.

Seddon, J. (2008) *Systems Thinking in the Public Sector, the failure of the reform regime…and a manifesto for a better way*. Axminster: Triarchy Press.

Strebel, P. (1996) 'Why do Employees Resist Change?', *Harvard Business Review*, May-June 1996, pp.86-92.

Trompenaar, F. and Prud'homme, P. (2004) *Managing Change across Corporate Cultures*. Chichester: Capstone Publishing.

PART THREE

CONCLUSIONS

CHAPTER 13:
Conclusions and next steps

Joanna Richardson

Introduction

This book has sought to underline the importance of focusing on the customer. There have been debates throughout, but particularly in chapter 1, on the concept of customer; and in spite of all challenges to its use – this book has unashamedly urged the reader to embrace a customer focus/ marketing approach to delivering social housing services. Of course the constraints to 'exit' and also even 'voice' in the sector have been discussed and there are real consequences. However, rather than deliberating on whether we really should use one term or another, the authors in this book have suggested ways forward in actually delivering a customer-focused housing service.

The case for a customer focus in social housing

A customer-focus, or marketing, approach is not just icing on the cake – it is a vital ingredient in the proper provision of social housing services. There are two key cases, particularly imperative in the current financial climate, to support a rationale for a customer focus:

1. Business efficiency case
2. Social needs case.

Business case

If an organisation knows who its customers are and what services they need, then it can target resources much more efficiently. In demonstrating its efficiency and good reputation it can attract better streams of revenue.

There have been innovative suggestions from social landlords for the future financing of housing organisations. Hyde Group announced plans to enter the bond market after being given an Aa2 rating; their hope was to raise £200 million in this way. Another housing association – London and Quadrant – had already made £300 million in a bond deal (*Inside Housing*, 2010). Unlocking innovative funding streams though depends on the reputation of an organisation, indeed a sector, to demonstrate its ability to deliver. For sceptics of customer focus and marketing approaches – there is a bottom line rationale too.

Social case

More efficient and better housing service delivery can make a difference to community cohesion too; some examples were seen in chapter 9 on social marketing. Particularly following a recession, there is a need for strong public services and social housing providers are in a good place to act as a hub for many of the most fundamental needs that people have.

In *The Cluetrain Manifesto* (2009) Levine *et al.* tell us that 'markets are conversations'. If we see what we do in the social housing sector as part of conversation with our tenants and other customers, then engaging a marketing approach is not such a strange concept.

Challenges to applying a customer focus

Not all customers have the skills necessary to engage with customer models such as choice-based lettings for example (e.g. computer skills, literacy and knowledge of services and support that is available in the area), and they will need the support and advice of public agencies, including social housing providers, to help access services. It should not be thought, though, that a customer focus precludes those with additional support needs; indeed this approach must enable and empower people. The approach has been used in health and social care services where users have been provided with personalised services and they have been able to utilise individual budgets.

In a volatile environment, with financial and regulatory pressures, a customer focus can help providers to market themselves, avoid costly mistakes and take opportunities to grow but it does not provide a magic bullet. It can help towards achieving greater diversity and sustainability and addressing the impact of residualisation and social exclusion but it does not necessarily offer solutions. Where greater tenure mix and social mix form part of the outcome being sought, with for example the development of 'intermediate' or 'bridging' areas to facilitate cohesion of particular communities, there is a need to take a bottom-up approach that will be capable of increasing positive social interaction. Engaging with communities in the development of plans for their future is the key to building social sustainability and creating links at neighbourhood level which can garner the necessary support for change and help build social capital in deprived communities and amongst vulnerable service users.

Therefore, rather than the challenges to 'customer focus' preventing us from taking this approach – they do instead provide a rationale for applying such a focus. If we can use a marketing approach to find out who the most vulnerable people in society are, how they are affected by the current economic climate, what services they might need and when – surely we are better equipped to deliver housing services to those in most need, than if we take a reactive stance and assume who our tenants are and that we are already delivering what is needed without asking first?

Impact of political context: likelihood for empowerment of customers?

The political rhetoric from the coalition government is one of empowering citizens, consumers and tenants by devolving power once held by central government and the regions, to a local level. Parvin (2009) warns quite presciently that decentralising power to communities can fail minority groups. This is an argument that I also made in relation to vulnerable groups following the financial crisis (see further Richardson, 2010) that certain groups who are not 'crowd-pleasers' will lose out in service provision and support. One such example is provision of accommodation for Gypsies and Travellers which would certainly face 'crowd-cutting' in more local debates on where resources should be spent. Government wish us all to engage in the 'big society' and they are encouraging Local Enterprise Partnerships to be piloted in some areas to show that local councils, citizens and voluntary agencies can work together to provide services efficiently. In addition to the concern raised by Parvin (2009) that some communities will lose out, there is also the question of how well partnerships and participation work together (Lowndes and Sullivan, 2004).

Key themes, conclusions and recommendations

Each of the chapters has looked at specific issues. In part one of the book, the first three chapters provided the context for examining housing and the customer, including the current political, economic and regulatory environment. Policies and issues were the focus of part two, and the topics included an examination of who the customer is, what they want, what customer satisfaction might look like and how Customer Insight can be achieved. Chapters in part two also examined the importance of brand, advertising, positioning, communications and change management, as well as the merits of social marketing.

The label of 'customer' was examined right at the start of the book in the context of 'tenant', 'consumer' and 'citizen'. Whilst there are issues and challenges with the use of the term customer, the aim of this book has been to show that the application of a customer-focused, or marketing, approach to housing service delivery can result in increased satisfaction and more efficient processes due to a better understanding of who would like to use our services and what exactly they need and want from us. The diversity of the customer base is apparent and it is important to remember the 'diversity within diversity' of housing customers – a 'one size fits all' approach is never going to be appropriate.

Establishing what customers want is an important aspect of a marketing approach for organisations. However, looking at this issue across the sector, and in spite of some of the challenges, choice is clearly something that customers want from their public service provider. How this will stack up following the announcements by the coalition government in 2010 regarding benefit reform, a review of 'lifetime' social tenancies and a sweeping change in the outlook for the regulatory furniture of the sector, remains to be seen. Whilst the detailed regulatory, policy-making and performance management frameworks underpinning customer voice (especially in England) face a period of uncertainty, it is clear that the principles are firmly embedded in the broader debates on, for example, localism, 'big society', co-production and personalisation and there will be continuing moves towards joined-up services for customers between organisations and sectors.

A marketing approach with its seven Ps marketing mix, branding strategies and advertising campaigns can provoke a hostile reaction from traditionalists in the sector. However, look beyond the marketing speak – as we have attempted to do in the book – and you will see a commonsense approach to finding out who needs what from our sector and a way of getting a message out – including a social marketing message – which may have benefits beyond the individual customer or housing provider to the community.

Customer voice has become one of the crucial issues for the social housing sector and yet some of the mechanisms for voice (such as the NTV) are under threat or have already had funding cut. The impact of the financial crisis on the ability of more vulnerable members of society (Richardson, 2010) to engage with service providers puts even more responsibility on the part of social housing organisations to focus on the customer – find out who they are and what they need. There are a number of big challenges for housing organisations in responding to the customer voice agenda. These include ensuring that principles and practice are applied to all of our customers – e.g. private tenants and owner-occupiers as well as social housing tenants. There are useful lessons that can be learnt from the Netherlands on customer voice and the policy-making and performance management system (including choice-based lettings of course!).

Quality of housing services is important and there are three key dimensions – product, process and perception of the organisation. The consequences of customer (dis)satisfaction will take one of three forms – loyalty, voice or exit. Housing organisations should reward loyal customers, encourage voice and analyse exit cases. Collecting robust information on customer satisfaction is a crucial task. The framework for measuring satisfaction may well change, but the need from a customer-focus and marketing approach, to understand tenants/customers' views of your service/brand is still important.

Communication is at the heart of a customer focus. It is the only way of hearing what customers want and of getting a message understood by tenants or staff. There is a lot of change following a recession and a new government, and communicating this change clearly and calmly can help ease the transition.

Complacency about the customer

In the introduction to this book I suggested that housing organisations collectively in the past had been guilty of taking advantage of a long-term (and sometimes difficult to exit) relationship with tenants. We have seen throughout this book a number of examples which show that the sector is no longer doing this and that for a range of reasons (higher satisfaction, greater efficiency) organisations are finding out who their customers are, what they want and how that can best be delivered.

Whilst some housing organisations have been at the forefront of innovation in Customer Insight and good service delivery, others have been led by a regulatory framework which asks housing and other public service providers to be mindful of customers and to focus on satisfaction. The regulatory framework is changing and the coalition government at the centre is focusing on less regulation and more of a DIY approach, largely through its idea of the 'big society'. The dangers of this have been outlined throughout the book, particularly the impact on vulnerable communities of reduction in vital public services. Some housing and support services may have to be cut altogether to make savings, but there is also a concern that the quality of overall services may reduce in the absence of regulation which focuses on customer satisfaction as a key driver.

There are examples across Europe of different regulatory regimes, and there will be many who say that top-down regulation does not work in the customer's best interests anyway. For example, in the Netherlands there is the system of collective self-regulation based on ten criteria which are similar to KLOEs that have been used in England, many of which have a customer focus. This is an industry-led initiative, as would any similar system that could be considered in England. The National Housing Federation (NHF) in its response to the TSA Review set out by housing minister Grant Shapps, underlined the need for a system of regulation which continued to inspire the confidence of lenders and they reiterated the importance of keeping separate the functions of investment and regulation. Whether a model such as the one from the Netherlands could work for the future of regulation in England, or whether it sets the customer-focus agenda back again by not inspecting customer satisfaction, or perhaps splitting regulatory functions between tenure again (rather than having one regulator regardless of who your social housing landlord is – LA or HA) will remain to be seen. The government should be advised though that not requiring social housing providers to focus on the customer is long-term loss for short-term gain.

Next steps

Public services and government are rapidly changing in light of a quick moving political and economic climate. The effects of smaller budgets and potentially larger numbers of people in need mean that housing organisations must focus on the customer – understand their diverse needs and find innovative ways of doing more with less and continuing to support the most vulnerable in society whilst maintaining a high degree of quality and professionalism.

References and Further Reading

Beuret, K. and Hall, R. (1998) *Marketing in Local Government*. London: Financial Times Management.

Clarke, J., Newman, J., Smith, N., Vidler, E. and Westmarland, L. (2007) *Creating Citizen-Consumers, Changing Publics and Changing Public Services*. London: Sage.

Cole, I., Kane, S. and Robinson, D. (1999) *Changing Demand, Changing Neighbourhoods: The Response of Social Landlords*. Sheffield: Centre for Regional Economic and Social Research.

Cole, G.A. (1996) *Management Theory and Practice*. London: Continuum.

Communities and Local Government (2008) *Communities in control: real people, real power*. White Paper. London: CLG.

DETR (2000) *Quality and Choice: A Decent Home for All*. Housing Green Paper. London: DETR.

Feinstein, L., Lupton, R., Hammond, C., Mujtaba, T., Salter, E. and Dorhaindo, A. (2008) *The public value of social housing: a longitudinal analysis of the relationship between housing and life chances*. London: The Smith Institute.

Flint, J. (2004) 'The Responsible Tenant: Housing Governance and the Politics of Behaviour', *Housing Studies*, Vol. 19, No. 6, pp.893-909.

Flynn, N. (2007) *Public Sector Management* (5th ed.). London: Sage.

Inside Housing (2010) 'Hyde sets its sights on £200m bond deal' *Inside Housing*, 5th February, p.2.

Le Grand, J. (2007) *The Other Invisible Hand, delivering public services through choice and competition*. New Jersey: Princeton University Press.

Lee, P. and Murie, A. (1999) 'Spatial and Social divisions within British Cities: Beyond Residualisation', *Housing Studies,* Vol. 14, No. 5.

Levine, R., Locke, C., Searls, D. and Weinberger, D. (2009) *The Cluetrain Manifesto* (2nd ed.). New York: Basic Books.

Lowndes, V. and Sullivan, H. (2004) 'Like a Horse and Carriage or a Fish on a Bicycle: How Well do Local Partnerships and Public Participation go Together?' *Local Government Studies*, 30(1), pp.51-73.

Mills, N. (2009) 'The Consumer and Social Housing' in Simmons, R, Powell, M and Greener, I (Eds.) (2009) *The Consumer in public services, choice, values and difference.* Bristol: Policy Press.

National Housing Federation (2010) *Submission to the Review of the Tenant Services Authority.* London: NFA.

Needham, C. (2006) 'Customer Care and the Public Service Ethos', *Public Administration*, 84(4), pp.845-860.

Newman, J. and Clarke, J. (2009) *Publics, Politics & Power.* London: Sage.

Parvin, P. (2009) 'Against Localism: Does Decentralising Power to Communities Fail Minorities?, *The Political Quarterly*, 80(3), pp.351-360.

Passmore, J. and Fergusson, S. (1994) *Customer Service in a Competitive Environment*, Coventry: Chartered Institute of Housing.

Richardson, J. (2010) (Ed.) *From Recession to Renewal: the impact of the financial crisis on public services and local government.* Bristol: Policy Press.

Sheaff, R. (2002) *Responsive Healthcare: Marketing for a public service* (chapter 2). Buckingham: Open University Press.

Shelter (2008) *Homes for the future, a new analysis of housing need and demand in England.* London: Shelter.

Shelter (2009) *Ground Breaking, New ideas on housing delivery.* London: Shelter.

Simmons, R., Powell, M. and Greener, I. (Eds.) (2009) *The Consumer in public services, choice, values and difference.* Bristol: Policy Press.

Walker, R. (2000) 'The changing management of social housing: The impact of externalisation and managerialism', *Housing Studies,* 15(2), pp.281-300.

Index

A

Accord Group, 169-70
Accountability, 8, 34, 68, 87, 102, 163, 213
ACORN, 12, 53, 113, 115
Advertising, 9, 13, 33, 38, 42, 112, 122, 128, 133, 151, 152, 153, 158, 182, 185-204, 226, 227
Affinity Sutton, ii, vii, 121, 130
Affordability, 42, 62, 73, 78, 80
Age, 22, 26, 29, 35, 41, 51, 52, 53, 54, 55, 58-9
AIDA model, 198
Allocations, 21, 22, 23, 24, 29, 75, 76, 77, 88, 109, 186
Apple, 129, 133, 135
Arnstein's ladder, 166-7
Ashfield Homes, 94
Aspirations, 33, 6, 9, 11, 12, 13, 50, 52, 55, 59, 61-2, 68, 69, 71-4, 84, 94, 101, 102, 108, 110, 112, 150, 156, 162, 215
Aspire Housing, 94
Asylum seekers, 55-6
Attitudes, 7, 41, 53, 69-95, 110, 126, 141, 142, 146, 150, 152, 155, 156
Attractiveness, 63, 84
Audit Commission, 75, 83, 90, 93, 99, 207-8, 211, 217, 218

B

Behaviour, 8, 12-13, 22, 33, 37, 41, 42, 52, 75, 91, 92, 94, 109, 113, 117-9, 126, 140, 141, 142, 145-159, 163, 170, 180, 185, 194, 215
Benefits, 6, 13, 22, 25, 29, 32, 34, 35, 36, 38, 39, 63, 70, 72, 73, 81, 84, 116, 118, 132, 134, 148, 156, 186, 187, 191, 194, 200, 208, 216, 227
'Big society', 10, 16, 17, 18, 19, 26, 29, 35, 91, 102, 158, 167, 209, 226, 227, 228
Brand, 9, 12, 25, 33, 45, 69, 101, 111, 125-143, 163, 167, 168, 182, 187, 189, 192, 195, 197, 201, 203, 226, 227
Brighton & Hove Council, 158

Business case, 3, 45, 106, 224
Business plan, 56, 63, 136, 139, 187, 189

C

Campaigns, 13, 110, 137, 139, 140, 145, 146, 147, 148, 150, 152-4, 158, 161, 167, 169-70, 171, 174, 181, 182, 183, 185-204, 210, 227
Cave review, 10, 17, 18
Change, 206-223
Change 4 Life, 152
Channels, 42, 45, 50, 59, 60, 136-7, 148, 169, 172, 173-7, 179, 189, 192, 197, 201, 202, 203, 204, 221
Chartered Institute of Marketing, 33, 107, 185
Choice, 4, 6, 11, 16, 18, 21, 24, 26, 29, 36, 38-9, 45, 60-63, 68-84, 88, 89, 96, 106, 109, 111, 112, 119, 128, 131, 151, 152, 156, 157, 161, 173, 186, 219, 226
Citizen, 4, 6-9, 17, 26, 34-7, 61, 63, 68, 87, 88, 89, 91, 101, 102, 115, 127, 140, 156, 157, 166, 177, 186, 226
City decay, 141
Cluetrain, 175, 225
Coalition government, 5, 10, 16, 17, 19, 21, 23, 27, 29, 34, 35, 44, 51, 54, 58, 78, 88, 90, 91, 102, 109, 153, 156, 158, 187, 206, 209, 226, 227, 228
Cognitive dissonance, 147, 152
Collaboration, 16, 26, 32, 139, 214
Communications, 9, 13, 18, 26, 119, 120, 122, 128, 137-9, 161-183, 186, 192, 221, 226
Communities and Local Government, 17, 56, 60, 90, 91, 158
Community cohesion, 9, 53, 56, 91, 112, 116, 120, 225
Competition, 27, 32, 83, 87, 131, 136, 139, 147, 158, 169, 178, 190, 193, 196, 203
Complaints, 18, 20, 22, 87, 88, 89, 90, 94, 100, 101, 113, 117, 174, 180, 187, 188, 191, 217

Comprehensive spending review, 5, 18, 23, 50
Conflict management, 217
Connexions, 158
Consistency, 8, 114, 151
Co-production, 11, 16, 27, 29, 88, 102, 146, 209
Co-regulation, 18
Cost, 20, 21, 22, 23, 26, 27, 36, 37, 39, 41, 53, 60, 62, 69, 77, 78, 81, 84, 87, 88, 89, 92, 93, 97, 100, 101, 111, 120, 131, 134, 143, 147-8, 158, 167, 182, 187, 189, 190, 204, 213, 225
Creative brief, 138, 196-7
Crowd-sourcing, 181
Croydon Total Place, 143
Culture, 13, 18, 34, 36, 55, 57, 69, 70, 101, 126, 130, 142, 148, 211-3, 215, 219, 221
Customer Insight, 9, 12, 41, 52, 57, 62, 94, 112, 115, 117, 121, 122, 139, 147, 148, 150, 168, 178, 226, 228
Customer journey mapping, 99, 120
Customer Relationship Management, 12, 41, 53, 105, 106
Customer service ethos, 7
Cuts, 6, 19, 21, 23, 25, 26, 29, 84, 88, 98, 102, 131, 139, 161, 183, 194, 206, 207

D
Data, 11, 12, 17, 25, 28, 51, 52, 57, 59, 72, 73, 90-100, 105, 107-9, 112-18, 121, 122, 146, 150, 168, 172-3, 175, 191, 193, 197, 200
Decision-making process, 37, 38, 100, 109-12, 214
Decision-making unit, 40
Demands and aspirations, 2, 3, 5, 6, 11, 12, 22, 23, 26, 27, 29, 39, 50, 55, 62, 89, 95, 96, 110, 113, 128, 131, 163, 167, 170, 185, 186, 187, 191, 200, 219
Demographics, 41, 52, 53, 117
Derbyshire Dales District Council, 155
Design, 18, 22, 23, 27, 29, 40, 43, 44, 87-9, 93, 94, 96, 99, 100, 102, 114, 126, 133, 135, 158, 169, 170, 175, 181, 203, 218

Digital exclusion, 59-60
Disability, 51, 53, 54, 59, 121
Diversification, 12, 63, 134
Diversity, 2, 4, 6, 9, 10, 11, 12, 19, 35, 45, 50, 54-5, 130, 178, 207, 218, 219, 225, 226

E
East Thames Group, 117
EasyBorough model, 35
Economic status, 51
Economy, 3, 4, 70, 150, 183
Efficiency, 3, 4, 6, 23, 32, 44, 45, 99, 114, 120, 121, 143, 177, 187, 207, 224, 228
Empowerment, 3, 4, 16, 18, 19, 24, 26, 56, 61, 79, 88, 109, 112, 115, 120, 161, 186, 217, 226
Equality, 53, 54, 56, 117
Ethnicity, 11, 35, 50-55, 109
Evaluation, 23, 37, 38, 61, 110-111, 177
Exit, 11, 18, 25, 28, 52, 62, 63, 87, 89, 141, 161, 210, 213, 224, 227, 228
Expectation, 11, 12, 22, 23, 37, 42, 61, 62, 63, 69, 75, 76, 80, 88, 96, 97, 101, 102, 109, 111, 117, 118, 120, 122

F
Fairness, 68, 95
Force-field analysis, 221, 217
Ford Retail, 119
Friendship Care & Housing, 199
Fundacion Secretariado Gitano, 153-4

G
Generational renter, 52
Governance, 3, 7, 8, 9, 20, 34, 129, 152, 173
Gypsies and Travellers, 13, 19, 51, 56-8, 109, 153-4, 218, 226

H
Harborough Home Search, 24
Harvest Housing Group, 166
Healthcare, 4, 9, 152
Heartlander, 120
Hills Report, 3, 26, 59, 77-78, 80

Hirschman, A., 11, 24, 25, 87
Home Connections, 26, 109
Homeownership, 6, 62, 167
Homes and Communities Agency, 20, 23
Housing management, 8, 93, 96, 136, 221
Housing stock, 5, 58, 62, 80, 131
Hull City Council, 94, 115

I
Identity, 54, 102, 120, 126, 130, 133, 138, 142, 143, 189
Image, 11, 69, 101, 126, 127, 131, 134-6, 140-1, 201, 219
Incentives, 73, 148, 149, 156, 157, 194, 213
Indicators, 11, 17, 18, 28, 34, 90, 97, 101, 114, 140, 142, 152
Individual budgets, 4, 9, 11, 24, 26, 50, 61, 88, 225
Inseparability, 43
Intangibility, 43
International comparison, 69, 80
Interpretation, 8, 36, 37, 98
Irwell Valley Housing Association, 25, 102, 194

J
Jam study, 109, 112
John Lewis model, 35

K
KWH label, 83

L
Leadership, 129, 133, 137, 206, 208, 209, 210, 211, 213, 218-9
Lego, 175, 181
Lettings, 6, 10, 22, 23, 24, 38, 54, 55, 61, 75, 76, 79, 80, 82, 88, 93, 109, 111, 117, 128, 139, 186, 225, 227
Lifestyle, 41, 52, 55, 82, 173, 192
Liveability, 28, 83, 140
Liverpool One, 141-142
Lobbying, 174, 204
Local Area Agreement, 10, 17, 18, 90
Localism, 10, 16, 17-18, 26, 29, 63, 102, 209, 227
Logo, 125, 126-7, 130, 133, 138, 139, 143, 152

M
Marginalised groups, 153, 181
Marketing mix, 10, 12, 13, 42-4, 146, 147, 149, 188, 189, 221, 227
Markets, 3, 10, 12, 27, 41, 45, 53, 55, 62, 63, 81, 105, 112, 125, 132, 134, 142, 148, 189, 225
Matrix Housing Partnership, 169
Measuring satisfaction, 100, 101, 227
Monitoring, 94, 112, 113, 136, 167, 171
MOSAIC, 12, 53, 113, 115, 117-8, 119, 178

N
National indicators, 17, 18
National Tenant Voice, 10, 19, 161
Netherlands, 11, 16, 25, 28, 29, 75, 76, 79, 80-84, 88, 155, 215, 227, 228
Networks, 7, 120, 162, 171, 174, 179, 180, 221
New-build completion, 5-6
Nimby, 154, 156, 210
Nudge, 146, 147, 148, 151, 155, 156-8

O
Ombudsman, 20, 87
Opening Doors project, 56
Outsourcing, 32
Ownership, 6, 23, 25, 43, 62, 63, 69, 70-74, 78, 79, 81

P
Participation, 8, 9, 75, 83, 97, 156, 165-6, 214, 218, 226
Partnerships, 17, 19, 26, 27, 57, 58, 131, 139, 167, 169, 203, 226
Pathways to Housing, 202
People, 43, 189
Performance management, 20-21
Perishability, 43
Personal agency, 119, 120
Personalisation, 4, 9, 11, 16, 21, 24, 26, 27, 60-61, 68, 88, 227
Persuasion, 151
PEST analysis, 207, 209
Physical evidence, 44, 188, 189
Place, 10, 18, 41, 42, 44, 50, 63, 69, 90-91, 93, 99, 100, 125, 126, 142, 145, 149, 188-9
Place-based budgeting, 18

Place branding, 139-143
Place shaping, 17
Places for People, 94, 111
Policy-making, 10, 16, 17-18, 21, 227
Portsmouth City Council, 23
Positioning, 9, 33, 41, 44, 45, 110, 127, 162, 193, 194-5, 226
Price, 32, 33, 37, 41, 42, 44, 107, 113, 133, 149, 156, 187, 188, 190, 194, 201, 213
Private sector, 5, 12, 24, 27, 29, 38, 39, 56, 62, 76, 78, 89, 102, 119, 207
Proactive communications, 169-70
Process, 3, 6, 8, 11, 20-23, 25, 33, 35, 36, 37, 41, 44, 52, 59, 95, 101, 109-12, 116, 175, 189, 211-2, 226, 227
Product, 3, 11, 20, 21, 25, 33, 36, 41, 42, 43-4, 125, 128, 134, 149, 188, 190, 227
Profiling, 3, 52, 57, 92, 112, 114, 116-20, 131, 162, 178, 185, 191-2
Profit, 33, 36, 45, 131, 185,186-7
Promotion, 333, 41, 42, 44, 149, 189, 196
Public service ethos, 7
Public service value, 8
Public value, 3, 11, 37, 42

Q
Quality, 6, 11, 16, 20-25, 27, 29, 43, 44, 62, 68, 73, 87-89, 95-6, 101, 143, 188, 194, 227, 228
Quasi-markets, 32, 63, 105

R
Reactive communications, 170-171
Reform, 3, 26, 68, 76-9, 84, 95, 206, 227
Refugees, 50, 54, 55-6
Regulatory framework, 10, 13, 16, 17-20, 53-4, 63, 228
Reluctant renter, 52
Reluctant user, 39
Repossession, 5, 203
Reputation, 23, 62, 126-9, 131, 136-7, 143, 168, 170, 171, 180, 189, 195, 204, 224
Resistance, 45, 148-9, 199, 208-10, 213-17, 221

Responsiveness, 68
Restorative Practices, 209

S
Satisfaction, 3, 16-7, 20, 21-6, 36-7, 69, 83, 87-102, 111, 114, 116, 119, 122, 182, 185, 187, 226, 227, 228
Security, 36, 43, 68, 78, 83, 120, 139, 195, 207
Seddon, J., 11, 21-2, 28, 95, 167
Segmentation, 12, 13, 33, 41-2, 52-3, 62, 115, 116-20, 147, 192
Shelter, 59, 167, 203
Social case, 9, 14, 225
Social marketing, 7, 12, 145-58, 193
Social media, 129, 136, 158, 168, 171, 174, 176, 177, 178-80, 182, 203
Solihull Community Housing, 121, 161, 218
Standards, 18-9, 21, 40, 52, 54, 62, 68, 96, 185, 186, 196
STATUS, 25, 52, 91-3, 96, 98-100, 142, 187
Stepping stone renter, 52
Stigma, 131, 134, 140-1
Surrey Police, 119
SWOT analysis, 190, 194
Systems thinking, 11, 22

T
Target, 2, 12, 17, 21, 32, 33, 40, 42, 45, 50, 59, 63, 71, 81, 96, 99, 106, 107, 112, 114, 116, 118, 126, 132, 136, 148, 161, 188, 193, 201, 211, 224
Tenant, 4, 6-9, 16-19, 25, 28, 45, 50, 51, 58, 61, 62, 68, 71-84, 88, 92, 93-8, 114, 121, 137, 148, 121, 137, 148, 152, 161, 164, 166, 176, 192, 221, 225
Tenant Services Authority, 10, 16-19, 25, 29, 53, 73, 91, 114, 180
Total Place, 18, 143
Total quality management, 22
Transformation, 76, 115, 142, 208, 209, 211, 213, 220

U
Unique Selling Point, 195-196
Up 2 Us project, 60

V

Value demand, 22, 23, 95
Value for money, 3, 4, 18, 20, 63, 96, 114, 117, 137, 188
Variability, 43
Victory Housing Association, 94
Vision, 127, 130, 132-3, 134, 137, 138, 142, 211-2, 217, 218
Voice, 10, 11, 16-30, 63, 87, 89, 94, 116, 138, 161, 167, 171, 216, 224, 227
Vulnerable groups, 51, 76, 119, 226

W

Wants, 36, 41, 45, 46, 77, 110, 113, 197
Welfare, 7, 9, 13, 23, 45, 80, 84, 87
Wellingborough Homes, 138
West Sussex County Council, 57
Wimby, 155, 215
Windsor & Maidenhead, 157-8
Winn's wheel, 174
Woonbron, 82, 83